Environmental Security and Quality After Communism

Published in cooperation with
the Institute of Central/East European
and Russian-Area Studies, Carleton University

Environmental Security and Quality After Communism

Eastern Europe and the Soviet Successor States

EDITED BY

Joan DeBardeleben and John Hannigan

Routledge
Taylor & Francis Group
LONDON AND NEW YORK

First published 1995 by Westview Press, Inc.

Published 2018 by Routledge
52 Vanderbilt Avenue, New York, NY 10017
2 Park Square, Milton Park, Abingdon, Oxon OX14 4RN

Routledge is an imprint of the Taylor & Francis Group, an informa business

A CIP catalog record is available for this book from the Library of Congress.

ISBN 13: 978-0-367-00467-5 (hbk)
ISBN 13: 978-0-367-15454-7 (pbk)

Contents

Tables and Figures

Tables

Figures

Acknowledgments

We wish to express our appreciation to the Norman Paterson School of International Affairs for sponsoring the conference on Environmental Security after Communism which provided the basis for the papers published here. The conference was funded as part of its Military Strategic Studies grant from the Department of National Defence of Canada. We express our special thanks to Professor Fen Hampson of the School. We are also grateful to Lisa Van Buren, Pamela Norris and Elizabeth James for their help in managing the numerous organizational details connected with the conference. Finally, we thank Professor Christopher Marsden of the Department of Spanish for providing camera-ready copy of the book.

Joan DeBardeleben
John Hannigan

Introduction

Joan DeBardeleben

Long before the collapse of communism, both Soviet environmentalists and Western observers warned that environmental problems in Eastern Europe and the Soviet Union had reached crisis proportions. Explanations for the situation, however, focused on deficiencies of the Soviet model rather than on common factors affecting both East and West.[1] For example, experts noted that the Soviet economic system placed a priority on expanded material output and was driven by an obsession with "gigantomania" and scientific-technical prowess, particularly in the heavy industrial and military industrial sectors. Economic incentives encouraged waste and rewarded fulfillment of narrow output goals rather than cost reduction and broad profit maximization. Second, Marxist-Leninist ideology, due to its grounding in the Marxist labor theory of value, was seen as devaluing natural resources.[2] Finally, political features of the system were noted. Especially important were censorship of information about environmental quality, unresponsiveness to local environmental hazards, and restrictions on the formation of independent environmental groups and on independent critiques by experts.

As in many other spheres, observers expected a brighter future following the collapse of the communist system. In this view, market incentives would encourage efficient use of natural resources, including energy, and this in turn would reduce pollution levels. Decentralization of political power would allow local authorities to respond to immediate environmental problems. Liberalization of the media and formation of independent environmental organizations would make the government and industry accountable to the public.

To some extent, the outburst of glasnost in the mid to late 1980s, particularly after the Chernobyl nuclear accident of May 1986, seemed to support these expectations. Glasnost brought increased public awareness of the dire state of the environment, and the Chernobyl accident raised the alarm all over the world about the hazards of environmental neglect in specific countries. Particularly in the more industrialized countries of Eastern Europe and regions of the Soviet Union, citizens began to organize themselves on the local level to demand improvements and, in some cases, offending plants were shut down, at least temporarily, under public pressure. Movements for national autonomy and independence in parts of the USSR (especially the Baltics and Ukraine) seized upon the environmental issue as a symbol of the degrading effects of Russian and Soviet control.[3] It appeared that an environmental awakening was at the doorstep, that local control would bring greater sensitivity to environmental issues, and that the public was attuned to the problem as a priority concern. The collapse of the USSR in late 1991 and the economic downturn which gripped the region interrupted the momentum, and the tide again seemed to turn against the environment. As in so many spheres of life, the promises of the post-communist future seem mere chimeras of past dreams. Just as the end of the Cold War has not brought the hoped-for stability and security to Europe, so the end of communism has not produced reordering of public priorities and redirection of public resources to restore some semblance of peace with nature.

Gorbachev's new thinking in foreign policy had conceived international security in largely non-military terms, and included a recognition of the potentially destabilizing effects of international isolation, global environmental degradation, and the sapping of economic well-being to support the arms race. In developing these ideas, Gorbachev was building on the work of Soviet scientists and philosophers who, already in the 1970s, were drawing attention of scholars and the elite to the reality of "global problems," among which environmental degradation held a primary position.[4] While these scholars were not able to issue an explicit critique of the Soviet model of development and the way in which it contributed to global environmental insecurity, they were able to legitimize concern with domestic environmental problems by linking it to a broader understanding of global issues. They grounded their concern with "global problems" in Marxist-Leninist understandings of Soviet internationalism and the progressive nature of the Soviet system in assuring the long-term well-being of humanity.

Gorbachev's new thinking in many ways set the tone for international relations in the late 1980s and 1990s. Politicians in both East and West expected that the end of the Cold War would bring an economic "peace dividend" which would free resources to address other pressing, but neglected, social problems, including environmental deterioration. The long-term effect would be both a local and global improvement in the quality of life and standard of living.

In embracing these hopes, politicians and the public were to a large extent victims of the exaggerations and misunderstandings generated during the Cold War. In the West, prevalent understandings of the Soviet system were unduly simplistic and failed to recognize both the contributions and deficiencies of that system. Since the dominant Western view attributed the failings of the system almost completely to the structure of communist power, the collapse of that system was expected to bring a positive reversal. If communism had repressed national self-assertion, then post-communism should bring a blossoming of national self-determination, in the Wilsonian sense. If communism had ignored consumer goods and agriculture, then post-communism should allow markets to respond effectively to consumer demands and free private initiative to increase production levels. If communism had set in place a centralized system of incentives and priorities largely hostile to the environment, then post-communism should see a revived capability of these liberated nations to improve the quality of life. Many leaders and citizens in the post-communist states adhered to these same illusions, as they engaged in a wholesale rejection of the Soviet past and an indiscriminating attempt to mimic Western values. In reality, of course, none of these optimistic outcomes has come to pass, at least not yet. Communism not only repressed national self-assertion, but also national hostilities. It not only imposed central priorities, but also assured enforcement of certain public values. It not only repressed consumer demands, but also organized a common economic space. With the collapse of communism some of the old security threats waned, but new ones quickly emerged. Nuclear proliferation, armed national conflicts, economic disorder, refugee flows, and localism have replaced the hazards of a spiralling U.S.–Soviet arms race.

In the scale of new and old security concerns, environmental degradation may seem to be a constant; in the fast-changing landscape of post-Soviet economy and society, the wounds inflicted on nature remain largely unaltered. But in other ways, with the collapse of old domestic and international regimes, the proliferation of new nations, and the demise of effective state authority, environmental problems pose even greater hazards than earlier. These are hazards both to international peace, in the strict sense, but also to human well-being and security, in the broader sense. First, the new states of the former USSR and the liberated countries of Eastern Europe have even fewer resources than previously to address the problems; at the same time, basic issues of material survival steal the attention of elites and the public alike. Second, the international cooperation which the leaders enforced in Eastern Europe has been replaced by new forms of international environmental competition and conflict. Many environmental problems are, by their nature, international, as they are not subject to the border controls and customs regimes that govern the economic sphere. Polluted rivers, lakes and air span national borders, and resource shortages easily translate into competition for shared natural wealth. Third, the decreasing capacity of many states in the region to fulfill basic regulatory functions means that in many cases pollution control and existing regulatory mechanisms have deteriorated, rather than improved. Pervasive corruption, resource shortages, and technological decline make even previously-existing structures for pollution control less effective. In the case of nuclear facilities or wastes, this decline in the regulatory capacity of the state (combined with shortages of money to maintain existing technology) produces heightened dangers of accidents with global implications. Finally, the general decline in living standards, including poor nutrition, a deteriorating social and material infrastructure, and poorer medical care, makes the health effects of environmental deterioration even more debilitating.

Some of these problems may be viewed as an inevitable stage in the larger economic, social, and political transition which is under way in the region, and therefore possibly of a temporary character. However, it is unknown whether the strains of the transition may themselves scuttle achievement of the long-term goals set out by policy-makers. At the same time, the expected "environmental dividends" of communism's collapse are barely evident. Market structures are slow in emerging. While rising prices for almost all goods have undoubtedly led to some reduction in natural resource consumption, this is in the context of a deep depression in many countries of the region. Economic depression does reduce resource expenditure and may even reduce pollution. As production declines, so do harmful emissions. These phenomena do not, however, mean that more rational modes of resource utilization have been internalized through the introduction of market structures. Shortages in many of these economies continue to encourage hoarding of goods, poaching, and non-optimal choices about natural resource use. Market principles function in only a distorted form in much of the region; whether market economics will develop successfully, with the hoped-for decrease in resource waste, is just not known. Furthermore, market structures, without effective regulatory regimes, could engender even greater pollution of the "commons," as enterprises seek to externalize costs to maximize profits.[5]

At the same time, economic crisis conditions have led local authorities to overlook past environmental concerns in the interests of keeping factories open, to stave off high levels of unemployment. They have supported the re-opening of production facilities closed for environmental reasons in the late 1980s. Short and medium-term conflicts between ecology and economics are generally being decided in favor of the latter. Thus decentralization in most cases has not resulted in increased sensitivity to local environmental problems, but rather in the bittersweet recognition that some difficult choices, previously made by central authorities, now rest in the hands of local politicians. Given dire material shortages, the environment falls low on the scale of priorities. Finally, media attention to environmental conditions, while theoretically possible, has declined. The public in most countries has become exhausted with the failure of public life, and thus enthusiasm for forming citizen lobbies and organizations has also waned as people are preoccupied with the travails of daily survival. Environmental groups which do exist are shackled by poverty, and often have to turn to commercial ventures for income, which divert them from their initial objectives. International cooperation and aid provide one of the few sources of material and moral support. New contacts and interaction are now not only possible, but essential to the vitality of the movements in these countries. In this way, Gorbachev's new thinking has, on a small scale, come full circle, becoming a reality at the grassroots level for some environmentalists in the region who look to the outside world for support as they struggle with the odds against them.

If environmental degradation threatens the health and well-being of the inhabitants of Eastern Europe and the Soviet successor states, is it likely to become a threat to global security as well? The answer is "yes," in at least three ways. First, by feeding discontent at home, the issue contributes to potential inter-regional or international conflict. An insecure population almost always poses a greater threat to neighboring countries. Second, accidents or localized environmental catastrophes can in themselves pose a threat to the security of far-away nations, and those are becoming more likely than previously. The Chernobyl accident is a graphic example, but dangers from nuclear waste leakage, global warming, and ozone damage are equally real. Finally, conflict over control of natural resources and their purity can, as the Yugoslav example demonstrates, contribute to actual armed conflict. It thus behooves us to examine both the domestic and international dimensions of the environmental crisis in Eastern Europe, for they may well become our own.

The chapters in this volume explore the linkages between environmental quality and security in the countries of the former Soviet bloc. Based on papers presented at a conference at Carleton University (Ottawa) in February 1993, the contributions have been updated to reflect developments through the end of 1993. In the first section of the book we explore direct linkages between the concepts of environmental quality and environmental security and in latter chapters more indirect ones.

The Environment as a Security Issue

Leigh Sarty reviews the debate about the notion of "environmental security" within the larger context of international relations theory. He analyzes ambiguities in the term itself and observes that it may evoke a perception of continuing "threat" from the former Soviet Union, and thus be utilized opportunistically to justify continued expenditures to support the infrastructure established in the West during the Cold War. Sarty concludes that the existence of such hidden agendas behind discussion of environmental security does not, however, negate the real dangers to both global and regional security that environmental hazards pose. One might also note that the rise of nationalism in Russia, evident in the support for Zhirinovskii in the December 1993 parliamentary elections, would provide an even clearer rationale for continued defense expenditures, whereas demands for "environmental security" would necessitate a shift in public spending in the West to various forms of non-military assistance rather than continued military competition. Thus, in the present context, a renewed competition between the defense establishment in the West and agencies addressing the new non-military threats reflected in the "new thinking" approach is a more likely scenario. Unfortunately, the chauvinistic rhetoric of the likes of Zhirinovskii could result in a set-back for these new security conceptions.

In Chapter 2, Peter Gizewski examines one of the most clear instances of environmental contamination that is linked to security concerns, namely, radioactive after-effects in the Arctic resulting from the military build-up of the Cold War. These include the contamination resulting from nuclear testing in Novaya Zemlya, accidents involving nuclear-armed or nuclear-powered vessels, and dumping of radioactive wastes in the Arctic. Gizewski notes that the short and long-term effects of these activities are insufficiently documented, but that continued international vigilance and action is required to assure control of existing damage and prevention of future increments to the already existing radioactive contamination of the North.

In Chapter 3, Barbara Jancar-Webster develops a tantalizing model for understanding the intersection among environmental degradation, regional security, and violent interstate conflict. She then reviews the way in which her model may impact variously on different parts of Eastern Europe, taking account of variations in culture, economic reform patterns, geophysical characteristics, and political developments. The core of her chapter applies the model to four specific case studies: the energy sector (with particular attention to the implications of nuclear power development), cross-border water resource issues (with a specific focus on the controversy between Slovakia and Hungary surrounding the development of the Gabcikovo-Nagymoros dams), attempts at reforming domestic environmental legislation and regional cooperation in the area and, finally, the role of natural resource and environmental issues in the Yugoslav conflict. The latter section brings to light an important but little-emphasized dimension of the Yugoslav war, as Jancar-Webster documents the important role that control of natural resource wealth plays in shaping the interests and actions of the various parties to the conflict.

One of Jancar-Webster's most thought-provoking conclusions concerns the role of international involvement in addressing environmental problems and regional environmental security. She concludes that international assistance plays and is likely to play a cardinal role in tilting the balance in favor of cooperative and constructive responses to environmental conflicts in the region. At the same time, however, she observes that many aid initiatives may reflect the values and agendas of the donor parties rather than constructively responding to the constraints and interests affecting the recipient nations.

Supplementing Jancar-Webster's argument, one might note that the environmental area offers promising opportunities for effective transmission of aid for a variety of reasons. First, in this area, East European technical expertise is relatively well-developed, thus allowing "aid" to take the form of genuine cooperation, reducing the stigma and arrogance often associated with assistance programs. Second, development of a structure of environmental regulation is an area where Western states have accumulated a variety of more or less successful experience over the past two to three decades. Rather than involving the wholesale transfer of an economic development model (such as is involved in the attempted "shock therapy" offered to these countries by Western "experts"), here Western governments can make available various models of regulation which may have a better "fit" with the traditionally broader role of state authority in these countries. Third, some of the regional cooperation initiatives cited by Jancar-Webster provide a ready mechanism for expanding regimes of international cooperation in this area, as new states seek a place in the international system or as old states (of Eastern Europe) seek to strengthen links with countries outside the former Soviet bloc. The former communist countries were, before the collapse of communism, involved in a host of international initiatives aimed at environmental cooperative linkages which can be built upon and strengthened, thus maintaining some continuity with the past. Finally, the existence of a broad range of independent grassroots environmental groups in the countries of Eastern Europe and the former Soviet Union provides a ready-made opportunity for citizen cooperation from both sides. For all of these reasons, the environmental arena is a fruitful avenue for building new cooperative relationships with the countries of the former Soviet bloc, free of much of the arrogance and ethnocentrism which characterize aid initiatives in other spheres. Here it is not so much a question of advancing Western models for adoption as it is a process of building new international regimes and domestic structures simultaneously under construction in the West.

Energy and the Environment: The Interface Between Security and Quality

The energy sector represents a particularly important interface between the problems of environmental quality and environmental security. The accident at the Chernobyl nuclear power station in May 1986 was the first and most graphic example of the global implications of a localized environmental accident. In his contribution, David R. Marples reviews the political aftershocks of the Chernobyl accident in the Soviet bloc, but reaches the sobering conclusion that the economic and political lobby supporting the continued operation of nuclear power plants of questionable safety has maintained its strength in Russia. The leaders of Belarus and Ukraine, the main recipients of Chernobyl contamination, also continue to view nuclear power as an important resource in their future energy balances.

There is little doubt that, whatever one's general attitude toward nuclear power safety, its application in the countries of the former Soviet bloc is riddled with hazards. This applies not only to plants utilizing the flawed reactor design of the Chernobyl-type RBMK reactors, but also to those using the more commonly used VVER-type in operation in both the former Soviet republics and the East European countries. Marples points out that, despite temporary set-backs for nuclear power development in the late 1980s, economic pressures have left leaders feeling compelled to maintain continued reliance on existing nuclear plants. In addition, plans for actual expansion of nuclear power are embraced by policy-makers in several countries. John M. Kramer notes that in Eastern Europe the future of nuclear power is somewhat uncertain, but that plans for new construction still seem to be on the agenda in the Czech and Slovak Republics, with continuing discussions in Romania and Bulgaria. More important for security considerations, existing Soviet-era plants will likely continue to operate in Lithuania, Bulgaria and the Czech Republic, despite major safety concerns; the Armenian plant, despite its location in unstable seismic conditions, is also slated to reopen. As Marples and Jancar-Webster point out, shortages of other energy resources and an end to Russian subsidies for other fuel resources make this approach a bittersweet attraction to political leaders of resource-poor countries. While Russia has other energy resources which could be developed, the countries of Eastern Europe for the most part have few domestic alternatives. In this area, Western aid and investment may be particularly crucial in assuring that the "peaceful atom" does not pose an international security threat.

John M. Kramer outlines the energy dilemmas facing the region in a broader sense. As Kramer's earlier work demonstrated, under Soviet rule, energy waste was encouraged by a system which under-valued natural resources and thus did not provide an economic incentive for their conservation. Western experts, including Kramer, have long argued that subsidies on energy resources (in the form of artificially low prices) encouraged this culture of waste. This resulted in the much higher expenditure of energy per unit of gross domestic product, compared to West European levels. Excess energy expenditure produced, in turn, higher pollution levels, particularly since domestic energy resources in these countries, especially coal, tend to be highly polluting. These specialists have long advocated price increases on energy resources, preferably to world levels, as a cardinal measure to reduce resource waste and pollution levels.

Now, indeed, these recommendations are becoming reality, as prices on energy resources are rising both domestically and in international trade in the region. What have been the effects thus far? Kramer suggests that market-determined prices have contributed in part to the decline in primary energy consumption in some parts of Eastern Europe. Increased prices on Russian oil and gas have produced an energy crisis throughout the former USSR, particularly in the Baltics and Ukraine. This has led these countries to seek other suppliers of these energy resources, but as noted above, has also fuelled regional interstate tensions, particularly between Ukraine and Russia. In early 1994, Turkmenistan cut off energy supplies to Ukraine for lack of payment, and Russia also temporarily cut back supplies dramatically to put pressure on Ukraine in the context of continuing squabbles over payment. Thus the immediate effect of increases in international petroleum prices in the region has been to fuel regional tensions and the economic depression. As in other spheres of life, the results of measures long supported by Western experts are more ambiguous than expected. As Kramer notes, the East European public may also be reluctant to accept the sacrifices which energy conservation requires. Present cut-backs in energy consumption may be more a product of economic depression than an indication of structural changes in energy consumption patterns.

Regional and Domestic Considerations

What used to be domestic problems have, in many cases since 1989, been elevated to the status of international relations. All three of the formerly federal states in the region have since splintered. The former Soviet Union has spawned fifteen independent countries, Czechoslovakia two, and Yugoslavia a yet undetermined number. Previously, each of these countries had a fairly viable state structure which provided a framework for regulating pollution and the use of natural resources among its constituent units. Now, the old regimes for regulating these affairs have collapsed and, as in other spheres, new ones have not yet crystallized. Furthermore, countries in Eastern Europe which previously had formal independence now have won a greatly expanded capacity to act autonomously in the international sphere. And Russia suffers from assertions of regional autonomy which also hinder the central state's capacity to enforce solutions to natural resource conflicts. Ultimately, the likelihood of effective international cooperation in the environmental area will depend on domestic policies in individual countries. In the last section of this volume authors examine how the changing landscape of state sovereignty and domestic state control are altering capacities for environmental amelioration and regulation in specific countries and regional settings.

The first two chapters in this section focus on recent developments within Russia, the dominant actor in the region. DJ Peterson examines the evolving institutional structure for environmental regulation both on a central and regional level in Russia. While he observes considerable regional variation in the effectiveness with which environmental problems are being addressed, Peterson also notes that the dominant trend involves bureaucratic and regional "empire-building," rather than development of effective policy responses. Conflicts over control and ownership of natural resources reduce possibilities to generate a unified and rational approach to resource management. Shortages of required experts, unclear systems of incentives, and minimal financial autonomy for regional units limit possibilities for regional environmental agencies to operate effectively. Peterson attempts to identify factors which lead some regions to develop more effective regulatory structures than others and, overall, is optimistic about the long-term possibilities which devolution of power offers for the amelioration of environmental pollution.

Western experience suggests that citizen watch-dog organizations are necessary to assure effective implementation of environmental regulations. This is a particularly important issue in the post-communist world, since state bureaucracies are riddled both with inefficiencies and corruption. Lisa Van Buren examines the important issue of citizen activism in Russia. She identifies factors which hinder the effectiveness of the activities of non-governmental organizations in this sphere, as well as those factors which facilitate it. One of the most debilitating conditions is the lack of material support for environmental groups, forcing many organizations to seek income from commercial ventures. Other problems include still deficient information about environmental conditions. Van Buren points out the role of international assistance in improving internal communication through electronic networking of local environmental initiatives.

The final two chapters in the book focus on problems in two regions of the former Soviet Union, the Baltics and the Central Asian republics. Water shortages are, of course, the key natural resource problem facing Uzbekistan, Tajikistan, Turkmenistan, Kyrgyzstan, and Kazakhstan. The focus of the water crisis is the Aral Sea and the devastating effects of its decline over the past decades. James Critchlow examines this and other environmental problems in the region, placing them in the context of the larger political situation. Here citizen activism is relatively undeveloped and generally discouraged by the governments. The legal infrastructure is weaker than in the European post-Soviet states and the severe environmental crisis surrounding the Aral Sea is intimately and inextricably connected to the structure of the economies, particularly the cotton mono-culture inherited from the Soviet past. The health effects of the crisis are both more visible and more intense than in most other countries. The governments of the region seem focused on aid from outside the region to assist them in addressing these problems.

An open question is the extent to which the Aral Sea and associated water problems will meet not only with governmental inertia, as Critchlow suggests, but also possibly be a spur to international conflict between these new nations. Since control of water is likely to play such a crucial role in defining future development possibilities for these nations, one might expect that, at least in border areas and perhaps on a broader scale, they could well cause heightened ethnic and national conflict. While some international involvement can be expected, it will likely be on a lesser scale than in the Baltics or some of the European areas of the former Soviet bloc; thus these countries may be left more to their own devices in resolving their domestic and international dilemmas. If Jancar-Webster's conclusions are correct, namely that international involvement plays a cardinal role in facilitating security-enhancing approaches to environmental problems, then the Central Asian case should perhaps elicit special concern in our examination of environmental quality and security.

In the Baltics, an international infrastructure for environmental cooperation was in existence before the collapse of communism, due to the active interest taken by the Federal Republic of Germany and by the Scandinavian countries in efforts to clean up the shared resource, the Baltic Sea. Juris Dreifelds documents in considerable detail the deleterious effects of pollution of the Baltic Sea and provides an in-depth examination of problems of air, water, and soil pollution in Latvia, Lithuania and Estonia. He also reviews efforts at domestic amelioration and international cooperation. While problems here are considerable, the availability of some international support presents prospects for a brighter future than faces the Central Asian republics.

Conclusion

The environmental crisis in Eastern Europe is likely to remain with us for decades to come. The positive impetus expected from the collapse of communism is not likely to be realized in the foreseeable future. Indeed, the socio-economic context of environmental decay in this region will probably retain a unique character. As state authority is weak, private interest in maintaining the quality of the resource base is also likely to remain feeble. Ownership rights to land and natural resources may well remain unclear and contested for some time to come, at least in the states of the former Soviet republics, and concern with long-term resource sustainability will probably continue to take a back seat to the desire for immediate economic returns. The polluting industrial and energy facilities of the past may well remain operative for many years, linking environmental amelioration to all of the complex problems of economic restructuring under conditions of economic depression. Whether multinational corporations and foreign investors will play a positive or negative role in the current destructive cycle is still unknown. In their desire to attract foreign capital, some of these governments may allow lax enforcement of environmental regulations, off-setting the benefits which might well accrue from the introduction of environmentally-friendly technology by foreign firms.

If security risks, broadly conceived, are to be minimized in this area, a concerted and focused involvement of international organizations and Western governments will be necessary. Benign neglect will, by inertia, only heighten the security dangers.

Notes

1. See, for example, Marshall Goldman, *The Spoils of Progress: Environmental Pollution in the Soviet Union* (Cambridge, Mass.: MIT Press, 1972); Philip R. Pryde, *Conservation in the Soviet Union* (Cambridge, England: Cambridge University Press, 1972); and Boris Komarov (pseudonym of Ze'ev Wolfson), *Destruction of Nature in the Soviet Union* (White Plains, N.Y.: M.E. Sharpe, 1980).

2. Goldman, *Spoils of Progress*, 47–48, 112–115; Pryde, *Conservation*, 42–44. For a critical analysis of this approach see Joan DeBardeleben, *The Environment and Marxism-Leninism: The Soviet and East German Experience* (Boulder: Westview Press, 1985), Chapter 8.

3. Joan DeBardeleben, "The New Politics in the USSR: The Case of the Environment," in John Massey Stewart, ed., *The Soviet Environment: Problems, Policies, and Politics* (Cambridge: Cambridge University Press, 1992), Chapter 6; and the roundtable discussion, "Panel on Nationalism in the USSR: Environmental and Territorial Aspects," *Soviet Geography*, 30 (June 1989), 441–509.

4. See, for example, D.M. Gvishiani, "Nauka i global'nye problemy sovremennosti," *Voprosy filosofii*, 3 (1981), 99–101; I.T. Frolov, "Filosofiia global'nykh problem," *Voprosy filosofii*, 2 (1980), 29–44; and the roundtable discussion on "Nauka i global'nye problemy sovremennosti," *Voprosy filosofii*, 9 (1974), 67–83, 102–24; *Voprosy filosofii*, 10 (1974), 46–60; and *Voprosy filosofii*, 11 (1974), 60–75.

5. On contradictory effects of market reform, see Joan DeBardeleben, "Economic Reform and Environmental Protection in the USSR," *Soviet Geography*, 31 (April 1990), 237–56.

PART ONE

The Environment as a Security Problem in the Post–Communist World

1

Environmental Security After Communism: The Debate

Leigh Sarty

The troubled course of world politics since the collapse of the Berlin Wall has long since affirmed John Mearsheimer's 1990 prediction that we would "soon miss" the Cold War.[1] Viewed against the backdrop of contemporary social, economic, and political upheaval East of the Elbe, the armed stand-off of the post-1945 era now conjures up alluring images of a simpler time, free of the paralyzing dilemmas that the West currently faces in Yugoslavia and the former territories of the Soviet empire. To be sure, nostalgia of this kind is somewhat misplaced. Whether the stability forged by the threat of nuclear holocaust and the forced subjugation of millions can be considered preferable to today's conflicts and uncertainties must remain an open question. Yet change, however welcome, can be a disquieting thing, especially for analysts and policy-makers who have been compelled to rethink long-held assumptions about international politics and East-West relations. The complex challenges of a post–Cold War world make it difficult not to look back with some fondness on the familiar trials of bipolarity. This urge must be resisted, however, if these new challenges are to be constructively engaged and successfully met.

In view of this, the theme of this volume – environmental quality and security after communism – merits close scrutiny. Coupling our study of the international dimensions of post-communist change with the term "security," however modified, evokes the thinking of a bygone era, when the communist "threat" to our values and well-being constituted the principal rationale for the West's concern with the USSR and its East European empire. Those who frame East-West relations after communism in terms of environmental security might be accused of engaging in a semantic sleight-of-hand in order to salvage the familiar analytical categories of the Cold War. This chapter seeks to anticipate and refute this charge by demonstrating how the concept of environmental security can be usefully applied to the post–Cold War agenda in East-West affairs.

The discussion is divided into three parts. The first part traces the recent evolution of scholarship on the nature and meaning of security in world politics and considers the ways in which environmental issues have been integrated into this work. The second part explores some of the hazards involved in linking the environment and security, focusing in particular on the problems that emerge when this linkage is introduced to the study of East-West relations. With these potential pitfalls established, this chapter concludes with identification of the merits of a properly qualified application of the concept of environmental security to a world transformed by the end of the Cold War.

Security in World Politics

In a field as topical as international relations, scholarship is invariably a product of the times, driven and shaped by the very events that it seeks to understand.[2] The emergence of environmental security as an issue for scholarly and policy debate is thus inextricably linked with the end of the Cold War, an event which liberated energies traditionally focused on the military/ideological competition between the superpowers to permit a reconsideration of basic concepts in the field.[3] The roots of this development stretch well beyond the recent changes in East-West relations, however, and are worth reviewing briefly in order to place the contemporary discussion in proper perspective.

From the late 1940s to the early 1960s, when the Cold War was at its height, understanding international security was a comparatively simple affair. Given an armed and (presumably) implacable Soviet foe, the principal threat to the West's health and well-being was perceived to be clearly a military one, to be met by military means. In the academic world, this apparent fact of international life secured wide acceptance of the Realist approach to world politics, which emphasized the centrality of interstate conflict and the primacy of "high" politics (military and security affairs) over such "low" issues as trade and international organization.[4] By the late 1960s and 1970s, as Cold War confrontation gave way to detente and the American debacle in Vietnam cast doubt on the efficacy of military power, "transnationalism" and "interdependence" emerged as the watchwords of an alternative "liberal" framework for understanding a world in which the clear-cut distinctions between high and low politics had become blurred.[5] At the same time, a growing awareness of global concerns that transcended state borders, such as air pollution, poverty, resource scarcity, and the host of other issues conjured up by the image of a fragile and finite "Spaceship Earth," was further eroding the military/state-centric outlook of Realist analysis.[6]

The unravelling of detente and the "new Cold War" of the early 1980s introduced a new dimension to this story. On the one hand, the salience of military issues and interstate conflict in the souring of East-West relations breathed new life into the Realist canon, a development codified by Kenneth Waltz's "elegant restatement of realism" in 1979.[7] The erosion of traditional concepts of power before the advance of global interdependence was a "myth," Waltz argued; the military and economic primacy of the two superpowers fundamentally shaped both the dynamics and the underlying stability of the international system.[8] The $1.5 trillion defense build-up initiated by the Reagan Administration, coupled with relentless deployments on the Soviet side, seemed to affirm that the familiar Cold War approach to security was alive and well in the 1980s.[9] In the meantime, however, the dramatic downturn in East-West relations injected fresh vigor into the quest for alternative approaches as well. In the fall of 1980, the Independent Commission on Disarmament and Security Issues, chaired by Olof Palme of Sweden, began the work that would culminate in its 1982 report, *Common Security: A Blueprint for Survival.* Rejecting the policy of mutual deterrence as amoral and ultimately futile, the Commission called instead for the adoption of the principle of "common security," which held that in an interdependent world armed with nuclear weapons, "true security" could be achieved neither unilaterally nor by military means, but only in cooperation with others.[10] Although the Palme Commission touched in passing on the opportunity costs of arms expenditures (in terms of foregone development) and the interconnections between human deprivation and international conflict, it fell to the World Commission on Environment and Development, which reported its findings in 1987, to spell out more fully the meaning and implications of a truly global, "common" approach to international security.[11] Its articulate identification of the close connections between "Peace, Security, Development, and the Environment" thrust the concept of environmental security into prominence in the contemporary discourse on global affairs.[12]

In the final analysis, however, it was the vicissitudes of world politics and public opinion that shifted these innovative approaches from the seminar room and the conference hall to the real world of international diplomacy. With the advent of Mikhail Gorbachev and "new thinking" in Soviet foreign policy after 1985, talk of interdependence, "mutual security," and the limits of military power entered the East-West mainstream. Levels of cooperation unthinkable in Brezhnev's time gradually entered the realm of the possible, casting the prospects for common security in a new light.[13] At the same time, a combination of scientific insight – the revelation of potentially hazardous atmospheric ozone depletion in 1985 – and circumstances – the nuclear accident at Chernobyl in 1986 and the hot, dry summer of 1988 – alerted policy-makers and the attentive public to the close connections between the state of the natural environment and their own well-being.[14] When the Cold War drew to a close at the beginning of the new decade, the stage was set for the concept of environmental security to come into its own.

Environmental Quality and Security

But what exactly is meant by environmental security? Does the term contribute to understanding, or merely make a complex situation even murkier? In the abstract, the argument for linking the environment and security is straightforward and makes sense. It is at the operational level that problems arise, however, since the variables involved and the interconnections between them are extremely complex. The discussion here will present both sides of the debate on these questions, with special reference to East-West relations after communism.

The case for linking the environment and security typically proceeds as follows. Because the life and well-being of the individual are the necessary preconditions for all human activity, the primary function of the state is to protect its citizens from bodily harm. Since the principal external threat to a populace's physical well-being has historically taken the form of organized interstate violence, the study of international security has traditionally – and, one might add, not unreasonably – focused on "the threat, use, and control of military force."[15] As a result of the political, technological, and physical transformations described above, however, non-traditional, non-military threats to individual and national well-being have proliferated, leading to demands that our conception of security be broadened to incorporate these new challenges.[16]

The environment enters into these deliberations in three respects. The first concerns the increased likelihood of interstate conflict over resources that are becoming scarce due to pollution and over-use. While the threat of resource wars is not new to international relations, this line of analysis points up the clear and growing connections between contemporary mismanagement of the environment and the security challenges of tomorrow.[17] A more refined variant of this theme was identified by the World Commission on Environment and Development and its supporters, which emphasizes the interrelationship between a diminishing quality of life brought on by environmental degradation and the probability of violent civil or interstate conflict. The sense here is that unchecked environmental destruction will "'ratchet up' the level of stress within national and international society, increasing the likelihood of many different kinds of conflict and impeding the development of cooperative solutions."[18] A newer potential threat, that posed by global warming, has been called "the major global security issue of the year 2000."[19]

What distinguishes this mode of analysis from traditional thinking is its sensitivity to the importance of "quality of life" in the security equation, and the role of the environment in determining it. The impact of this variable can be understood either in traditional terms, by singling out the connections between drastic changes in the quality of life and the prospects for violent conflict, or non-traditionally, by framing, for example, the effects of global warming on peoples' health and well-being as a threat to security in and of itself. There is a potential problem here, however. As one observer has put it, "if everything that causes a decline in human well-being is labelled a 'security threat', the term loses any analytical usefulness and becomes a loose synonym of 'bad'."[20]

For this reason, the concept of environmental security is best defined in terms of the probable linkages between environmental degradation and the outbreak of violent civil or interstate conflict. Thomas Homer-Dixon of the University of Toronto has done some very interesting pioneering work along these lines. Although his focus is on the particular vulnerabilities of Third World states, the linkages he identifies between environmentally sensitive variables such as agricultural production, economic decline, and displaced populations, on the one hand, and the disruption of legitimized institutions, growing relative deprivation, and the potential for violence, on the other, clearly have a bearing on the "Second World" as well.[21]

Yet for those who study the states of the former communist bloc, an approach to the region's environmental problems that emphasizes the connection between these issues and the outbreak of military conflict within the region carries potentially troublesome implications. The field of Soviet and East European studies blossomed in the postwar era due to government and private foundation largesse that was sought and justified on grounds of the need to "know thine enemy."[22] By framing the environmental challenges of the post-communist era in terms of "threats" and interstate conflict, post-Soviet studies might open itself to the charge of perpetuating the "us vs. them" mentality of bygone days as a means to maintain the distinctiveness and funding levels that this area of inquiry enjoyed during the Cold War. Perhaps more importantly, as one critic of the environment/security link has argued, the competitive, zero-sum mindset that the terms "threat," "security" and "conflict" conjure up is antithetical to the sense of global interdependence and common destiny on which substantive solutions to the current environmental crisis depend.[23]

The question of opportunism is certainly a valid concern. The existence of the Cold War generated a massive constituency within government, business, and academia that is now scrambling to define a *raison d'être* in the post-communist era, and tapping into popular anxiety about the environment is one obvious way of doing this.[24] This potential drawback is not sufficient grounds for dismissing the concept of environmental security, however. The fact that some might exploit the term for their own personal ends does not invalidate the range of intellectual, political, and technological developments that have brought the links between environment and security into the public policy mainstream. As far as East-West relations are concerned, it is true that the divisive language of "threats" and "national security" carries connotations that may seem outdated and even counterproductive when weighed against the global challenges that our interdependent world now faces. Yet the fact is, in an environmental sense, the divide between East and West is as great as it ever was. The Cold War is over, but the East remains a significant threat to the West's health and well-being.

This introduces a further dimension to the problem of environmental security after communism. For in addition to the relationship between current environmental conditions and the prospects for future conflict, students of this issue must also take into account the environmental and security impact of forty years of past East-West conflict. Here again, this impact can be understood both in terms of its contribution to the conditions that breed civil and interstate violence, and in terms of the direct effects of Cold War ecological damage on the quality of life in the international community.

As a number of the contributions to this volume make clear, it is in this latter sense that the case for framing contemporary East-West relations as a challenge to environmental security is most persuasive. To inhabitants of the northern hemisphere, the legacy of Soviet nuclear testing, submarine accidents, and radioactive dumping in Arctic waters poses a much more tangible hazard than did abstract Cold War tensions at their peak.[25] Thus, although the threat to planetary survival posed by a potential nuclear exchange has diminished, both the infrastructure that nurtured this peril and the process of dismantling it continue to pose awesome environmental challenges.[26] Likewise, a future accident in one of the Chernobyl-type nuclear reactors scattered throughout Eastern Europe would pose an immediate threat to populations on both sides of the former iron curtain, a threat which, while not directly attributable to the Cold War, is nevertheless a constant reminder of the enduring significance of the East-West divide.[27]

Conclusion

The link between the ecological legacies of the Cold War and the future well-being of both East and West is real and constant. The difficulties involved in analyzing this link should not inhibit us from at least making the attempt. Scholars and policy-makers must address the ways in which environmental degradation contributes to the general climate of economic decline, to the erosion of institutions, and to a sense of relative deprivation among the peoples of the former Soviet bloc; for the exacerbation of current conditions could lead to an escalation in inter-ethnic and interstate conflict, creeping authoritarianism, further environmental decay, and destabilizing refugee flows to the rest of Europe and beyond. Problems of environmental degradation are thus an integral part of the broader social, economic, and political challenges inherent in the transition from communist rule.

This conclusion will undoubtedly dismay those who believe that the concept of environmental security is overloaded enough as it is. Whatever the analytical pitfalls, however, drawing attention to the linkages between the environment and problems of post-communist development serves a critical function in the ongoing debate on East-West relations after the Cold War. One of the obligations of students of the former Soviet bloc is to alert decision-makers and the attentive public to the West's stake in seeing the difficult transition from communist rule proceed in a stable and peaceful fashion. This objective cannot be achieved without addressing the environmental legacy of the Soviet era. This is not to say that the environment can or should take priority over politics or economics. But to paraphrase a remark that the President of the World Bank made in Poland a few years ago, it seems clear that economic progress alone will do little to alleviate the prospects for social dislocation and violence for those in the region "who cannot breathe, or drink the water, or avoid toxic assaults on their physical well-being."[28] It is therefore critical that the environment win pride of place in the post–Cold War agenda of East-West relations; the concept of "environmental security" is a valuable means toward this end.

Notes

This paper was prepared while the author was funded by a Postdoctoral Fellowship from the Social Sciences and Humanities Research Council of Canada.

1. John J. Mearsheimer, "Why We Will Soon Miss the Cold War," *The Atlantic*, 266, 2 (August 1990), 35–50. A fully documented, scholarly version of this article appeared as "Back to the Future: Instability in Europe After the Cold War," *International Security*, 15, 1 (Summer 1990), 5–56.

2. This is especially true of security studies. See Stephen M. Walt, "The Renaissance of Security Studies," *International Studies Quarterly*, 35, 2 (June 1991), 211–39.

3. Thomas F. Homer-Dixon, "Environmental Change and Acute Conflict: A Research Agenda," paper submitted to the Global Environmental Change Committee, Social Science Research Council, March 1991, 5.

4. The classics of the Realist genre include E.H. Carr, *The Twenty Years' Crisis 1919–1939* (New York: Harper and Row, 1964) and Hans J. Morgenthau, *Politics Among Nations: The Struggle for Power and Peace* (New York: Alfred A. Knopf, 1948).

5. Seyom Brown, *New Forces in World Politics* (Washington, D.C.: The Brookings Institution, 1974); Robert O. Keohane and Joseph S. Nye, *Power and Interdependence: World Politics in Transition* (Boston and Toronto: Little, Brown and Company, 1977).

6. For a concise summary of the emergence of global environmental politics in the 1970s see Barbara Jancar, "Environmental Studies: State of the Discipline," *International Studies Notes*, 16/17, 3/1 (Fall 1991/Winter 1992), 25–26.

7. Kenneth N. Waltz, *Theory of International Politics* (New York: Random House, 1979). The description is Joseph Nye's, in "Neorealism and Neoliberalism," *World*

Politics, 40, 2 (January 1988), 235–51, at p. 240. See also Walt, "The Renaissance of Security Studies," 216–21.

8. Waltz, *Theory of International Politics.*

9. A good summary of these developments can be found in Raymond L. Garthoff, *Detente and Confrontation: American-Soviet Relations From Nixon to Reagan* (Washington, D.C.: The Brookings Institution, 1985), 1009–67.

10. The Independent Commission on Disarmament and Security Issues, *Common Security: A Blueprint for Survival* (New York: Simon and Schuster, 1982).

11. The World Commission on Environment and Development, *Our Common Future* (Oxford and New York: Oxford University Press, 1987).

12. *Ibid.*, 290–307. See also Gareth Porter and Janet Welsh Brown, *Global Environmental Politics* (Boulder, Colo.: Westview Press, 1991), 109–10.

13. Porter and Brown, *Global Environmental Politics*, 110–11.

14. Thomas F. Homer-Dixon, "On the Threshold: Environmental Changes as Causes of Acute Conflict," *International Security*, 16, 2 (Fall 1991), 79–81. On the nature and international significance of ozone depletion, see Fen Osler Hampson, "Climate Change: Building International Coalitions of the Like-minded," *International Journal*, 45, 1 (Winter 1989–90), 39–44.

15. Walt, "The Renaissance of Security Studies," 212. On the primacy of security in politics see Richard H. Ullman, "Redefining Security," *International Security*, 8, 1 (Summer 1983), 130.

16. See especially Jessica Tuchman Mathews, "Redefining Security," *Foreign Affairs*, 68, 2 (Spring 1989), 162–77; Ullman, "Redefining Security," 133–35; and Sean M. Lynn-Jones, "International Security Studies," *International Studies Notes*, 16/17, 3/1 (Fall 1991/Winter 1992), 53–54.

17. Peter H. Gleick, "Environment and Security: The Clear Connections," *The Bulletin of the Atomic Scientists* (April 1991), 19–21; Ullman, "Redefining Security," 140ff.

18. Homer-Dixon, "Environmental Change and Acute Conflict," 4; see also Mathews, "Redefining Security," 166.

19. Jim MacNeill, "The Greening of International Relations," *International Journal*, 45, 1 (Winter 1989–90), 7.

20. Daniel Deudney, "The Case Against Linking Environmental Degradation and National Security," *Millennium: Journal of International Studies*, 19, 3 (Winter 1990), 463–64.

21. Homer-Dixon, "On the Threshold," 91ff. On the applicability of this mode of analysis to the former Soviet empire, see Barbara Jancar-Webster's contribution to this volume.

22. Stephen White, "Political Science as Ideology: The Study of Soviet Politics," in Brian Chapman and Allen Potter, eds., *W.J.M.M. Political Questions. Essays in Honour of W.J.M. Mackenzie* (Manchester: Manchester University Press, 1974), 252–68; Stephen F. Cohen, "Sovietology as a Vocation" in his *Rethinking the Soviet Experience: Politics and Ideology Since 1917* (New York: Oxford University Press, 1985), 8–19.

23. Deudney, "The Case Against," 465–69.

24. Deudney cites the example of Senator Sam Nunn's 1990 "strategic environmental research program, which earmarked $200 million for environmental research and monitoring by the U.S. military. *Ibid.*, 462.

25. See Peter Gizewski's contribution to this volume and William J. Broad, "Russians Describe Extensive Dumping of Nuclear Waste," *The New York Times*, April 27, 1993, A1, C8.

26. See Murray Feshbach and Alfred Friendly, Jr., *Ecocide in the USSR: Health and Nature Under Siege* (New York: Basic Books, 1992), 170–79.

27. See the contribution in this volume by David R. Marples.

28. Feshbach and Friendly, *Ecocide in the USSR*, 254.

2

Military Activity and Environmental Security: The Case of Radioactivity in the Arctic

Peter Gizewski

Introduction

The Arctic has long been viewed as a distant, pure, natural frontier. In reality however, it serves as the location of considerable military activity. During the Cold War, adversarial relations between the United States and the Soviet Union bred vigorous military deployments in the region in the name of deterrence. On the Soviet side, the region provided a crucial base for Soviet naval power as well as a large portion of Moscow's sea-based nuclear deterrent. For the West, it served as the location for air defense systems dedicated to the early warning and assessment of an impending Soviet attack. Moreover, the region witnessed both an active Soviet nuclear testing program, and an often intense cat-and-mouse game under the seas as the superpowers probed each other's capabilities with hunter-killer submarines.

Today, the political rationale which drove much of this activity – both in the Arctic and elsewhere – has virtually evaporated. The Cold War is over and, with it, the ideological competition which so embittered East-West relations. In this diminished threat environment, security can be preserved at much lower levels of military force. Furthermore, political conditions now favor increased cooperation among states which are no longer adversaries. This cooperation embraces both a non-military and a military agenda.

Central to a new agenda in the Arctic are efforts to remove the environmental legacies of the Cold War. Although a great deal of Arctic-based pollution is attributable to industrial and commercial activity, the military has clearly contributed its share, and there is increasing concern that past military activities may produce greater destruction in the future.

Particularly notable is mounting evidence of environmental damage created by the former Soviet Union. While by no means the sole polluter of the North, reports increasingly indicate that the Soviet Union's efforts to achieve superpower military status may have been purchased at the price of ecological catastrophe both within and beyond its borders.

The fact that a high concentration of U.S. and Russian military power still exists in the region makes worries over the future health of the Arctic environment and its inhabitants even more urgent. Indeed, with the Arctic encompassing eight nations and an even greater number of distinct nationalities, the consequences of its environmental degradation extend beyond any one state, and may heighten tensions and the prospects for future interstate conflict in the process.

Military Activities/Radioactive Threats

A variety of military activities may be cited for their environmental effects on the Arctic. Military maneuvers on land and sea, tree-top aircraft overflights, and other types of activity disturb fish spawning grounds, reindeer pastures and herds, and negatively affect people, animals and Arctic ecosystems generally. PCBs (polychlorinated biphenyls) left by transformers used in the Distant Early Warning (DEW) and North Warning Systems (NWS) threaten the food chain.

Yet three types of activity stand out: (1) nuclear testing, (2) naval accidents involving nuclear-armed/powered vessels, and (3) the dumping of radioactive materials in the ocean. Together, these activities raise the specter of the radioactive contamination of the North, and as such represent a particularly serious threat to the health and welfare of the states and the peoples who inhabit them. A discussion of the extent to which damage has occurred in the region (or may occur in future) follows.

Nuclear Testing

From the earliest days of the Cold War both the United States and the USSR have pursued vigorous nuclear testing programs aimed at ensuring the reliability, safety and modernity of their respective nuclear arsenals. For both, testing was viewed as essential to nuclear deterrence, as deterrence was crucial to national security. For the United States, much of this activity was conducted in Nevada, while the Soviets chose Semipalatinsk in Central Asia as the site for most of their explosions. Yet a significant portion of testing has also occurred in the Arctic.

Arctic testing has taken place at two sites, Amchitka in Alaska and on and around the two islands of Novaya Zemlya off the Arctic coast of the USSR. Little public information is available on the effects of U.S. testing at the former. The few statements that exist simply cite the environmental impact of the Amchitka program as negligible or zero.[1]

Data on the Soviet testing program at Novaya Zemlya are more plentiful. Between 1955 and 1990, the islands were the site of approximately 132 nuclear tests.[2] Of these, over 90 were atmospheric while 42 occurred underground following the conclusion of the Partial Test Ban Treaty (PTBT) in 1963. The last test occurred in October 1990.

During the late 1950s and early 1960s, the islands represented Moscow's testing center, and marked the site of some of the world's largest test explosions – including the detonation of a 58-megaton multi-stage thermonuclear device off the coast on October 30, 1961. While the site only accounts for 25 per cent of all testing done by the USSR, the aggregate yield of all tests in the area is estimated at 273 megatons – roughly 94 per cent of the total megatonnage yield for all Soviet tests.[3]

Indeed, testing on Novaya Zemlya represents the greatest single source of artificial (i.e., man-made) radioactive contamination in the Arctic. From 1958 to 1962, the large number of high-yield atmospheric tests on the islands not only resulted in radioactive contamination locally, but also in Alaska and northern Canada. In fact, fallout from all previous atmospheric weapons testing still represents a major source of plutonium isotopes in the Arctic Seas.[4] The severity of contamination declined dramatically in the wake of the PTBT. Thereafter, most Soviet test activity shifted to Semipalatinsk, and virtually all was underground and of lower yield.[5]

The possibility of underground nuclear tests venting radionuclides due to inadequate containment practices nevertheless remained a source of concern. For years, the U.S. government criticized Moscow for taking inadequate precautions against venting and has detected traces of radioactivity from 20–25 per cent of all Soviet underground nuclear tests. In 1987, an incident of venting at Novaya Zemlya reportedly resulted in the release of fission products throughout Sweden, producing the highest levels recorded in northern Sweden in 15 years, apart from the Chernobyl incident. Three years later, a second case of venting produced similar results.[6]

Moscow's decision in 1989 to close its main test site at Semipalatinsk and shift all remaining testing to Novaya Zemlya increased worries over the possible dangers which testing poses to the Arctic. Canada, Norway, Sweden and Finland all expressed concern to Moscow, as did the Inuit Circumpolar Conference (ICC), an international organization representing the aboriginal peoples of Alaska, Canada, Greenland and, more recently, Russia. In the Soviet Union, the Association of Polar Explorers called upon the government to end Arctic nuclear testing.

Notwithstanding such concern, studies of the extent to which underground testing represents an appreciable environmental risk have yielded ambiguous results. In April 1991, an international symposium conducted by the Canadian Center for Global Security aimed at examining the environmental effects of underground nuclear testing found "no observed impact on plant and animal life that could be directly ascribed to the effect of underground nuclear explosions."[7] Indeed, it concluded that there was "no evidence that underground tests had any impact on the Arctic biosystem, with the exception of the area that has been directly disturbed by the industrial activity associated with the testing program."[8]

On the other hand, a satellite study conducted by researchers at the Norwegian Institute for International Affairs has highlighted possible geological problems at the Novaya Zemlya site.[9] Testing activity at one site, for instance, produced craters in the earth's surface, indicating the destruction of the entire permafrost layer under the explosion site and the formation of a so-called chimney over the destruction cavity. This raises new possibilities of radioactive residues leaking from the caverns caused by the test explosions into the groundwater and eventually into the sea.[10]

This eventuality may seem remote given current U.S. and Russian moratoria on nuclear testing, and recent moves toward the negotiation of a Comprehensive Test Ban Treaty (CTBT). Yet strong constituencies in both countries continue to maintain that nuclear testing is necessary for national security, and recent developments in other nuclear-weapon states could strengthen their argument. France is currently observing its own self-imposed moratorium, but has come under severe pressure from its defense establishment to resume testing.[11] And on October 5, 1993, China ignored international pressure and conducted its 39th nuclear test at Lop Nor (in the Xinjiang Uighur region of Western China).[12]

These developments threaten to reverse the momentum for a test ban, and could in fact unravel the unilateral testing moratoria currently observed in Moscow and Washington. The result could ultimately be a resumption of nuclear testing by the United States, and perhaps also by the Russians at Novaya Zemlya.

Accidents at Sea

Accidents involving nuclear-armed and/or nuclear-powered vessels mark a second source of concern. Throughout the Cold War, American and Soviet nuclear submarines engaged in continual undersea military maneuvers in the Arctic. While Soviet attack submarines endeavored to protect their northern waters and ballistic missile submarines, their U.S. counterparts continually attempted to shadow and monitor the Soviet vessels.

From 1945–88, more than 20 naval accidents involving nuclear-armed or nuclear-propelled submarines or warships occurred in northern seas.[13] In February 1992, a U.S. Los Angeles-class nuclear-powered submarine collided underwater with a Russian Sierra-class submarine in the Barents Sea just off the coast of Russia, causing damage to both vessels. Reports indicated that both were carrying nuclear torpedoes and that if they had collided at a different angle, both would have sunk instantly, eliminating the opportunity to shut down safely their nuclear reactors.[14] The result could have been an environmental catastrophe in the Barents Sea. A second collision, involving the American nuclear-powered attack submarine U.S.S. Grayling and a Russian Delta-class nuclear submarine on routine patrol, occurred off the coast of the Kola Peninsula in March 1993.[15] According to one report, had the U.S. submarine been five seconds slower, it would have struck the Russian vessel's missile bay, and thereby could conceivably have sunk the submarine and scattered its nuclear warheads over the ocean floor.[16]

This interaction of U.S. and Russian nuclear-powered attack submarines, and its attendant risks, seem destined to continue despite the fact that Russian naval activity is declining. While the recent submarine collisions have led the United States to restrict naval operations in the Barents Sea and to begin reviewing naval activities in the region, nuclear-powered attack submarines continue to patrol beneath the Arctic ice.[17] Even as the U.S. Navy is shifting from a focus on global threat to regional challenges and opportunities, recent doctrinal statements illustrate that it remains intent on maintaining a forward presence in the region.[18]

Other incidents have bred additional concern. Most notably, technical malfunctions have left a number of U.S. and Soviet nuclear submarines – along with the nuclear warheads they carried – at the bottom of the ocean.[19] Over the past three decades, the U.S. Navy has lost two nuclear submarines, the Thresher and the Scorpion, and has admitted to dumping one nuclear reactor from the Seawolf, in 1959.

More recently, in April 1989, a ship-board fire resulted in the sinking of the Komsomolets, a Soviet (Mike-class) nuclear-powered attack submarine carrying two nuclear-armed torpedoes. Since then, the vessel has been the source of much controversy, largely due to the prospect of radiation leaking into the surrounding ocean, thereby threatening the environment.

The vessel currently lies under 1,450 meters of water, 240 kilometers southwest of Bear Island. It is leaking cesium 137, a carcinogenic isotope which can be stored in biological tissues. While investigations have so far shown a radiological situation consistent with predicted background levels, scientists have expressed concern about future leaks of radiation and their long-term effects on Arctic ecology and the food chain. Some scientists contend that by 1995, a more intense leakage of radioactive materials into the marine environment may begin.[20] Reports from Russian scientists have indicated that the submarine's hull is damaged, the torpedoes are no longer watertight, and that they could eventually begin leaking plutonium.

A number of scientists have noted that even if plutonium leakage occurs, it will be absorbed by the sediments on the ocean floor and remain localized.[21] Other reports suggest that strong currents could result in the spread of such material throughout the region, adding that currents in the area of the wreck may be "more violent than was originally thought."[22] They also note that other radionuclides, such as cesium 137, are mobilized much more easily and could ultimately become widely dispersed throughout the Arctic ocean.

Officials from Norway and the Russian Navy have denied that there is any immediate danger, but continue to monitor the submarine closely. In August 1993, a U.S.-Russian research team undertook a full investigation of the sunken vessel and concluded that the dangers of contamination were negligible: any leakage of radioactive material would most likely settle on the sea floor near the vessel.[23]

One month later, however, other Russian officials announced that Moscow had decided to seal off the corroding nuclear torpedoes with a polymerizing gel to avoid even an outside risk of plutonium leakage. Work is scheduled to commence by the summer of 1994 "with or without Western financing."[24]

Radioactive Dumping

Compounding concern over radioactive contamination is a litany of revelations about the past dumping practices of the Soviet Navy. Since 1991, a number of scientists, environmental activists and Russian environmental officials have charged that the Soviet Navy and ice-breaking fleet had dumped large amounts of radioactive material into the waters of the Barents and Kara Seas for over three decades. Much of the dumping was associated with Soviet nuclear weapons production, and was thought to be located at about five sites in the area, with the largest located in shallow waters off Novaya Zemlya.

Until recently, attempts to document the nature and extent of the dumping were either prohibited or highly circumscribed by Russian military authorities. The result has been delays in the capacity to formulate an effective response. In the fall of 1992, for instance, the Greenpeace ship Solo was stopped by Russian coastguard authorities when it attempted to examine submarine reactor dumps off the coast of Novaya Zemlya.[25] Other researchers and journalists attempting to undertake investigations of the area have encountered similar obstacles.

By October 1992, mounting international and domestic pressure had nevertheless worked to secure the creation of a 46-member multi-departmental Russian Commission to investigate the nature and extent of Soviet and Russian dumping practices. Established by Russian President Boris Yeltsin and chaired by Alexei Yablokov, the Commission's findings proved long in coming, as bureaucratic infighting continually delayed access to required information. By March 1993, however, the Yablokov Commission's report was released in limited form.[26]

The Commission calculates that, since 1965, the USSR dumped a total of 2.5 million curies of radioactive waste into ocean waters.[27] Among the items dumped are 16 nuclear reactors from submarines and an icebreaker in the shallow gulfs off the eastern coast of Novaya Zemlya.[28] Seven of the reactors still contain highly radioactive nuclear fuel, and some date back to the 1960s, when more plutonium was used per reactor. In each case, the reactor core suffered damage that prevented removal of the spent nuclear fuel.

Approximately 11,000 barrels of liquid and solid radioactive waste were dumped in the same region. Some containers were punctured to facilitate sinking.[29] According to Andrei Zolotkov, a legislator from Murmansk who was party to some of the documentation on dumping, a container registering high levels of radiation washed onto the shores of Novaya Zemlya in 1984, only to be tossed back into the ocean when discovered.[30] The report also observes that the Soviet Navy sank two empty reactors in the Sea of Japan off eastern Russia, as well as additional barrels of radioactive waste there, and in the Pacific Ocean.[31]

Ocean dumping of radioactive waste is by no means unique to the USSR. Over the years, other nuclear nations such as the United States, Britain, France, Germany and Japan have engaged in their own disposal of such waste at sea.[32] Yet the Soviet dumping is more than double the combined amount reportedly disposed by all the other nations over the last 45 years.[33]

More importantly, much of the activity documented in the Yablokov Commission's report has occurred in waters ranging from 200 to 1000 feet in depth. As such, it contravenes provisions established by the 1972 Convention on the Prevention of Marine Pollution by Dumping of Wastes and Other Matter, commonly known as the London Dumping Convention (LDC).[34] This accord outlaws the dumping of high-level wastes at sea, initially restricting the disposal of low-level radioactive wastes to ocean basins greater than 12,000 feet, and then establishing a legally non-binding moratorium on all radioactive dumping in 1985.[35] The USSR ratified the LDC in 1976, and while it had abstained on the vote for the 1985 moratorium,[36] Moscow consistently maintained that radioactive waste material had never been dumped, notwithstanding occasional Western suspicions to the contrary.

Further dumping has also occurred inland. In August 1992, in testimony before the Senate Select Committee on Intelligence, Director of the CIA Robert Gates noted that during the early days of the Cold War, radioactive waste from the Soviet Union's first nuclear weapons at Chelyabinsk was discharged into the Techa River, severely contaminating its watershed for thousands of miles.[37]

After 1951, activities at the Mayak military complex in the southern Urals led to similar waste being dumped in Lake Karachai, where the radiation is reportedly so great today that as little as one hour's exposure at the shoreline could prove fatal. Radioactive contamination in the ground water has spread two to three kilometers from the lake and, in 1957, an explosion from a waste tank reportedly contaminated over 23,000 square kilometers of land in the region.[38] According to recent reports from the Vernadskii Institute of Geochemistry and Analytical Chemistry in Moscow, subsurface pollution from Karachai is presently moving toward the nearby Misheliak River at a rate of about 80 meters per year and will soon reach the river.[39] The Mayak facility also has 200,000 curies of radioactive waste stored in a system of reservoirs that are in danger of overflowing.[40] Water from the region ultimately drains into the Ob' River, which then flows north into the Arctic Ocean. At present, Western scientists know little about the extent of radioactive pollution of the Ob' River. Russian scientists are investigating the problem, but have not yet issued a report.

Assessing the Threat

Data provided by the Yablokov Commission and others amply chronicle the location and extent of Soviet and Russian dumping practices. Yet the information available is still insufficient to reveal the exact composition of the radioactive refuse, and little is known about whether the containment vessels are intact or leaking. Nor is there any mention of the plutonium contained in nuclear warheads lost through submarine sinkings, or any discussion of the possible radioactive pollution resulting from atmospheric, undersea or underground nuclear testing at Novaya Zemlya.

Not surprisingly, speculation persists about the potential impact these activities may have on the Arctic environment. The past few years have witnessed a wealth of reports suggesting that these activities may already have had damaging effects on humans and other mammals in the region. In the Russian Arctic, environmentalists and scientists have claimed that there has been a definite decrease in health quality over the last 15–20 years. Increases in mortality rates, cancer, blood, skin and oncological diseases have been reported in the Arkhangel'sk Oblast.[41] The Russian Academy of Medical Sciences recently observed that the cancer death rate in Chukotka jumped from 10 per cent in 1970 to 27 per cent in 1988.[42] That same year, Mary Simon, President of the Inuit Circumpolar Conference (ICC), reported on pleas for help among members of the Soviet Union's 26 northern indigenous peoples, who claimed that people were becoming ill from radioactive contamination in the environment.[43] And, in April 1992, scientists noted that thousands of seals were dying off Russia's northern coastline as a result of the radioactive pollution of the seabed.[44]

More recently, and with specific reference to nuclear dumping, Norway and Russia (two of the world's largest fish exporters) have expressed concern about the impact of such activity on their fishing industries. Concern is especially high in Russia, where the fishing industry remains a vital source of hard currency in economically desperate times. A reduction in sales of fish and reindeer meat could also have a negative impact on the living conditions of indigenous peoples, who are highly dependent on the export of both products.[45]

Many officials representing governments in the region contend that the immediate risks to humans and major forms of Arctic life are small, and note that none of the dump locations are reported to be near important fishing or spawning grounds. The Kara sea remains frozen for nine months of the year and contains little biological activity, and the fishing grounds of the Barents, White and the Norwegian Seas are hundreds of miles away.[46] Furthermore, much of the dumped material may by now have lost much of its radioactivity, amounting to perhaps less than one million curies.[47]

In fact, officials contend that ocean dumping may be safer than land burial, where the potential for the poisoning of underground water is always a possibility.[48] Some add that alarm bells coming from Moscow are grossly exaggerated, and have more to do with leveraging Western aid to finance the cleanup of a Russian problem, than with the description of a genuine regional threat.[49] Nevertheless, most admit that the longer term effects may be more worrisome. As containers break down and as submarines corrode, the materials within could pollute marine life and possibly disperse radioactivity into the ecosystem. Thereafter, strong currents could carry contaminants into fishing grounds or the feeding areas of sea mammals and birds.[50]

Non-governmental sources convey a greater sense of urgency, making less of a distinction between short- and long-term effects, in the hope of mobilizing relevant political constituencies to address the problem more forcefully. For instance, Greenpeace researchers have argued that countries cannot afford to adopt a "wait-and-see attitude" toward this problem and react only when and if the situation becomes serious. Wastes must be quickly removed from the oceans and buried on land.[51]

Calls for prompt action are given added credence by the prospect that past dumping may represent only part of the problem. There are approximately 90 older Russian nuclear submarines that have been decommissioned, and about 50 or 60 in the Northern Fleet that are due for disposal over the next decade. Submarine reactors requiring disposal will thus amount to well over 200. The poor reactor design and safety record of Soviet naval propulsion reactors has led some to speculate about the potential for "maritime Chernobyls" occurring later.[52] Discharge of the radioactive byproducts of decommissioned vessels represents another possibility. In this respect, a powerful argument for action comes from the Yaboklov Commission itself, which warns that since there are currently no on-shore storage sites for the radioactive waste and no reprocessing facilities, the Russian Navy will be unable to halt the dumping immediately.[53]

As if to underscore the point, a Russian ship discharged 900 tons of low-level radioactive waste from submarine engine coolants into the Sea of Japan in mid-October 1993. And while protests from the Japanese, the United States and other states have led Moscow to suspend plans for further dumping, Russian officials have stated that foreign financial assistance is urgently needed for the construction of a nuclear waste-processing plant to prevent a resumption of such practices in future.[54] According to Russian estimates, the cost is considerable.[55] Other countries may seek similar means of disposal for their own submarines.[56] In this regard, both Britain and France must soon decommission a number of their own submarines and power stations and could seek to resume dumping practices in the future.

Meeting the Challenge

Given available information, it is clear that the current risks posed by nuclear testing, sunken nuclear submarines, and radioactive dumping to the Arctic environment are somewhat uncertain. Data are incomplete, and in some cases, inaccessible.

Nevertheless, the information at hand clearly justifies the growing concern and the need for a prompt response. Without concerted efforts to address these issues, the risks to the Arctic environment may increase, along with the prospects for political tension and conflict among the actors who inhabit the region. Indeed, it is worth noting that, whether it is the result of nuclear testing, nuclear accidents at sea, or dumping, the release of radioactive materials into the ocean or the atmosphere will not respect national borders. The waste dumped by one country will almost certainly enter the waters of another.

Even in the absence of a clear threat, the need for action remains. Without devoting greater attention to these issues, policy-makers may face a political-psychological climate which may eventually restrict even legitimate military activity in the North, not to mention a relatively inexpensive means of waste disposal.[57]

A growing recognition of the potential consequences of such practices and the vulnerability of the Arctic environment has already led to some efforts aimed at protecting it and repairing the damage done. Meeting under the aegis of the Arctic Environmental Protection Strategy (AEPS), the eight Arctic states adopted, in 1992, the Arctic Monitoring and Assessment Program (AMAP), an Arctic-wide monitoring plan to add information on the extent of environmental risks, including those posed by radioactivity. AMAP consists of an Overall Implementation Plan as well as individual National Implementation Plans for each Arctic country.[58] Linkages are also being established with a number of international organizations capable of supporting the goals of the program. Working in cooperation with the International Atomic Energy Agency (IAEA), and enlisting the support of national governments and other bodies such as the European Community's Radiation Protection Program (CEC/RPP) and the NATO-based Committee on Challenges to Modern Society (CCMS), AMAP is coordinating an agenda of activities aimed at addressing these issues. These activities – some are already under way – are scheduled for completion in 1996–97.

In February 1993, a three-year international program was created for assessing the existing and possible future radiological and environmental impact of the dumping as well as the need for remedial action. Known as the International Arctic Seas Assessment Project (IASAP), the program is being run by the IAEA in cooperation with a Norwegian-Russian group of experts.[59] Recently, the expert group launched an expedition to inspect the condition of dumped material and to collect samples from dump sites and surrounding areas to assess possible leakage. Information is currently being analyzed, and will eventually be provided to AMAP.

As for future initiatives, the Radiation Protection Program (RPP) of the Commission of the European Community's (CEC) plans to undertake a project on marine ecosystems in the Arctic region with special reference to the behavior of transuranics and long-lived radionuclides. The CCMS has recently organized a study within the framework of the Brussels-based North Atlantic Cooperation Council, to identify radioactive contamination and health risks associated with defense-related activities in the Barents, Laptev and Baltic Seas.[60] And the U.S. government, through the Office of Naval Research, is sponsoring activities to support an initial assessment of radionuclide levels in Arctic and North Pacific waters, an initial assessment of dumped material in these waters, predictions on the fate of contaminants if release occurs, and information to guide the selection of monitoring sites.[61]

Other organizations have pledged their support for these initiatives. Indeed, both the Nuclear Energy Agency of the Organization for Economic Cooperation and Development and the recently created Barents Euro-Arctic Council have registered a strong commitment to the cause of Arctic environmental protection in general, and a willingness to address the problem of radioactive pollution in particular.

Finally, efforts are under way to extend the London Dumping Convention's moratorium on the ocean dumping of all radioactive waste to an outright ban. In July 1993, Denmark proposed a total ban based on the principle of a "precautionary approach." This approach holds that, in light of the incomplete state of knowledge on these issues, and the relatively short period over which data have been collected, caution must govern decision-making, and irreversible measures should be avoided. In the specific case of radioactive dumping, this entails the prohibition of all such activity unless and until those engaging in the practice can convincingly demonstrate that sea-based disposal is safe.[62] Adoption of the proposal would follow a two-thirds vote of the 70 countries that have ratified the Convention. Parties to the LDC have agreed to hold an Amendment Conference in the summer of 1994, following a consultative meeting in early November 1993 to formulate amendments for formal adoption at that time.[63] At present, international support for the ban is running high, but it still faces opposition. In particular, officials in the U.S. Department of Defense oppose the initiative on the grounds that it may unduly restrict future operations of the U.S. Navy.[64]

The Need for Further Measures

The initiatives undertaken thus far underscore the fact that much remains to be done. The chief task is to acquire more detailed information concerning the extent of the problem. In the case of dumping, this process is currently under way and will, it is hoped, include additional data on the location of all dump sites, the type of waste dumped, when such dumping occurred, and the types of containment used.[65] Yet similar efforts are needed in the area of nuclear testing and with regard to sunken nuclear warheads. Soviet records and/or the conduct of detailed scientific surveys are crucial to these enterprises. Consequently, the Russian government should continue to be pressed to release all information about radioactive waste, whatever its source, as quickly as possible.

Beyond this lie challenges associated with the assessment, clean-up and disposal of radioactive waste. Even if adequate data are made available, raising the material and disposing of it safely are likely to cost billions of dollars.[66] Issues such as the prioritization of threats, organizing a detailed plan of attack, and effectively implementing the measures decided upon are just some of the challenges that will need to be addressed.

Given the numerous other problems that Russia currently confronts, it would be unwise, if not foolish, to expect Moscow to tackle such challenges alone. Sustained international financial and technical assistance will be required. Equally important is the need to ensure close coordination of any multinational response that emerges.

Steps must also be taken to prevent additional dangers from emerging. As noted above, the activities which have contributed to the existing problems of radioactive pollution in the Arctic could continue in the future. Nuclear testing may resume, nuclear-powered submarines will go on patrolling the Arctic, and incentives to dump radioactive material are likely to endure. To ensure more fully against the future environmental dangers that these activities present, a number of preventive measures warrant consideration.

First, the LDC's moratorium on the dumping of radioactive waste in the oceans must be transformed into an outright ban. Such a ban should be informed by a *precautionary approach* to dumping, which places the burden of proof as to the safety of any future sea-based disposal on those who plan to engage in the practice.

Second, all necessary steps should be taken to prevent a resumption of nuclear weapon testing in the Arctic. In fact, the United States and Russia, as well as the three other nuclear-weapon states (France, China, and the United Kingdom) should hold to the negotiation of a comprehensive test ban as soon as possible. In the meantime, existing moratoria on testing should be extended, and China and the United Kingdom should be encouraged to implement their own respective moratoria, until such time as a CTBT is signed and enters into force.

Third, the United States and Russia should consider a negotiated reduction in the number of nuclear-powered attack submarines (SSNs) they possess.[67] Reduced numbers of SSNs would force the U.S. and Russian navies to concentrate their remaining submarines on primary missions: for Russia the defense of its Arctic waters, and for the United States the protection of its carrier battle groups for regional contingencies. The result, accordingly, would be a greater separation of these forces and a reduction in, if not an end to, dangerous underwater confrontations in the Arctic.

Fourth, in order to help ensure against irresponsible disposal practices in the future, the international community must move to establish guidelines for the safe disposal of nuclear submarines and the handling of nuclear waste, and do everything it can to ensure that all countries, Russia in particular, subscribe to them.[68]

Finally, it is time for the nations of the Arctic to adopt a circumpolar perspective on Arctic security.[69] This is based on the belief that today there are common regional interests among the eight Arctic states and the people living in them, and that all circumpolar nations, not just the United States and Russia, have a responsibility for ensuring the peaceful development of the region. Crucial to this development is a recognition that the concept of security encompasses not only military, but social, economic and, indeed, environmental dimensions as well. With the end of the Cold War, the United States and Russia must once and for all adapt military activities to the new political realities. The Arctic must no longer play host to military activity based on the logic of a bygone era. Not only are the military threats too low, but the environmental risks may well be too high.

Notes

1. Details on the history of U.S. nuclear testing can be found in Thomas B. Cochran, William M. Arkin, Robert S. Norris and Milton M. Hoenig, *Nuclear Weapons Databook Volume II: U.S. Nuclear Warhead Production* (Cambridge: Ballinger Publishing Company, 1987), especially 41–54.

2. Figures on Soviet testing were presented by Professor Victor N. Mikhailov, former Deputy Minister of Atomic Energy and Industry of the USSR and current Russian Minister of Atomic Energy, at the symposium "Environmental Effects of Underground Nuclear Testing" held by the Canadian Center for Global Security (formerly the Canadian Center for Arms Control and Disarmament) in Ottawa, April 1991. See, Canadian Center for Global Security, *Containment of the Environmental Effects of*

Underground Nuclear Testing: Proceedings of an International Symposium (Ottawa: Canadian Center for Global Security, forthcoming in 1994). Slightly lower figures are given by Lynn R. Sykes and Steven Ruggi in Thomas B. Cochran, William M. Arkin, Robert S. Norris and Jeffrey I. Sands, *Nuclear Weapons Databook Volume IV: Soviet Nuclear Weapons* (New York: Harper and Row, 1989), 332–81. According to Sykes and Ruggi, the Soviet Union conducted some 120 nuclear explosions on the islands, slightly under 20 per cent of all nuclear explosions conducted by the Soviet Union.

3. Mikhailov, "Environmental Effects of Underground Nuclear Testing."

4. Arctic Monitoring and Assessment Task Force, *Report to Ministers: Update on Issues of Concern to the Arctic Environment, Including Recommendations for Action*, AMAP Report 93:4 (Oslo: Arctic Environment and Assessment Program, September 1993), 21.

5. According to Mikhailov, "Environmental Effects of Underground Nuclear Testing," approximately 467 explosions occurred at the Semipalatinsk site, for an estimated total of 16 megatons – roughly 5.5 per cent of the yield of all Soviet testing.

6. Arctic Monitoring and Assessment Program, *Report to Ministers*, 21.

7. Canadian Center for Global Security, *Containment of the Environmental Effects of Underground Nuclear Testing* (forthcoming).

8. *Ibid.*

9. Johnny Skorve and John Kristen Skogan, *The NUPI Satellite Study of the Northern Underground Test Area on Novaya Zemlya: A Summary Report of Preliminary Results*, Research Report No. 164 (Oslo: Norwegian Institute of International Affairs, December 1992).

10. *Ibid.*, 41–42.

11. As reported in R. Jeffrey Smith, "China Reported to Plan First Atom Test in a Year," *International Herald Tribune*, September 19, 1993, 1.

12. *Ibid.*

13. Compilations of these and other types of naval accidents are provided in William A. Arkin and Joshua Handler, *Naval Accidents: 1945–1988*, Neptune Papers No. 3 (Washington, D.C.: Greenpeace/Institute for Policy Studies, June 1989) and Joshua Handler, Amy Wickenheiser and William M. Arkin, *Naval Safety 1989: The Year of the Accident* (Washington, D.C.: Greenpeace/Institute for Policy Studies, April 1990).

14. "Subs Nuclear-Armed, Moscow Says," *The Toronto Star*, February 28, 1992, A21.

15. "Russia Blames U.S. Manoeuvres for Subs' Collision," *The Toronto Star*, March 23, 1993, A3.

16. Jon Bowermaster, "The Last Front in the Cold War," *The Atlantic Monthly* (November 1993), 36.

17. *Ibid.*, 44.

18. U.S. National Security Strategy, August 2, 1990, and U.S. Navy, *From the Sea: Preparing the Naval Service for the 21st Century*, Navy and Marine Corps White Paper (Washington, D.C.: U.S. Government Printing Office, September 1992).

19. Such mishaps have reportedly left some 38 nuclear warheads on the ocean floor. See Joshua Handler, "Soviet Subs – A Neglected Nuclear Time Bomb," *Christian Science Monitor*, December 18, 1991, A1, and Steven Erlanger, "Russians Tell of '61 Atom Accident on Submarine," *New York Times*, December 27, 1992, A9.

20. Danielle Bochove, "Submarine Threatens Sea Life," *Globe and Mail*, November 30, 1992, A4. For a detailed preliminary assessment, see Greenpeace International, *The*

Sinking of the Soviet Mike Class Nuclear Powered Submarine (London: Large and Associates, April 1989).

21. Paul Raeburn, "Soviet Sub Leak," Associated Press, November 25, 1992.

22. As reported in Anne McIlroy, "Soviet Nuclear Dump Threat to North," *Ottawa Citizen*, December 4, 1992, A3.

23. William J. Broad, "Hazard is Doubted from Sunken Sub," *New York Times*, September 6, 1993, A7.

24. William J. Broad, "Russians to Seal Sunken Torpedoes," *New York Times*, September 19, 1993, 20.

25. Greenpeace, "Greenpeace Ship Fired Upon, Crew Arrested in Kara Sea," *Press Release*, October 12, 1992.

26. Office of the President of the Russian Federation, *Facts and Problems Related to Radioactive Waste Disposal in Seas Adjacent to the Territory of the Russian Federation* (Moscow: Office of the President of the Russian Federation, 1993).

27. *Ibid.*, 32. A curie is the amount of radiation released by one gram of radium and, in any nuclear material, is equal to the disintegration of 37 billion atoms per second.

28. *Ibid.*, 24, 27.

29. For details see *ibid.*, 20–27.

30. "Soviets Dumped Radioactive Waste: Leaky Containers Sunk in Arctic Seas, Official Says," *Globe and Mail*, August 24, 1992, A12.

31. Office of the President of the Russian Federation, *Facts and Problems*, 29–32.

32. William J. Broad, "Russians Describe Extensive Dumping of Nuclear Waste," *New York Times*, April 27, 1993, A8.

33. R. Monastersky, "Hazard from Soviet Nuclear Dumps Assessed," *Science News*, 143, May 15, 1993, 311.

34. The Convention was signed on December 29, 1972, entered into force on August 30, 1975, and currently boasts 70 parties.

35. The 1985 moratorium was established through resolution LDC.21, and was adopted by a vote of 26 in favor, 5 against and 7 abstentions. For further details see, Clifton Curtis, "The London Convention and Radioactive Waste Dumping at Sea: A Global Treaty Regime in Transition," in *Proceedings: Radioactivity and Environmental Security in the Oceans: New Research and Policy Priorities in the Arctic and North Atlantic*, June 7-9, 1993 (Woods Hole, Massachusetts: Woods Hole Oceanographic Institute), 542–44.

36. The other states that abstained were Japan, Italy, Portugal, Greece, Belgium and Argentina. The United States, Britain, France, Switzerland and South Africa all voted against the moratorium. *Ibid.*, 552.

37. Robert Gates, Testimony Before the Senate Select Committee on Intelligence, U.S. Senate, University of Alaska (Fairbanks), Fairbanks, Alaska, August 15, 1992.

38. *Ibid.*

39. Monastersky, "Hazard from Soviet Nuclear Dumps Assessed," 311.

40. *Ibid.*

41. The data were presented in greater detail by M.P. Roshevsky, Director of Physiology of the Urals Branch, Russian Academy of Sciences, at the conference "Ecological Problems in the Arctic and the Prospects for Nuclear Disarmament," held in Arkhangel'sk, Russia, October 14–18, 1992. The sponsors were: the Arkhangel'sk

Oblast Administration, Goskomsever, the Popular Movement "Towards Novaya Zemlya," the Russian Committee of the International Physicians for the Prevention of Nuclear War and the Russian Peace Fund.

42. Tim Parker, "Russian Nuclear Mess Threatens Arctic," *Daily News-Miner*, August 16, 1992, A1.

43. Milo Cernetig, "Ailing Arctic Ocean Focus of Inuit Talks," *Globe and Mail*, July 20, 1992, A1.

44. "Nuclear Test Fallout Killing Russian Seals," *Toronto Star*, April 4, 1992, A25.

45. Arctic Monitoring and Assessment Task Force, *Report to Ministers*, 25–26.

46. As reported in William J. Broad, "Russians Describe Extensive Dumping of Nuclear Waste," *New York Times*, April 27, 1993, A8.

47. *Ibid.*

48. *Ibid.*

49. William J. Broad, "Russians to Seal Sunken Torpedoes," *New York Times*, September 25, 1993, A6.

50. David White, "Interview with E.F. Roots, Science Advisor Emeritus, Department of the Environment, Canada," CBC Northern (Whitehorse), August 19, 1992. Also, Arctic Monitoring and Assessment Task Force, *Report to Ministers*, 26–27.

51. McIlroy, "Soviet Nuclear Dump Threat to North," A3.

52. See for instance, Vladimir V. Stefanovsky, "Their System Still Needs Victims," and Rear Admiral (retired) Thomas A. Brooks, "Soviet Weaknesses are U.S. Strengths," *U.S. Naval Institute Proceedings*, August 1992, 64–68, and 68, respectively. Also Joshua Handler, "No Sleep in the Deep for Russian Subs," *The Bulletin of the Atomic Scientists* (April 1993), 7–9.

53. Office of the President of the Russian Federation, *Facts and Problems*, 50.

54. Craig R. Whitney, "Russia Halts Nuclear Waste Dumping at Sea," *New York Times*, October 22, 1993, A9.

55. *Ibid.*

56. Bronwen Maddox, "Last Stop for Britain's Nuclear Submarines," *Financial Times of London*, September 28, 1992, A8.

57. In this regard, certain forms of non-radioactive dumping may present no appreciable risk to the environment and at the same time be more cost effective than disposal on land. If efforts to inform the public more fully about the nature, extent and possible effects of radioactive dumping practices are not forthcoming, there is a danger that the stigma surrounding them will be extended to all forms of dumping, constraining a cost-effective, environmentally-sound means of disposal as a consequence.

58. M.A. Lange, et al., *Audit Report: Arctic Monitoring and Assessment Program, First Implementation Plans*, AMAP Report 93:5 (Oslo: Arctic Monitoring and Assessment Program, 1993), 5–6.

59. Arctic Monitoring and Assessment Task Force, *Report to Ministers*, 26. Details of the first IASAP meeting can be found in International Atomic Energy Agency, *Working Material: International Meeting on Assessment of the Actual and Potential Consequences of Dumping of Radioactive Waste into Arctic Seas* (Vienna: International Atomic Energy Agency, 1993).

60. *Ibid.*

61. *Ibid.*, 27.

62. For a good discussion, see Clifton Curtis, *The London Convention*, 544–46.

63. David E. Pitt, "Pentagon Fights Wider Dumping Ban," *New York Times*, September 26, 1993, A8.

64. *Ibid.*

65. In this regard, the most recent report of the Arctic Monitoring and Assessment Task Force notes that "even though knowledge has been gained on the behavior of radionuclides in the Arctic region ... there are still severe gaps in the scientific information that have to be filled if long term assessments on future consequences are to be obtained within reasonable uncertainties." In particular, the report notes that there is an urgent need for information on potential leakage from disposal sites. Arctic Monitoring and Assessment Task Force, *Report to Ministers*, 26.

66. McIlroy, "Soviet Nuclear Dump Threat to North," A3.

67. For an extended discussion see Tariq Rauf, "Post–Cold War Naval Arms Control in the Arctic Region: Reductions in U.S. and CIS General-Purpose Nuclear Submarines," in Tariq Rauf and Peter Gizewski, *Naval Arms Control: Implications for the Arctic Ocean Region of Limits on Attack Submarines and Cruise Missiles*, Aurora Papers 14 (Ottawa: Canadian Center for Arms Control and Disarmament, September 1992), 1–34.

68. This proposal has been advanced by the North Atlantic Cooperative Council, a joint NATO and former Warsaw Pact members' forum. Movement toward its adoption has yet to occur.

69. On this point, see David Cox and Tariq Rauf, *Security Cooperation in the Arctic: A Canadian Response to Murmansk*, Report of the Panel on Arctic Arms Control (Ottawa: Canadian Center for Arms Control and Disarmament, 1989) and Peter Gizewski, *Arctic Security After the Thaw: A Post–Cold War Reassessment*, Report of the Panel on Arctic Security (Ottawa: Canadian Center for Global Security, January 1993). In addition to the call for a circumpolar perspective, both reports advance arms control proposals similar to those discussed above.

3

Environmental Degradation and Regional Instability in Central Europe

Barbara Jancar-Webster

This chapter examines the relationship between environmental degradation and regional instability in Central Europe. The point of departure is the research of Thomas Homer-Dixon, who examines the potential for environmental degradation to contribute to political and economic disruption, more particularly linkages between "environmental stress" and "acute conflict."[1] The extent and seriousness of environmental degradation in Central Europe clearly has the potential to generate conflict among nations, while national rivalries and political and economic instability (e.g., in the former Yugoslavia) have already contributed to large-scale ecological disruption. In the broader view, environmental devastation may also affect prospects for political stability. It is still unclear whether the democratic transition will increase or decrease environmental risks.

Recent findings from the natural sciences have profoundly altered our understanding of the nature of ecosystems, their resilience and adaptability to changing circumstances. Previously, we had thought of "nature" as neutral, immune to the impact of human intervention. Unmanaged or ravaged land "went back to nature" and nature then took care of it. During the sixteenth century, Europeans began to see nature as one vast machine that operated like giant clock-work. If man could understand how nature worked, he could in a sense harness nature to his needs. This view impelled the industrial and agricultural revolutions. Only recently have we realized that human activities have a decided impact on nature. Nature does not just passively "take it," but reacts in often unpredictable ways with "surprise."[2]

Response to surprise creates its own problems. History suggests that after an initial period of innovation and exploration, all technological development tends towards monoculture. As a technological monoculture matures, the network of institutions that diffuse it becomes increasingly rigid, denying the system the flexibility to respond quickly to surprise. When humans finally do take action, they intervene in a dynamic, not static, environment. Intervention that directly addresses one environmental issue may contribute to the deterioration of another environmental area, or exacerbate a related social or economic problem. Even more dangerous, a course of intervention set in motion at one historical moment may produce, at some time in the future, highly negative political, socio-economic or environmental consequences that could not be predicted when the choice to intervene was made. Choosing solutions to their very serious environmental problems poses especially high risks to the Central European countries because their social, economic and political institutions have collapsed under the weight of economic and environmental "surprise" resulting from the rigidities of the former system. Entire societies are seeking to develop new institutions on the ashes of the old. Institutional immaturity (too much flexibility) gives the new governments insufficient resilience to manage effectively the dislocations arising during the transition: a continuing rise in pollution, unemployment, lack of capital, impoverishment of large sections of the population, and resurgent ethnic rivalry. Throughout the region, instability rules.

The Model

The relationship between environmental degradation, regional insecurity, and the possibilities for war may be visualized in a three-dimensional relationship as set forth in Figure 3.1. The optimal solution to all three sets of problems should be located in the decision space in the upper right quadrant of the figure. The worst-case solutions are found in the lower left quadrant. Geophysical, political, economic and socio-cultural factors are key variables affecting the outcome in any case. We shall briefly discuss each one of these in turn and then attempt to examine their interaction in four specific environmental problem areas.

The Geophysical Factor

As elsewhere in the world, the environmental problems of Central Europe are linked one to another. But the problems are compounded by the small size of the countries, multiple borders and the disintegration of previous political entities. The Czech Republic, Slovakia and Hungary are also land-locked. All of these factors make issues of trans-boundary pollution a crucial factor in the nexus of environment and security.

FIGURE 3.1 Linkages Between Environmental Quality and Security

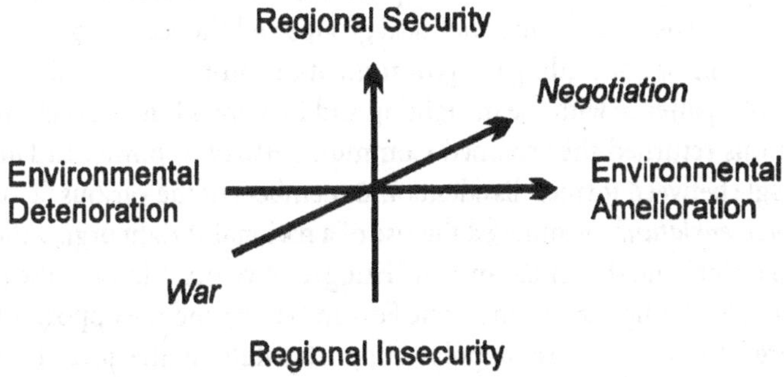

The dieback of the forests in the Krkonose National Park, on the frontier of Northern Bohemia where Poland, the Czech Republic and Germany meet, is testimony to the problems faced by small countries in their attempt to handle trans-boundary pollution generated within the region. The radioactive fallout from Chernobyl provides the most sinister evidence of the region's cross-boundary vulnerability to pollution generated outside the area. In addition, few waterways lie wholly within one East European country. The Elbe rises in the Czech Republic and empties into the North Sea at Hamburg, Germany. The Danube rises in Germany, and flows through six European countries before it empties into the Black Sea in Romania. Conflicting national demands upon the use of these waterways have increased rather than abated pollution.

Since environmental degradation most often transcends national borders, the economic and social problems it engenders are also intra-regional in character. One state alone typically cannot solve a given environmental problem, nor can that state compel neighboring polluters to take action. Most often, several countries are the polluters. In some cases, countries see attempts to control trans-boundary pollution as a threat to national independence or domestic self-determination. Obstacles to international cooperation must therefore be sought in the political, economic and social spheres as well.

The Political Factor

Since the end of communist rule, there has been fierce jockeying for power between the various forces of the former communist elite. The key issue has been the pace of "decommunization," i.e., the transfer of man-made industrial assets and natural resources into private hands. In Czecho-Slovakia,[3] the 1992 election of a pro-market reform minister in the Czech Lands and a go-slow nationalist in Slovakia precipitated the break-up of that country in January 1993. In Poland, 1992 saw not one but three governments, all locked in a struggle with the presidency over constitutional questions and with each other over the pace of reform. The splintering of political groups and the accusations and counter-accusations of not ridding the government of communists resulted in the loss of public patience with the in-fighting and in demands for new elections.[4] The elections returned the renamed Communist Party to power. In Hungary the struggle between former dissidents and members of the various factions of the old *nomenklatura*[5] encouraged the rise of a nationalist right urging the defeat of the old elites and the renaissance of "Hungarian values."[6] In 1992, the two largest parties, the Hungarian Democratic Forum (HDF) and the opposition Alliance of Free Democrats, lost popular support, while at the local level, former Communists, in the renamed Hungarian Socialist Party, staged a political comeback.[7]

This pattern of in-fighting is being repeated in all the other Central European states. With the exception of the Czech Republic, in all cases, the former communist elites are reemerging with a strengthened personal hold over the industrial and natural resources of their constituency. The public knows that the old oligarchic and patron/client networks are still functioning. It sees bureaucratic power being converted into economic assets,[8] and feels helpless to do anything about it. The elite retention of the "commanding heights" of the economy has done little to lessen the distance between the rulers and the ruled, and quite possibly has increased it.

The in-fighting plays a highly negative and divisive role in regional efforts at environmental amelioration. Not enough time has elapsed since the fall of communism for the education of a new elite generation, raised and trained in a democratic system. Many leaders view elections as a one-time expression of popular opinion and have no concept of the responsibility of the elected to the electorate. Public office continues to be viewed as an invitation to garner privilege, not as a public trust. Many, particularly at the local level, are inexperienced in providing leadership. Trained to follow orders, they are unfamiliar with the mechanics and politics of decision-making. The national governments tend to promulgate contradictory economic and environmental regulations, without establishing clear priorities. It is not surprising that in most cases the regulations are ignored. At the very most, they are used as bargaining chips in the deals local elites are trying to make with foreign investors. Local leaders have few "role-models" to follow who encourage change. They also lack access to international meetings, where they could establish the international collegial contacts that would help them reform their jobs and reach out for community support. With most political effort invested in the struggle for power, environmental problems become just one more item for manipulation on the power agenda.

On the intra-regional level, the power struggle has promoted the reassertion of national identity. As politicians seek to reinforce their positions among an increasingly alienated public, they turn to nationalism to garner support. A new variety of intolerant chauvinist nationalism has effectively divided Moldova into two states, encouraged irrendentism in Hungary and Romania, splintered the Caucasus and brought atrocities to the former Yugoslavia that have not been seen in Europe since the Second World War. Neo-nationalism may have its roots in the traditional nationality concerns of the region, but it is better understood as the elites' new-found ideological weapon in their struggle to control natural resources and technology. As such, the new nationalism is divisive rather than inclusive, splitting people from one another, creating jealousy of prerogatives and jurisdictions, and insisting on exclusive closed spaces. Such a mindset does not augur well for international cooperation, particularly the kind of cooperation that entails relinquishing national sovereignty to address intra-regional environmental problems.

The Economic Factor

Central Europe is fast entering the North-South dichotomy. In the North, Poland, the Czech Republic, Hungary, and Estonia are making slow but steady progress towards a market economy.[9] Latvia and Lithuania are following suit. The South is less prepared to make the transition to a market economy. Slovakia, Bulgaria, Romania and Serbia were to a large extent industrialized under communist regimes. In none of these countries has privatization taken off. Bulgaria's stabilization program has been hampered by difficulties in constructing the institutional infrastructure of a capitalist system. Romania is faced with triple digit inflation, a $600 million balance of trade deficit and high unemployment. Almost one half of the population is now considered to be living below the poverty level, and one Romanian in seven is barely subsisting.[10] Slovakia faces a very uncertain future. War has set back any moves towards economic improvement in all the republics of the former Yugoslavia, Moldova, and the Caucasus. Ukraine is on the verge of bankruptcy.

In such an economic setting, environmental issues play a secondary role. In the South, the struggle for survival dominates. In the North, concerns focus on moving the economy forward. In 1988-89, the region seemed to be leading the world in popular demands for environmental action through regime change. Once the regimes did change, it became clear that environmental degradation was viewed as a symbol of regime arbitrariness[11] rather than as a serious problem demanding a serious solution. There is little understanding of environmental issues outside the major cities, and what understanding there is, is submerged beneath the day-to-day struggle to remake one's life.

The Socio-Cultural Factor

Political culture affects the states' receptiveness to international cooperation. Here again we find the North-South dichotomy. All the northern tier countries played formative roles in the religious, scientific, economic and political revolutions of the last five hundred years that created modern Europe. All learned and benefitted from political behaviors that operated "within system." At the turn of the century, all developed conservation movements that operated across borders. All these states today see integration into the European Union as a guarantee of their national independence. All proclaim the primacy of environmental values even if they do not act upon them. Even before the fall of communism, these countries were joining regional environmental initiatives and reaching out across frontiers. In the former Yugoslavia, the two Yugoslav republics with the closest contacts to the West were once lands of the Austro-Hungarian Empire, Slovenia and Croatia. Slovenia was the first of the Yugoslav republics to hold free elections and the first to develop an organized republic-wide environmental movement.

By contrast, Romania, Bulgaria, Serbia, Macedonia and Albania experienced the "otherness" of the non-European, Islamic civilization of the Ottoman conquest.[12] Successful political behavior was perceived as possible only from outside the existing imperial system, and relations between peoples and cultures in the Balkans were typically characterized by confrontation and conflict rather than negotiation. As a result, regional concerns relating to nationality and national space have most often been resolved through war. In this context, environmental quality becomes one with national space.

The two different cultural experiences cannot help but influence the progress of environmental remediation in Central Europe. The northern states are better prepared for the transition to a Western-style polity. They have closer ties with the West. Western capital, including funds for environmental remediation, flow into the region. Environmental officials and activists from environmental grassroots organizations move easily between the major West European cities and Prague, Warsaw and Budapest. By contrast, the South remains trapped in its ethno-cultural conflicts.

These four factors (the geophysical, the political, the economic and the socio-cultural) determine the parameters of the decision space in our model for inter-regional stability in Central Europe. No one factor operates exclusively along one axis. However, the geophysical factor has special reference to the environmental axis, the economic and socio-cultural factors operate primarily along the regional security axis, and the political factor is decisive in defining the points on the war/negotiation axis. For example, it is difficult to create functioning international regimes (political factor) in the absence of mutual confidence and trust (socio-cultural factor) on the part of the signatories. Conflict (political factor) has wrought ecological havoc (geophysical factor) in much of the former

Yugoslavia, and at the same time has undermined the will or desire to cooperate (socio-cultural factor) in environmental rehabilitation.

To obtain a more precise understanding of how these factors interact, we first look at two issues where environmental degradation has been a cause of tensions: energy and water, with a special focus on the Gabcikovo-Nagymoros controversy. Then we examine two issues located on the war/negotiation dimension: progress in domestic legislation and regional environmental cooperation, and the civil war in Yugoslavia.

Case Studies

Energy

Since the reactor exploded at Chernobyl, nuclear power has been a highly visible issue.[13] The accident gave a special stimulus to the expansion of independent environmental groups all over the region. Chernobyl virtually created *Rukh*, the opposition movement in Ukraine, and thanks to the accident, environmental and public protests forced the abandonment of several nuclear energy projects and a declaration of a moratorium by the Ukrainian government on the construction of new reactors. Among the power stations closed were those in the disputed Crimea.[14] In Poland, there was a veritable explosion of grassroots groups after the accident. In Bialystok, Wroclaw and Krakow, thousands of workers signed protests against atomic energy. In May 1986, the newly founded Independent Ecological Committee in Lublin began regularly to inform the public of environmental hazards in the Lublin area. In an open letter to the Sejm (the Polish parliament), the Polish Ecological Club appealed to the legislators to place nuclear energy under public control and subject its continuing use to a national referendum. In Czechoslovakia, Austrian Greens protested in Prague and Bratislava against the construction of Temelin just miles from the Austrian frontier. Young Czech sympathizers were immediately arrested.[15] But Chernobyl probably had its greatest impact in Yugoslavia, where popular attention was already focused on a nation-wide debate over the construction of four new nuclear power plants. Starting in a high school in the suburbs of Belgrade, moving to Llubljana and then across the whole country, protest mounted to stop nuclear power completely. In December 1988, the federal Parliament voted in favor of a moratorium on nuclear power until the year 2000.[16]

The issue was so salient that it figured prominently in the first free election campaigns in Lithuania, Slovenia and Czechoslovakia. Lithuania's Sajudis Party promised that, if elected, it would close the plant at Ignalina. The Czech Civic Forum promised that, if it were elected, Temelin would be closed. Vaclav Havel personally endorsed this position. In Slovenia, one of the battle cries of the newly-formed Green Party was to close down Krsko, the nuclear power plant whose energy is shared between Croatia and Slovenia. In all cases, the victorious parties quickly went back on their campaign promises. Faced with hard Russian bargaining over oil and other deliveries, the Lithuanian authorities found it impossible to close Ignalina. Havel quickly announced that it was unrealistic to close Temelin. The country needed a cheap, domestically produced source of energy. In an interview with the author in the summer of 1990, the new Slovenian Minister of Energy, member of the Green Party, described the building of Krsko as a policy of the "time of irresponsible gigantomania," made possible by the political monopoly of the Communist Party. But, he continued, the truth is that the Slovenians cannot afford to close the facility.

The revelation that the nuclear plants in the former German Democratic Republic (GDR) were more unsafe than had been previously thought heightened fears about the safety of all nuclear plants in Central Europe. In March 1992, the announcement of an accident at the nuclear power plant near St. Petersburg received wide attention in the national media, and the plant authorities went to great pains to demonstrate that the accident bore no resemblance to that at Chernobyl. The news touched off a flurry of concern about Chernobyl, where the Ukrainian State Atomic Inspectorate subsequently found serious violations of safety procedures and low work morale. Unfounded rumors proliferated. The most exciting one was that there had been an accident in the first reactor at Chernobyl in December 1991, but news of it had been suppressed.[17] In May 1992 a commission of experts from the Group of Seven (G-7) countries recommended that all the old RBMK (graphite-moderated) models be closed.[18] Then on May 19, a turbine was damaged at the Khmel'nitskii-1 plant in Ukraine, causing a three-hour shut-down. The damage was followed by a subsequent rise in humidity levels due to heavy rains which caused a circuit breakdown in the reactor's generator. During the summer, there were reports of similar small accidents at other Ukrainian nuclear plants.

In Bulgaria, the nuclear plant at Kozloduy continues to present problems, despite attempts to upgrade safety practices from the slipshod safety habits of the communist regime. The two new reactors already meet most Western safety standards, and the Bulgarians are trying to meet Western criticism of the four old ones. However, inspectors from the International Atomic Energy Agency (IAEA) in 1990 found radioactive contamination of ground water around the plants and instances of excessive exposure of workers to radiation.[19] In January 1993, experts from the Group of 24 (G-24) developed countries declared that the plant would be the first in the area to receive substantial foreign aid to update equipment and improve safety.[20] The Slovak nuclear power facility faces the same criticisms. The risk of a serious accident from all these plants is admittedly very high. Colleagues in St. Petersburg told the author that the only thing preventing a catastrophe at the nuclear plant there was the training and caliber of the personnel.

Despite the public airing of nuclear problems since the end of communist rule, demonstrations and protests against nuclear energy no longer occur. Economic considerations prevail. Without nuclear power, in many cases production would decline even further and living conditions would become intolerable. Electric power is not only necessary at home. It can also be sold for hard currency abroad. At one time, Kozloduy produced not only 40 per cent of Bulgaria's electricity but a small surplus which the government was able to sell to the Austrians. Chernobyl produced power not only for the Ukraine, but also for Belorussia (now Belarus), Slovakia and Hungary. The Ignalina power plant in Lithuania continues to export electric power to Kaliningrad Oblast in Russia.

The post-communist governments are faced with very hard choices. International experts recommend closing the old plants. Public opinion is sympathetic. But, as yet, there is no viable alternative to nuclear energy. Russian oil must now be purchased for hard currency. Coal-fired plants are the number one cause of acid precipitation and forest die-back in the region. Equally important, nuclear plants are also a bargaining chip in international negotiations. Since Belarus cannot buy electricity from Ukraine, the government plans to build its own nuclear plant. The energy going to Kaliningrad from Ignalina means that the Russian government cannot totally disregard Lithuanian views on other issues, such as the removal of Russian troops from Lithuania.

Problems with the import of other energy resources accentuate the problem. Belarus and Ukraine squabble with Russia over the prices and supply of oil and natural gas imports. Ukrainians see Russia dictating terms of trade despite the fact that Ukrainian money and manpower went into developing Tyumen' and other oil fields.[21] At the same time, Russia has been under constraints from the International Monetary Fund (IMF) to raise the price of oil to world market levels, but Ukrainians prefer to believe that the Russians are deliberately "doing" them in.[22] Who can assure them that is not the case? Russia also exerted pressure on Estonia in 1990 by shutting off supplies of power to the country.

There is little the new governments can do to help themselves. Some help has come from Western Europe, notably through the European Community's Program of Assistance to Poland and Hungary for Economic Reconstruction, or, as it is known by its French acronym, PHARE. As its title suggests, the program was initially set up to aid Poland and Hungary in economic reconstruction, but it has expanded its activities to include all the northern tier countries. It donated about $4.7 million to evaluate the nuclear facilities in Czechoslovakia and to help upgrade their technical standards.[23] Representatives from the IAEA and Western, particularly French, firms are highly visible in all the countries. Proposals by General Electric to upgrade the reactors at Temelin have been met with loud protest by Austrian environmental groups. But in this author's opinion, the West has not yet taken seriously enough the risk that Central European nuclear plants pose to Europe and the world. Russian and

Ukrainian experts feel isolated in their efforts to address safety issues. The costs are more than any government can bear. Money from G-7 or other Western sources so far has been coming only in small amounts. In this context, it is understandable that President Kravchuk has procrastinated in signing the START treaty. START deprives Ukraine of its most formidable weapons, while seemingly bringing nothing in return.[24] Procrastination has brought renewed attention from the Clinton administration and promises of financial assistance to dismantle the weapons. For its part, the United States is not eager to appropriate funds to assist in the Chernobyl clean-up. The Freedom Support Act of December 1992 clearly states that the U.S. taxpayer will not pay to clean up pollution in the former Soviet Union. And the author was told privately that U.S. agencies are reluctant to sink money into what looks like a vast pool of corruption, preferring to select smaller, more manageable problems, like air pollution monitoring, where a small investment may yield immediate and visible returns.

The environmental risk posed by nuclear energy and nuclear weapons becomes doubly serious when coupled with the general energy problem. Failure to solve the energy issue in all the former communist countries will result either in continued reliance on highly polluting coal or international bids to expand the construction of nuclear plants. Either solution threatens to increase instability in the region. Pollution from coal combustion has pushed northern Bohemia close to the ecological barrier where no further development can take place. Air pollution emissions in Krakow exceed national standards most of the year. Life expectancy at birth in all the Central European countries is on average five years below that in Western Europe and the United States, due in no small part to the effects of a polluted environment. Further deterioration in living conditions resulting from increased ecological degradation can only add to the pervading disenchantment with the transition and encourage demagogues with simplistic nationalist solutions like reconquest of the Soviet empire, ethnic repatriation, or ethnic cleansing. Another result may be increasing out-migration from the region, already greater than at any time since the Second World War. Dismal as these prospects appear, the encouragement of nuclear power is not necessarily the most appropriate answer. Another nuclear disaster will have untold consequences for the region, for Europe and for the world.

In the case of energy, then, environmental deterioration is contributing to regional (and global) insecurity, as the geophysical factors of either poor or polluting energy sources undermine public health, lower the quality of life and contribute to out-migration. The points on the environmental and stability vectors are on the negative side. The points on the negotiation/war axis at first might seem to be positive, but are probably closer to zero. Discussions are under way to upgrade existing plants and Western nuclear firms are interested in extending their expertise. However, the desire of the national governments to be as energy independent as possible means that economic, socio-cultural and political factors will encourage them to pursue the nuclear option until or unless some other energy solution becomes available. The interaction between our four factors thus projects a decision space tilting negatively into the area defined by environmental deterioration, war and regional insecurity.

Water

After energy, water ranks second as an environmental area that raises important security issues in Central Europe. The years of communist rule were characterized by rapid deterioration in water quality. In Poland, by 1986 only four per cent of all surface water was classified as being drinkable after disinfection; 39 per cent was classed unfit for any purpose. In Czechoslovakia, although only 27 per cent of the major waterways have been put in class IV, the worst class, the Elbe and Berounka Rivers were considered 100 per cent polluted by 1980. One of the last demonstrations in Prague before the fall of the communist regime involved a group of mothers protesting the fact that there was no safe drinking water for baby formula. In Hungary, the Danube has long ceased to be blue, and the Tisza River is heavily polluted. In the former Yugoslavia, the Sava River was called a dead river in 1980. The Dniester and the Don are similarly polluted.

Water problems in Central Europe's northern tier have been and continue to be a source of friction. One example is the Oder River, which rises in Bohemia, crosses the border and empties into the Vistula River in Poland. Waste from Czech plants upriver has caused heavy metal and other forms of pollution across the border in Poland. In 1987 Polish nightly television news carried reports of a demonstration in Wroclaw involving ecological groups and students protesting the accidental discharge of heating oil into a tributary of the Oder by a lime and cement factory near the Czech town of Ostrava. The Poles asked for compensation. The Czechs refused.[25] Unfortunately, cleaning up the Oder water system required money, which neither side had at the time.

Fortunately, water quality has now been recognized as a serious problem in virtually all of Central Europe and there appears to be good will on all sides to solve water problems. A few of the many regional initiatives follow:

- The Elbe River has long been used by all the riverine countries to dump waste. In 1990, Czechoslovakia took the lead in forming an Elbe Commission with representatives from that republic, the Federal Republic of Germany, the GDR, and the Commission of the European Community (EC). In 1992, the EC funded two projects relating to Elbe water quality in the Czech lands: the development of a monitoring system, and the construction of an incineration system to burn the sludge now being dumped into the Vltava, which flows into the Elbe, to reduce pollution of the main river and decrease sedimentation at the port of Hamburg.[26]

- To help clean up Polish waterways that end in the Baltic Sea, Sweden has allocated $40 million to Poland for sewage treatment on the Vistula and Oder Rivers. Discussions are under way to apply the Elbe Commission model to the Oder to resolve the Polish-Czech dispute; this model may also eventually be applied to the Danube.
- The Baltic Marine Environment Protection Committee is one of the oldest initiatives, formed in 1980. In 1988, the member countries agreed to reduce the 1987 emission levels by 50 per cent in 1995. The agreement was reconfirmed in 1990 by the signing of a declaration by the Baltic states and a representative of the European Commission. The declaration calls for the establishment of an action plan for 100 priority sites, where the best available technology will be installed at both industrial plants and municipal sewage treatment facilities. Four international banks have agreed to fund the initiative: the World Bank, the European Investment Bank, the European Bank for Reconstruction and Development, and the Nordic Investment Bank.[27]

Some of the most interesting developments have been cross-border initiatives at the local level. Before the Soviet Union fell apart, there was agreement between the Ukrainian and Moldavian republics on management of the Dniester River basin. This agreement has been renegotiated. Before Yugoslavia collapsed, Croatia and Slovenia were active participants in the Alps-Adria project that spanned republican and local governments in Yugoslavia, provincial and local governments in Italy and Austria, as well as the national governments. Croatia and Slovenia continue to participate in the project, which involves information gathering and sharing. Yugoslavia also signed the Mediterranean Basin Agreement.

There have thus been strong thrusts towards cooperation to secure water quality. But cooperation cannot be taken for granted. Water can be an effective weapon in regional politics. It is generally little known that the Crimea has no water of its own. All the water comes by canal from a reservoir on the Dnieper River, one very good reason why Crimea remains part of Ukraine.

To refer again to our model, while the seriousness of water pollution indicates a negative point on the environmental vector, the general recognition of the problem, the intra-regional steps taken to form water regimes, and the support of European countries outside the region are all positive developments. The decision space for water therefore is found somewhere within the area defined by environmental deterioration, regional security and negotiation.

The Gabcikovo-Nagymoros Controversy. The Gabcikovo controversy exemplifies the tension that may be produced by decisions involving multiple use of one waterway. The origins of the controversy go back to the first decades of this century, with the first investigations by hydrologists of the possibilities of utilizing the Danube for power. In 1913, a Swiss firm was awarded the concession for developing a project to utilize the river between Bratislava and Gyor, but the First World War brought cessation of all plans. In 1946, the Hungarian Authority of Water Energy initiated research regarding the possibility of building a dam at the Danube bend. In 1951, the pre-war plans were revived when the Hungarian and Czechoslovak governments started joint research for power development on the Danube between Bratislava and Budapest. In 1956, the Council for Mutual Economic Assistance (CMEA) approved a plan for the comprehensive utilization of the Danube from the Slovak and Austrian border to the Black Sea. Included in the plan was the concept of the Gabcikovo-Nagymoros dam complex. In 1963, the Czechoslovak and Hungarian governmental representatives agreed on a joint investment project with a 50 per cent share for each side. The Slovaks assert that the Czechoslovak President at the time, Antonin Novotny, objected to proceeding with the project because of its cost and the matter was put on hold until 1971. Novotny was a Czech, they argue, and saw no immediate need for a new power plant in Slovakia. During the interval, research was undertaken on alternatives to the dam, and scientists from both sides checked out the design.

Following the 1968 Soviet invasion of Czechoslovakia, Slovak Gustav Husak became President in 1969. In 1971, the Hungarian-Czechoslovak Committee on Economic, Technical and Scientific Cooperation (CETSO) set up a Joint Technical Committee on the project. This committee adopted the outlines for a joint investment project as it was conceived in the earlier inter-state agreement in 1973. The next year, both governments approved developmental goals for the project. 1977 brought a definitive interstate agreement between the two governments with both parliaments voting their approval. In 1978, the Slovaks started construction on the upper part of the dam. At the beginning of the 1980s, the Hungarians asked for partial interruption of the construction because of financial difficulties. CETSO agreed to an environmental impact assessment and on altered deadlines. The assessment was coordinated by the water management authorities of the two countries and endorsed by the Hungarian government in 1985 with small modifications of the original project. The Hungarians then restarted construction on their part of the dam. In 1986, Hungarian and Austrian banks negotiated a private agreement with the approval and guarantee of both governments on the extension of Austrian credit of about $600 million for construction at Nagymoros. The loan was to be repaid by electricity between 1996 and 2016. With the Austrian loan, construction began in earnest at Nagymoros. Construction was again approved by the Hungarian Parliament in 1988.

Events, however, had already gone beyond the Hungarian government's control. From the early 1980s on, Hungarian biologist Janos Vargha mounted a concentrated opposition to the dam; in 1986 he received the alternative Nobel

Peace prize for his efforts. Opposition to the dam drew increasing numbers of Hungarians into the semi-legal protest movement, one of the few outlets for political opposition at the time. Vargha's "Danube Circle" expanded into demonstrations with thousands of participants. In early 1989, the Hungarian government urged the Czechoslovak government to accelerate construction. But massive protest in the streets brought the formal suspension of construction on the Hungarian side in May 1989,[28] and stoppage of all construction at Nagymoros in October.[29]

The very age of the project, and the years during which it was discussed, rediscussed and then finally approved, indicate the strength of the political and economic forces behind the dam construction. When the Hungarians abandoned the project, the Slovaks were furious. Their part of the dam was already built. They had been counting on it, as had the so-called Hungarian water lobby.

The geophysical values of the project are debatable. Proponents of the scheme argue that hydro-electric power is clean and cheap, and that the dam is not environmentally disruptive. It merely harnesses the natural flow of the river for human purposes. Opponents argue that the energy is not cheap since the whole river bed has to be diverted, and that the river is part of a vital ecosystem. The operation of the dam will change water levels, impacting on available supplies of drinking water and water for agricultural use. The changed flow would alter the BOD content in the river, requiring the rebuilding or new construction of sewage treatment plants. Finally, and most importantly, a single dam, like the one at Gabcikovo, cannot provide sufficient energy on its own. To get adequate water flow, the river would have to be held back and the water released at peak times. Holding the water back would further reduce water levels, making the river virtually unnavigable; hence the need for the second dam at Nagymoros. Thus, if the Hungarians abandon Nagymoros, the Slovaks have to abandon Gabcikovo.

Before Slovak independence, Vaclav Havel went on record in support of the Slovak dam. While Czechs generally have been opposed to the dam, support among Slovaks has been high. The one group in Slovakia solidly against the dam is the Hungarian minority, centered in Komarno. The Slovaks accuse the Hungarian government of deliberately inciting the Hungarians in Slovakia. Tensions on both sides are high, the more so because many Slovaks interpret the Hungarian position as a return to the inter-war policy supporting the territorial reconstitution of the Hungarian kingdom as it was before the First World War.

Gabcikovo and the Hungarian minority in Slovakia may not be issues for which Slovakia or Hungary is willing to risk its international reputation. Both governments have agreed to a review of the project by the European Community (EC), and have indicated they would abide by the findings. Toward this purpose, the EC under the PHARE program has provided some $3 million.

However, the question remains whether either side will accept findings that undermine its position on the issue.[30] Slovakia's move to complete the divergence of the Danube by the end of 1992 signaled its continuing commitment to the original project. Hungary also has not sounded overly eager to compromise. In an interview with *East European Reporter* in the summer of 1992, Hungarian Deputy State Secretary responsible for Central and Eastern European Regional Co-operation and National Security, Ivan Baba, called the issue a problem of environmental security:

> Our position is that the project is a bad investment and a bad heritage that we should sort out on a bilateral basis, but if this is not possible then we should try to come to a multilateral solution involving EC experts. … What we cannot accept is the solution proposed by the last Slovak government by which the Danube is diverted. For, although the river is principally significant in terms of shipping, it also demarcates the border between our two countries. Any compromise we reach must allow the Danube to remain the same size and take the same course as today.[31]

Environmentalists are not taking any chances. In 1990 a new environmental movement was formed from the remnants of Vargha's Danube Circle. Once again located in Hungary, it is called ISTER, the Greek name for the Danube River. One of the movement's first priorities is to push forward a proposal for the creation of a protected environmental region along the Danube on the border of Slovakia, Austria and Hungary. The area would be an international park under trilateral management with the objectives of securing drinking water supplies, improving quality of life, maintaining shipping lanes, and protecting the ecosystem.[32]

The EC evidently believes the controversy sufficiently explosive to take an active part in its resolution. How the Community deals with this highly sensitive issue may help establish criteria for other cases as well as guidelines for EC arbitration of similar conflicts in the future.

The Gabcikovo-Nagymoros controversy in many ways is illustrative of the negative impact of our four factors. As in the other cases we have examined, geophysical constraints are paramount. Slovakia simply has no other substantial energy resources. The economic downturn associated with Slovakia's independence has done nothing to increase popular support for the current Slovak government. Indeed, Slovak television has become increasingly critical of the Meciar regime. The most viable political recourse is an appeal to nationalism, with its deep socio-cultural roots. Nationalism incites nationalism, with the resulting Hungarian charge that the changed borders produced by the construction of the Slovak part of the hydro-project raise the issue of Hungarian security. On the positive side, the two countries have agreed to remediation, thereby setting in motion a process of negotiation that, with sufficient support from the EC and outside countries, may eventually resolve the dispute, although a final solution is by no means clear. We may locate the decision space for the controversy within an area described by the end points: regional insecurity, environmental amelioration and negotiation.

National Efforts at Reforming Environmental Legislation and Regional Cooperation

Since 1989, environmental legislation in Central European countries has been subjected to extended review and considerable revision. Several observations may be made about the review process. First, the reform of legislation and environmental administration has progressed slowly and unevenly, even though all the countries, including the Baltic states, are committed to adapting to EC standards. Central and East European environmental professionals are frequent and regular visitors to Brussels. The Czech Republic has perhaps gone farthest to bring its new environmental legislation into conformity with EC regulations. In 1990, Czechoslovakia passed a landmark law on waste management, providing for the first time a statutory basis for waste management regulation. Time and commitment are the two difficulties most often cited by officials when queried on the status of the legislative review process. Officials interviewed at the newly created Environmental Ministry of the Czech Republic in 1990 told the author that they were overwhelmed by the demands made upon them. On the one hand, they were under a great deal of pressure to draft new legislation, including a comprehensive law on the environment, at the same time as they were charged with up-dating branch law already in existence. On the other hand, the focus of the government was on economic renewal, and environmental legislation was a low priority. During 1992, both Czechs and Slovaks were occupied with the "velvet separation." Hence, much of the proposed environmental legislation, such as an Environmental Impact Assessment Act, as well as new branch regulations, have been put on hold.[33]

In Hungary, the Ministry of the Environment and Water Resources has been reorganized into the Ministry of Environmental Protection and Regional Development. Water resource projects were assigned to the Ministry of Transportation, and the new environmental ministry was given responsibility for Hungary's five national parks, the National Meteorological Office and the National Preservation Agency. However, as elsewhere, jurisdiction over enforcement and regulations remains scattered among a variety of agencies. For example, the environmental ministry has jurisdiction over emission levels, but regulation of soil and water pollution is under the Ministry of Social Welfare.[34] Aside from the reorganization, Hungary has done little to upgrade its laws. Most in need of redrafting is the Comprehensive Law passed in 1976.

As each country emerged from under the communist regime, steps were taken to enforce the collection of air and water pollution penalties and water-use taxes. These have been used in virtually all the countries to establish a national environmental fund to help pay for pollution clean-up. The new environmental administrations have experienced considerable difficulty in collecting the monies. Industry has questioned both the legitimacy and legality of the penalties, while legislatures have fought with the environmental authorities over where the money is to go and how it is to be distributed. Although the fines themselves may provide some income for environmental clean-up, they are far below the level that would dissuade industry from further pollution and encourage companies to invest in pollution control.[35]

Environmental practitioners in the region are adamant in their assertion that environmental conditions will not improve unless the new governments take a different attitude towards the environment. According to Jacub Szacki of Poland's Institute of Physical Planning, what is necessary is a strategy based on the concept of environmental foresight, compliance with the principle of the long-term use of the environment, a ban on further environmental degradation, implementation of "the polluter pays" principle, incorporation of environmental impact assessment (EIA) procedures, and compliance with international legal norms on environmental protection.[36]

In the opinion of environmental professionals, governments do not consider the environment a first priority. With an apathetic public, there is no popular domestic force pushing legislatures or executives to take action, and there is little money to carry out improvements. All predictions foresee a worsening of environmental conditions in the 1990s before the economic situation will have sufficiently improved so that governments can turn to the environment.

For their part, the new environmental agencies have yet to demonstrate an ability to mobilize public opinion and exert influence. It is the author's impression that the relative influence or ability to act of any given agency continues to be based on pre-transition bureaucratic politics. In most cases, environmental personnel have changed little from the communist period, except perhaps in the top positions. Many have been working in the environmental bureaucracy for at least a decade and are thoroughly acquainted with national problems and priorities. Likewise, many are simply continuing or expanding programs begun under the communist regime. There has been remarkably little change in thinking about environmental problems.

Legislative reform is a case in point. There is much talk about drafting new laws "to reflect" the new reality but, with the possible exception of the Czech law on solid waste, no new law has yet been written that either reflects or responds to market conditions. The Russian law passed in December 1991 and made public in March 1992 is in the spirit of the old legislation. The concept of taxing industry for whatever pollution the enterprise emits, whether within norm or above norm, comes straight from the thinking of the 1980s. The tax is set to equal only a certain amount of the industry's profits, not exceeding nine per cent, in order not to put the industry out of business. The rational response of industry, as research at Moscow State University demonstrated, was for a factory to continue to pollute, secure in the knowledge that the government would not close it down and that some day all the money it was paying into the environmental fund as pollution taxes would be returned to it to pay for new equipment.[37] The Russian legislation has served as a model for all the Central Asian Republics and, to some extent, for Ukraine and the Baltics. Because research and methodology were highly centralized under the Communist regime, these capabilities are weak or absent in most of the new republics. The situation is more serious because the worst polluters tend to be the large, still state-owned, enterprises that have resisted privatization. The lack of a solid legal framework not only hampers implementation and enforcement of pollution policy, it renders efforts in that direction ineffectual. A second and equally serious impediment to effective implementation is the continuing inflation plaguing most countries, decreasing the value of environmental funds.

On the inter-regional and international levels, there has been a surprising amount of activity. In addition to agreements noted above, there are new inter-regional agreements.

- In 1990, with West European backing, Czecho-Slovakia, Hungary and Poland signed a free trade and standardization agreement known as the Visegrad Triangle. With the formation of Slovakia as an independent state, this group has now expanded into a very loose organization called the Central European Initiative. The Initiative aims to provide the region with common environmental standards.
- In February 1993, Poland, Hungary, Slovakia, Ukraine and Romania signed an agreement creating a Carpathian Euroregion. Joint development projects within the region aim to attract foreign investment and improve the local economies. Long before the agreement was signed, however, frontier communities in Ukraine, Hungary, and Poland were already cooperating in a common effort to develop a single regional environmental management plan for the Carpathian mountains. The signing of the agreement opens up possibilities for direct Western funding to the area as well as Western assistance in the development of technical and organizational skills necessary for the transition to a democratic, market-based community.[38]
- Information-gathering and exchange have been facilitated by the establishment in September 1990 in Budapest of the Regional Environmental Center for Central and Eastern Europe with seed funding of $12 million (commonly known as the Bush Fund, because President Bush

inaugurated the Center). The Center is non-governmental and acts as a clearing house for the dissemination of information about any and every aspect of the environment, including environmental technologies and administration, and how to set up independent non-profit environmental organizations or governmental institutions.

The key to any environmental initiative has been Western funding and Western support. While some might argue that the funding has been modest, as of June 1993 the G-24 countries had committed $60 billion in assistance to Central and Eastern Europe, of which around eight per cent can be considered for environmental purposes.[39] The major Western environmental organizations and foundations have actively contributed to the restructuring of environmental management and policy. These include the World Wildlife Fund, Friends of the Earth, the Institution for European Environmental Policy, the Environmental Law Institute, the World Conservation Union, Greenpeace, the Environmental Development Fund, the Rockefeller Brothers' Fund, the MacArthur Foundation, and the International Institute for Applied Systems Analysis (IIASA) in Austria. If there is a negative aspect to the assistance provided by these organizations, it is quite simply that each has its own agenda and objectives. That agenda may have integrity, but does not necessarily reflect the very complex needs of the region.

For example, financial support for the opposition to the Gabcikovo-Nagymoros project has come from the World Wildlife Fund/Conservation Foundation, which has long advocated the abandonment of the entire project and the establishment of a regional park along the Danube.[40] Although one might wish that the Danube could be returned to its original state throughout the length of the 17-mile construction site, the cost would be prohibitive.[41] The central Slovak concerns are flood control and energy supply. Western environmental organizations may argue that Slovakia can generate more energy by conservation than by dam construction, but to do so requires the reconstruction and modernization of its economy. While modernization may be the long-term savior of the Central European environment, it is an expensive and difficult process requiring critical decisions on the import of technology.[42] In this author's reading of the documents, the international environmental organizations have shown an insensitivity to local needs and a rush to impose solutions possible in the United States but not available given local conditions.

If Western governmental, environmental, and financial institutions are to advance environmental protection in Central Europe, they must study the local situation and options, not dictate the agenda. Western organizations should also understand that environmental conflicts are potentially threatening to regional security. National emotions in Central Europe are very close to the surface, and the authority and legitimacy of the new governments are weak. A perception of environmental injustice or the use of an environmental issue to promote revanchist or national gains could be the match that ignites the tinderbox of violence, triggers a governmental crisis, or results in mass migration from the region.

Given the extent of intra-regional and international negotiation, the solution space for our third case would at first seem to lie entirely within the positive area formed by the three vectors. But domestic economic and political factors preclude a hasty assignment. So far, regional governments have visibly failed to take the initiative in rewriting environmental legislation and developing appropriate implementation and enforcement procedures. For them, economics has priority over the environment, because economics is the chief determinant of election outcomes. The intra-regional environmental regimes are functioning largely because of funding and support from institutions and countries outside the region. Were this support to cease, regimes like the Elbe Commission or the Carpathian Euroregion might well become non-functional. For these reasons, the points on the regional security axis must run negatively through zero towards regional instability. The decision space is thus defined by negotiation, environmental amelioration and regional insecurity.

War and the Environment: The Yugoslav Case

We have one tragic case of acute conflict in Central Europe, the former Yugoslavia. The central environmental concern is control of land and territory. For example, the *krajina* is a region along the north side of the Sava River in what used to be the old Hapsburg border zone. In the eighteenth century, to defend her empire from the Turks, the Empress Maria Theresa offered land on the Austrian side of the river to any Serb that had the courage to defend it. The Serb could keep his land on the one condition that he protect it with his life from any Turks who dared cross the river. Serbian peasants crossed the river and settled. During the Second World War, they formed the backbone both of Tito's Partisan Army and Mihailovic's Chetniks. They also bore the brunt of Croatian Fascist violence. The proclamation of Croatian independence, with its emphasis on Croatian nationalism, re-awakened the old fears. Serbs had lived in the region for generations. They consider this land to be Serbian, to be tilled by Serbs.

Second is the question of control of natural resources, as exemplified in the fighting along the Dalmatian coast. Serbia does not have a port on the Adriatic. Montenegro, which remains part of the rump Yugoslavia, has Bar, but the harbor at Bar or Budva is inferior to that at Split. Without a larger harbor, the new Yugoslavia becomes a landlocked country. A final settlement in Bosnia depends upon a harbor not only for the Serbs but for the Moslems as well. The Bosnian Moslems may reluctantly agree to the division of the country on the condition that they receive a pathway of land to the sea and an appropriate harbor.

Finally, there is the question of water, energy, and mineral resources. In February 1993, the Croatians broke the terms of the United Nations monitored cease-fire that was to expire that month, to retake a bridgehead on the national highway linking the Zadar peninsula to the mainland, and most importantly to re-establish Croatian control over the Peruca Dam. The dam is one of a chain of dams on the lower Cetina River that were built in the 1950s and 1960s to provide water and electricity for the Dalmatian coast. It is about 50 kilometers east of Split. Downriver from it are three more dams, the oldest of which is at Kraljevac. The total installed capacity of these plants is 615.2 megawatts (MW), with a mean average annual production of 2,972 gigawatt-hours. Peruca itself is an earth and rockfill structure with a central clay core 65 meters (213 feet) high. The installed capacity of the plant is only 41.6 MW, but the dam performs the important function of regulating water flow downriver to the two plants below.[43]

The dam and hydro-plant were taken by Serbian forces on September 17, 1991. During and after that engagement, the Croats argue, the Serbs deliberately set explosives under the dam with the intent to destroy it. The Serbs allowed no one near the dam for one year after the occupation. The ceasefire in August 1992 brought United Nations forces to the dam, but the Croatians were not allowed to assess damage. As time ran out for the United Nations to fulfill the conditions of the ceasefire, the Croatians decided to launch their own offensive and recapture the dam, claiming that the condition of the dam was precarious. If the clay works had been undermined by explosives, and water were not let out before the autumn rains, the earthwork structure might not hold. If it broke, some 50,000 people downstream would be flooded out. Power has not been produced at Peruca since the Serbian occupation and the lines that joined Peruca to the power grid, including the entire Dalmatian Coast, have been cut. Nevertheless, the plants downstream have been operating. Croatian authorities told the author that while the system had lost much of its power generation capacity, the Croatian Electricity Board was still able to generate enough electricity to keep the city of Split in operation. Their real concern was with flooding and water supply. Flora and fauna, particularly crayfish in the Cetina River, have been destroyed because of irregular water supply. Agriculture has suffered because there has not been sufficient water for irrigation. Since the Croatian recapture, British engineers have been invited to the site. According to their report, it will take at least two years to rebuild the dam. New outlets have been made in the dam and the water is being let out in preparation for repairs. With the war far from over, it is highly doubtful that reconstruction will start soon.

The Peruca Dam is but one instance of the significance of natural resources as objects of war. Since the ceasefire in Croatia, the Croatian Ministry of Environment, Town Planning and Housing has attempted to ascertain the status of the country's national parks and protected areas now occupied by the Serbs. The evidence is incomplete, as Croatians have not been allowed near the areas. The Ministry fears that the limestone barriers around the Plitvice Lakes may have been mined, trees felled and wildlife killed "uncontrollably." In the marshland of the Kapackirit Park, destroyed industrial plants in the nearby towns as well as uncontrolled wastes from local pig farms may have polluted the groundwater. As at Plitvice, there has been widespread felling of trees and killing of wildlife. The full tally of the effect of the war on Croatia's protected natural areas will only be known when the war is over.[44]

The former Yugoslavia was not rich in natural resources. While 30 per cent of its land was arable, cropland was not equally distributed among the republics. The same was true of mineral and fossil fuel reserves. All sides know where they are and know their value. A nearly impossible dimension of the Bosnian crisis is to find a way to divide the country so that one side does not "benefit" from Bosnia's resources at the expense of the other two. While Serbia may talk loudly about the Battle of Kosovo Field in 1389 and the importance of Kosovo as the traditional Serbian home, Serbs are well aware that the majority of the former Yugoslavia's coal reserves lie in Kosovo. Similarly, the Vojvodina in the Danube flood plain of northern Serbia is one of the few areas in this mountainous region suitable for large-scale farming. Historically, it was occupied primarily by Hungarians and during communist rule the population continued to be largely Hungarian. Fears are now rising that a new ethnic cleansing may appear to Serbia the best available means to secure Serbian control of the fertile region.

Bloody national clashes taking place in Yugoslavia are not purely or even primarily the product of centuries of ethnic hatred. Real environmental objects and real territory are at stake. With the virtual breakdown of governmental capacity in the region, valuable natural resources have become objects of conquest, as they were when the barbarians descended upon the Roman Empire. With reference to our model, the decision space for the problem is located totally within the worst-case solution defined by environmental deterioration, war and regional insecurity. In such a situation, a durable peace would seem possible only with the victory of one side and the annihilation of the other, a prospect too painful to contemplate.

Conclusion

This chapter offers only an initial investigation into the complex relationship between environmental stress and regional stability in Central Europe. The brief review of energy, water, national and international legislation and agreements, and the impact of war suggests the following summary findings.

1. Environmental stress is "built into" regional relations because the region as a whole is geophysically characterized by highly unequal access to natural resources and ability to control regional pollution.

2. Where there is a perception of severe geophysical constraint, as in the Gabcikovo-Nagymoros controversy, or extensive trans-border water or air pollution, environmental stress may increase tension in the political and socio-cultural spheres. This tension may be manifested by precipitous drops in public health, increasing inter-ethnic clashes, forced or voluntary out-migration and heightened international friction.

3. Where the political system has broken down, as in the former Yugoslavia, natural resources, energy, water, and land become important military objectives, the aim being to destroy the enemy's economic and socio-cultural foundations and to secure one's own resource future.

4. The ability of the region's states to develop a comprehensive environmental legal framework is highly dependent on economic, technical and political assistance from the European Community, the international lending institutions, and the United States. This assistance, however, has tended to reflect the political, economic and environmental agenda of Western governments and organizations.

5. Perhaps the most important finding of this research is that there was no decision space located within the positive parameters of the model without the presence of data showing support for regional activities from outside the region. The research thus suggests that negotiation, environmental amelioration and regional stability in Central Europe may not be objectives the region can achieve on its own. The West plays a critical role in influencing the direction decisions take through the kinds of management strategies it chooses to support in the environmental, economic and political spheres. The European Community appears to have developed the most effective working relations with the northern tier of Central European states. Closer West European ties to the northern tier are largely a product of a common socio-cultural history. EC arbitration of the Gabcikovo-Nagymoros controversy will provide a clearer idea of the degree to which Western Europe actually understands those aspects of East European culture and society that are not based on West European cultural values but on East European needs. In the former Yugoslavia, the kindest interpretation is that the West failed miserably to understand the depth of the cultural clash between Bosnian Moslems, Bosnian Serbs and Bosnian Croats. The worst interpretation is that Western non-decision was a deliberate action wilfully permitting the destruction of the Bosnian environment and society as non-relevant to Europe.

If Western support is decisive, then the West must assume greater responsibility than it has to date for what happens in the region. The findings suggest that Western input may have its optimal impact through more careful monitoring and coordination of assistance programs designed for maximum effectiveness along all dimensions of the model. Given the exceedingly high vulnerability of the region to political and economic collapse, it is especially important to target for in-depth study the most severe existing inter- and intra-nation environmental problem areas with the aim of finding the best fit between environmental stress and regional management capabilities.

Notes

1. Thomas Homer-Dixon, Jeffrey H. Boutwell and George W. Rathjens, "Environmental Change and Violent Conflict," *Scientific American* (February 1993), 38–45. See also Leigh Sarty's discussion of Homer-Dixon's research in his contribution to this volume.

2. For more discussion of this process, see Barbara Jancar, "Technology and Environment in Eastern Europe," in James P. Scanlan, ed., *Technology, Culture and Development: The Experience of the Soviet Model* (Armonk, N.Y.: M.E. Sharpe, 1992), 171–78. See also Thomas F. Homer-Dixon's discussion of this point in his unpublished paper, "Environmental Change and Acute Conflict: A Research Agenda," submitted to the Global Environmental Change Committee, Social Science Research Council, March 1991. The article cited above in *Scientific American* is a shortened version of that report.

3. In 1990, the federal Parliament formally changed the name of Czechoslovakia to Czecho-Slovakia. In January 1993, the two nations split to become the Czech Republic and the Republic of Slovakia.

4. Anna Sabbat-Swidlicka, "Poland: A Year of Three Governments," *RFE/RL Research Report, 1992: Experimenting with Democracy*, 2, 1 (January 1, 1993), 102–07.

5. Editors' note: Under communist rule the *nomenklatura* were those persons selected by responsible Communist Party bodies for important positions in all spheres of social, economic and political life.

6. "Political Storm in Hungary," *RFE/RL Research Report*, 1, 40 (October 9, 1992), 15–29.

7. For a review of Hungarian politics in 1992, see Judith Patacki, "Hungary: Domestic Political Statemate," *RFE/RL Research Report, 1992: Experimenting with Democracy*, 2, 1 (January 1, 1993), 92–95.

8. For a brilliant presentation of this thesis, see Elmer Hankiss, "Reforms and the Conversion of Power," *East European Reporter*, 3, 4 (Spring-Summer 1989), 8–9.

9. *Christian Science Monitor*, January 13, 1992, 4.

10. Data taken from *RFE/RL Research Bulletin*, 10, 1 (January 4, 1993).

11. Barbara Jancar, "Chaos as an Explanation of the Role of Environmental Groups in East European Politics," in Wolfgang Rudig, ed., *Green Politics Two* (Edinburgh: Edinburgh University Press, 1992), 164–71. Also, Jancar, "Technology and Environment in Eastern Europe," 184–85.

12. Huntington calls areas where two cultural traditions meet the "fault lines of civilization." Samuel Huntington, "The Clash of Civilizations," *Foreign Affairs*, (Summer 1993).

13. On the impact of Chernobyl in the Soviet Union and its successor states, see the chapter by David Marples in this volume.

14. David Marples, "Chernobyl and Nuclear Energy in Post–Soviet Ukraine," *RFE/RL Research Report*, 1, 35 (September 4, 1992), 54–55.

15. *Rude pravo*, May 28, 1986.

16. For more detail on the movement, see Barbara Jancar "Ecology and Self-Management: A Balance Sheet for the 1980s," in John B. Allcock, John H. Horton, and Marko Milivojevic, eds., *Yugoslavia in Transition: Choices and Constraints* (Oxford: Berg Publishers, 1992), 337–64.

17. Radio Moscow, December 17, 1991.

18. *Izvestiya*, July 1, 1992.

19. Malcolm W. Browne, "Bulgaria Must Fix Run-Down A-Plant," *New York Times*, December 8, 1992, A13.

20. *RFE/RL News Briefs*, 2, 5 (January 18–22, 1993), 10.

21. A senior official of Ukraine's state Oil and Gas Committee told Reuters on January 12, 1993 that Kiev may ask Moscow to pay world salaries to the 200,000 workers in Russian oilfields if Moscow insists on world prices for its oil. As reported in *RFE/RL News Briefs*, 2, 4 (January 11–15, 1993), 3. In the summer of 1993, Ukraine was ready to sell its part of the former Soviet Black Sea fleet back to Russia in exchange for oil but, on pressure from the Ukrainian parliament, the government denied such an agreement had taken place.

22. A. Hatchynsky, "Oil as a Means of Diktat," *Demokratychna Ukraina*, March 31, 1992.

23. Information from the Czech Ministry of the Environment. Also, Stanley J. Kabala, "EC Helps Czechoslovakia Pay Debt to the Environment," *RFE/RL Research Report*, 1, 20 (May 15, 1992), 56–57.

24. At the January 15, 1993 summit in Moscow, Yeltsin stated that Russia was ready to guarantee Ukraine's security and that the "text of the guarantee would come into force" as soon as Ukraine ratified the START-l Treaty and the Nuclear Nonproliferation Treaty. *RFE/RL Research Report*, 2, 5 (January 18–22, 1993), 1. As of this writing, Ukraine has neither accepted Russian security guarantees nor officially said it would dismantle its nuclear weapons, despite Western and U.S. offers of financial assistance for this purpose.

25. Barbara Jancar, "Environmental Politics in Eastern Europe," in Joan DeBardeleben, ed., *To Breathe Free: Eastern Europe's Environmental Crisis* (Washington, D.C.: The Woodrow Wilson Center Press and the Johns Hopkins University Press, 1991), 44–45.

26. Kabala, "EC Helps Czechoslovakia," 56; "International Treaty to Protect Elbe signed by Germans, Czechs, EC Official," *International Environmental Reporter*, October 24, 1990, 436–37.

27. The World Bank, "Poland Environment Strategy Study," *Conclusions and Recommendations* (Washington, D.C.: The World Bank, 1991), iii. For more information on the Baltic Sea region, see Juris Dreifelds' contribution to this volume.

28. Barbara Jancar, "The East European Environmental Movement and the Transformation of East European Society," in Barbara Jancar, ed., *Environmental Action in Eastern Europe: Responses to Crisis* (Armonk, N.Y.: M.E. Sharpe, 1993), 192–219.

29. The chronological history of the Gabcikovo-Nagymoros controversy was adapted from Miklos Persanyi, "Danube Dams or Democracy," in Jancar, *Environmental Action*, 134–57.

30. After a meeting on January 14, 1993, between Slovak, Hungarian and European Community experts, Dominik Kocinger, a Slovak government commissioner, told reporters that the Hungarian and Slovak views were still very far apart. According to Kocinger, each side had raised different demands regarding the future of the dam project. *RFE/RL News Briefs*, January 11–15, 1993, 20.

31. "Interview with Ivan Baba," *East European Reporter*, 5, 4 (July-August 1992), 55–56.

32. "The Blue Danube" (Interview with Tamas Fleischer), *The East European Reporter*, 4, 2 (Spring/Summer 1990), 79.

33. For a discussion of the old form of environmental legislation and problems in making the transition to the new, see Eva Adamova, "Environmental Legislation in Czechoslovakia," in Jancar, ed., *Environmental Action*, 42–57.

34. Karoly Okolicsanyi, "Hungary: Antall's Government Proves Less than Green," *RFE/RL Research Report*, 1, 33 (August 21, 1992), 65–69.

35. The Department of Natural Resource Use of the Economic Faculty of Moscow University conducted a two-year review in 1990–1991 of industrial compliance in the Moscow area with payment of pollution penalties. The review concluded that if the level of the fines were set high enough to encourage investment in pollution control, the enterprise would go out of business.

36. Jakub Szacki, et al., "Political and Social Changes in Poland: An Environmental Perspective," in Jancar, ed., *Environmental Action*, 21–23.

37. Viktor Loksha, Thesis for *kandidat nauk* (Ph.D. equivalent), Department of Natural Resource Use, Faculty of Economics, Moscow University, Moscow, December 1992.

38. The development of cooperation in the Carpathian Euroregion is being promoted by the Institute for EastWest Studies with offices in Prague, Budapest, Warsaw, New York and Atlanta, Georgia. Institute for EastWest Studies, *Annual Report 1992–93*, 17–18, 26.

39. Institute for EastWest Studies, *Annual Report*, 23.

40. For a discussion of what the Czechoslovak government clearly considered interference by "local unbiased environmentalists," the green lobby, and external groups such as Eurochain, Global 2000, and WWF, see *Vodohospodarska vystavba Bratislava* (Bratislava Water Authority), "Gabcikovo-Nagymoros Project: Standpoint of the Czecho-Slovak Side and Answers to Questions," April 1992 (mimeographed).

41. *Ibid.*

42. On this point, see *The Economist*, February 15, 1993.

43. T. Megia, "The Effect on Peruca Dam of the War in Croatia," *International Water Power and Dam Construction* (January 1993).

44. Details from Republic of Croatia, Ministry of Environment, Town Planning and Housing, "Report on the State of Damaged Natural Heritage of Croatia" (Zagreb, 1991), unpublished.

PART TWO

The Environment and the Energy Sector

4

The Post-Soviet Nuclear Power Program

David R. Marples

In the 1980s, the Soviet Union embarked on an ambitious program to construct new and expand existing nuclear power capacity to meet planned electrical power requirements for the 1985–2000 period. According to the program, nuclear energy would, by the end of the century, provide about 30 per cent of Soviet electricity production and over 50 per cent in certain republics (including Lithuania and Ukraine). The program was curtailed abruptly in the wake of the 1986 Chernobyl disaster. A powerful environmental movement developed in Ukraine that eventually forced the Ukrainian government to declare a moratorium in 1990 on the commissioning of any new reactors in that republic. In 1991, a second decision was made to take the Chernobyl station off line completely by the end of 1993. In Russia, the program also was halted, mainly as a result of local protests from communities close to the reactors under construction. After the disintegration of the USSR in December 1991, some observers assumed that the Soviet successor states would continue the general policy line that prevailed during the USSR's final years: energy programs would not involve significant reliance on nuclear power generation.

Such an assumption, however, did not anticipate the calamitous events of 1992. In that year, industrial output plummeted and the attempt to switch the former command-administrative economy of the Soviet Union to market-oriented structures brought rapid price rises, including in the energy sphere. These price rises in Russia soon affected neighboring republics. The selling price to Ukraine of Russian oil from Siberia rose by 300 times in 1992, despite the fact that Ukraine had, in the Soviet period, contributed to Siberian oil development with labor and materials. Even these prices were not at world levels. The price of gas increased by 100 times. Inflation stood at more than 2,000 per cent.[1] The Republic of Belarus also experienced rapid price rises throughout 1992 that outpaced wage increases. This republic has long been dependent on nuclear energy to meet its electricity needs, but from stations outside its borders: Rovno in Ukraine, Ignalina in Lithuania, and Smolensk in Russia.[2] Thus the energy situation became critical in the region as a whole.

In the turbulent climate of hyperinflation and rapid rises in energy costs, a new trend soon emerged, namely, a strong movement advocating renewed dependence on civilian nuclear energy. This movement was spearheaded by officials of the Russian Ministry of Nuclear Power and Energy but it extended beyond the borders of Russia. A strong pro-nuclear element developed within the government of Belarus (a republic that had never put into operation a nuclear power station, though one had been under construction in the 1980s), in Ukraine, Armenia, and other areas. Here we will examine past and present trends in nuclear energy development and provide an assessment of the Russian, Ukrainian and proposed Belarusian nuclear energy programs.

The Soviet Nuclear Energy Program

The former Soviet Union was well endowed with natural resources, possessing well over one half of the world's potential coal reserves based on geological structure. It occupied first place in the world for the production of oil and natural gas; and first or second for coal. Advocates of nuclear power, however, advanced several arguments for its increased exploitation, such as the high costs of organic fuel development, the concomitant pollution of the atmosphere with nitrogen and sulfur oxides, regional fossil fuel imbalances, high conventional energy transportation costs, and the need to preserve hard currency earnings from oil and natural gas exports.

The Soviet Union's nuclear development dates from 1954, with the commissioning of the world's first (experimental) civilian nuclear reactor at Obninsk.[3] The two main reactor designs are well known: the graphite-moderated (RBMK) reactor and the pressurized-water (VVER) reactor. The first civilian reactors in the USSR designed for regular operation went on line in the 1960s at Beloyarsk (100 megawatt [MW] capacity, RBMK), and a 210 MW station at Novovoronezh (VVER). However, a major program of expansion took place only in the 1970s. The RBMK program was further developed at the Sosnovyi Bor station near Leningrad (now St. Petersburg) in 1973 and the VVER program at Novovoronezh. A standardized VVER-440 design was later replaced with a 1,000 MW version also pioneered at Novovoronezh.

At the time of the Chernobyl accident, the existing RBMK stations were at Sosnovyi Bor, Kursk and Smolensk, in Russia; Chernobyl, in Ukraine; and Ignalina, in Lithuania. VVER stations, on the other hand, were located at Novovoronezh, the Kola Peninsula and Balakovo, in Russia; Rovno, Zaporozh'ye and Nikolayev, in Ukraine; and Metsamor, in Armenia. The Chernobyl accident did not halt the commissioning of new reactors. For example, two went into service in Ukraine (Rovno-3 and Zaporozh'ye-3) later in 1986. By January 1, 1987 there were 43 operating reactors in the Soviet Union, with a total capacity of 30,000 MW.[4]

Approximately 36,000 MW of capacity were under construction at that time. For the most part, this expansion was to be based on a standardized design, namely, the VVER-1000, which was also to be used widely in Eastern Europe and other allied countries, such as Vietnam, Mongolia, and Cuba. In addition to the new VVERs, existing RBMK stations were to be completed, with the exception of Chernobyl, where reactors 5 and 6 (85 per cent and 15 per cent complete, respectively, on April 26, 1986) were to be mothballed. The RBMK program's fulfillment entailed the commissioning of Kursk 5 and 6, Smolensk 3 and 4, and Ignalina 2 and 3. A new station was envisaged in Kostroma, central Russia. By 1987, the RBMK had come under heavy criticism from nuclear experts because of its positive void coefficient and design flaws, deficiencies already recognized by some experts in the 1970s.[5] An exclusively Soviet design, it had been regarded within the Soviet nuclear industry with pride and there was great reluctance to abandon it completely. The fact that it can be refuelled on-line renders it economical, and it has a relatively short maintenance period. In addition to the RBMK, the nuclear authorities also intended to expand their small program of "fast breeder" reactors at Beloyarsk with the BN-800 and BN-1600, a highly controversial design.[6]

Nuclear Power for Heating and Nuclear Energy Development in the Twelfth Five-Year Plan

As a result of the pre-Chernobyl confidence in nuclear power, plans also were under way to construct a series of heat-supply (heat-only, or AST) stations at Gor'kii (now Nizhnii Novgorod), Voronezh and Arkhangel'sk, with twin reactors based on a 500 MW version of the VVER design. These are known as "single-purpose district heating nuclear plants," and were to be built within five kilometers of major towns.[7] A second variant is nuclear power and heating stations (ATETs), also to be located near major cities such as Odessa, Khar'kov and Minsk. These units would involve twin VVER reactors (1,000 MW each) based on new turbine units. The original Soviet plan called for the start-up of these stations by the year 2000. Their construction was to follow the harnessing of nuclear power stations for heating purposes in several locations, including Rostov, Tatarsk, and the Bashkir station, albeit at projected costs not appreciably less than the operation of plants based on organic fuel.[8]

An early example of such use of nuclear power was the Bilibino station in the Arctic region, south of the East Siberian Sea, which has been in operation since 1974. The costs of providing heat from such reactors were said to be 2-2.5 times less than regular heat supply based on fossil fuel and/or from AST units, when the reactor is used exclusively for heating purposes. They were to be located within 20 kilometers of major cities.[9] Total electricity production for the Soviet economy in the period 1985–1990 was to be raised from 1,545 billion kilowatt hours to 1,840–1,880, with the contribution of nuclear energy to rise from 170 to 390 billion kilowatt hours (from 11 per cent to 21 per cent of the total).[10] Thus the total increase in capacity expected by the end of the plan period was to have been 41,500 megawatts.[11] From the outset, the plan was very optimistic. Even without the Chernobyl disaster, it is extremely unlikely that it would have been fulfilled. As it turned out, total capacity rose by only 11,500 megawatts by the end of 1990.[12]

More significant than the overall increment to electricity production that was to have been achieved through the plan was the saving on conventional fuel that such an addition to power would have entailed. The Soviet coal industry was in the process of re-siting its investment and resources from the European coalfields of the Donbass to Kazakhstan and East and West Siberia, whereas oil and gas reserves were to be maintained as a present and future source of hard currency. This left the more populous European portion of the country at risk of an energy shortfall. Nuclear energy was to fill the gap as it could be generated close to the consumer, as rapidly as possible, and in guaranteed supply, unlike fossil fuel supplies, which fluctuate according to labor productivity and geological conditions and are costly to transport to locations of consumption.

The Impact of Chernobyl

The 1986 disaster at Chernobyl, has been covered in detail elsewhere.[13] Suffice it to say that the accident contaminated a vast area (over 100,000 square kilometers) in Belarus, Ukraine and Russia, and has been responsible for some serious health problems among the populations living in contaminated zones. The economic impact of Chernobyl is still felt today; governments have been unable to deal financially with the public health and clean-up operations, and are now reliant on international aid.

There have still been no official disclosures of the casualty toll from Chernobyl, and the authorities restricted access to the relevant health information for a period of three years. The Soviet reports to the International Atomic Energy Agency (IAEA) always maintained that strict attention was being paid to safety at existing nuclear power units. They also maintained an official air of optimism with regard to nuclear safety, even at times of the heaviest criticism from environmental and other pressure groups. Thus a Soviet team of experts reached the following conclusions in a review published for the accident's first anniversary.

> The causes which led to the reactor accident are associated primarily with errors by plant personnel, who violated established operating regulations. These causes in and of themselves do not have a specifically nuclear

character and thus cannot be considered fatal to nuclear power development.[14]

Moreover, in the post-Soviet period, the Chernobyl station not only continued operating, but relied until recently on the first-generation reactors at units one and two. (Chernobyl-1 is still on line, but unit two has since been dismantled permanently.) Despite official demonstrations of confidence from the nuclear authorities, the station has been riddled with problems, including one potentially serious mishap in 1990.[15]

Despite official reassurances following the Chernobyl accident, environmentalists and political activists mounted an effective campaign to prevent new nuclear reactors from coming on stream. As a result, building and design work were stopped on some 60 Soviet reactors, bringing the nuclear energy program to a standstill. In 1990, the RBMK reactor Smolensk-3 was the only one to come into service.[16] Those at Crimea and Chigirin were abandoned largely as a result of public protests, and the Rostov station was the subject of an official inquiry. Strong protests also occurred at Balakovo, directed at the cessation or suspension of construction of the fifth and sixth reactors there.[17]

Concern over seismic activity in Armenia, after the December 1988 earthquake, led to the mothballing in March 1989 of the only nuclear station (with two reactors) in that republic. In addition, all the nuclear power and heating stations were abandoned by late 1988 on the grounds that it was too risky to build edifices close to major cities. (The Odessa station was already close to completion.) Anger against the ATETs soon spread to the ASTs, and the Arkhangel'sk AST was removed from the grid in early 1990. In response to protests, the Soviet authorities had permitted the IAEA to inspect the Gor'kii station in 1989, and the inspectors evidently gave their approval for start-up. Yet this proved an impossibility in the face of public furor.[18]

In Lithuania, the Ignalina station was the focus of the largest anti-nuclear demonstration to date. More than 280,000 people signed a petition opposing continued operation of the station, and demonstrators formed a ring around the RBMK complex.[19] In Ukraine, the Green World ecological association spearheaded the protests, led by Yurii Shcherbak, a doctor who had visited Chernobyl shortly after the accident and interviewed several of the eyewitnesses at the site.[20] In August 1990, the Ukrainian government introduced a moratorium that prohibited any increase in capacity over that which was in place on August 1, 1990. Decommissioning of the Chernobyl station, originally scheduled for completion by 1995, was to be realized by the end of 1993. The moratorium was scheduled to last for five years.[21] Thus Chernobyl was the catalyst for the emergence of an anti-nuclear movement in the glasnost period of the late 1980s.

The Energy Alternatives

Opponents of nuclear power for the most part advocated increased energy savings through conservation rather than supply-side alternatives. They could point to abundant instances of waste; for example, in Russia the levels of power consumption were virtually unchanged despite a dramatic downturn in economic activity.[22] Russia's Ministry of Fuel and Energy estimates that domestic energy consumption could be cut 20–25 per cent by 2010 through the introduction of more energy-efficient technologies and other conservation measures.[23]

Energy savings depend in large part on imported equipment and technologies. Since funds are insufficient for this, supply-side alternatives are emphasized. Hydro-electric potential has already been developed to nearly its fullest extent in the European republics. Thus, thermal-electric power stations fueled by coal, oil, or gas offer the major alternatives to nuclear.[24] There are not, however, readily available supplies of any of these resources in the regions of major consumption. This fact was given new emphasis by the coal strike of 1991 in Siberia and Ukraine, and by subsequent strikes and catastrophes in the various coalfields in the period 1991–93.[25] One observer has estimated that in the coal mines of Russia, there is one death for every million tons of coal extracted.[26] The attempts to modernize the coal industry have been hindered by an acute shortage of funds and by the militant attitude of the miners themselves. Thus the cessation of the nuclear power program, in the absence of equivalent declines in energy consumption, has resulted in an energy crisis in Soviet successor states.

In the post-Soviet era, the situation has been complicated by disputes between the major states, Ukraine and Russia in particular. Ukraine raised strong objections to being forced to pay higher prices for Russian oil and gas in 1992–93 and, in protest, attempted to impose a tariff on Russian fossil fuel resources transported through Ukrainian pipelines. In mid-1993, Ukraine agreed to pay Russia $80 per ton for oil with an increase to $100 by the end of the year. The world price at that time, however, was approximately $120 per ton.[27]

The Russian oil industry also began to experience difficulties at the beginning of the 1990s. Like other sectors of the Russian economy, the oil industry experienced a drop in output that would have been considered catastrophic in the Soviet period. In 1991, oil production stood at 461.1 million tons, but in 1992, it fell to 395.8 million tons, a drop of 14 per cent in a single year. The anticipated output for 1993 was less than 350 million tons,[28] a reduction of at least nine per cent from 1992. In such circumstances, Russia's primary concern lies in preserving its oil for hard currency exports and for essential uses at home. Thus, Ukraine cannot be reliant on future supplies from Russia, even assuming that it could raise the hard currency required to purchase them. Instead, apart from its nuclear power plants, Ukraine is heavily reliant on the coal industry of the Donbass region for its energy supplies.

All of these questions have provided ammunition for campaigns by nuclear authorities in Russia and Ukraine for the establishment of new energy programs. By 1990, although nuclear power was ostensibly at its lowest ebb, steps were being taken to ensure its future. A campaign of "openness" was inaugurated, for example, in which nuclear "incidents" in the former Soviet republics and every commissioning or start-up of reactors would be reported on the front page of the government daily newspaper, *Izvestiya*. One source suggests that such measures originated as early as 1988, with the establishment of an Interdepartmental Council on Public Information and Relations in Moscow, the object of which was to enhance the public's understanding of nuclear power.[29] The Council was established as a result of nuclear proponents' perceptions that the media were more responsive to the anti-nuclear movement, which provided sensational articles and reports.

The New Russian Nuclear Power Program

In December 1992, the Russian Ministry of Nuclear Power and Industry, led by Viktor Mikhailov, announced an ambitious nuclear power program which was the natural culmination of four years of intensive activity and propaganda. The projected expansion of nuclear power generation startled observers and elicited instant criticism about safety concerns and financing. The new plan did, however, have the approval of the government of the day.

In January 1993, Yevgenii Reshetnikov, the First Vice President of the state organization *Rosatomenergii* (Russian Atomic Energy) noted that no country could survive without an adequate supply of energy, but that only two reactors had been commissioned in Russia since 1986.[30] Clearly the nuclear authorities were taking advantage of the energy problems in Russia to reassert themselves. In an attempt to assuage criticism, Aleksandr Lapshin, also of *Rosatomenergii*, stated at a press conference that the Ministry of Nuclear Power must receive approval from three different agencies before new reactors could be commissioned: the Russian State Committee for the Safe Operation of Nuclear Energy, the State Sanitary Supervision Committee, and the Ministry of Ecology. In his confused description of the overlapping functions of these agencies, however, he implied that the powers of the Ministry of Ecology (which opposes planned nuclear expansion) are limited.[31]

The first section of the program declares that reactors which had been at advanced stages of construction (Balakovo-2, Kalinin-3, and Kursk-5) would be completed by the end of 1995. Regarding the Kursk reactor, a RBMK-1000, Reshetnikov attempted to reassure the public about its safety with the rather opaque comment that:

> It is nominally classified as the RBMK-1000 reactor, but it has been totally rebuilt compared to the units that were installed at the station at first. Its safety margin has been expanded considerably and it will be examined for its ecological safety this year.[32]

The Kursk station was built as a twin to Chernobyl and experienced similar construction and design problems from the outset. The attempt to complete construction there is further indication of the new confidence of the nuclear authorities. One can only assume that modifications have been made to the existing reactor design rather than a total reconstruction, given the extreme difficulty involved in replacing one former Soviet design with another in midstream. It is probable that the authorities have reduced the shutdown time, upgraded the safety features, increased the uranium enrichment, and incorporated similar measures, rather than (as implied above) changing the reactor design itself. Reshetnikov attempted to explain the decision, but in terms reminiscent of the doublespeak used by the former Soviet bureaucracy:

> The point is that we are not beginning new construction, but rather we are undertaking a thorough feasibility study to explore the possibility of building a station acting on the basis of appropriate requests from the local administration.[33]

Reshetnikov then commented on the second section of the program. In certain regions of Russia which are facing energy shortages, "local authorities" had decided to build nuclear power plants in the region based on a new design and size (600 MW capacity). New units were planned at various sites, including the Kola Peninsula, St. Petersburg (at the Sosnovyi Bor site), Khabarovsk, and Kostroma.[34] Later, statements made clear that two new units are also planned for the Novovoronezh station, the staff of which is to be comprised partly of former employees of the Ignalina station who could not obtain Lithuanian citizenship. Smaller units are to be built in remote regions – the original premise for the Bilibino station in the Arctic. Moreover, there are to be discussions about siting future stations across the country as new questions arise over energy needs, again with concentration on the more remote regions of the country.[35]

The program also entails the building of infrastructure for the industry, such as housing and social amenities, including in the remote regions. Feasibility and ecological studies are to be carried out in each area designated for new nuclear power stations. In all the regions, Reshetnikov declared, other possible sources of energy had been considered and ruled out. During the press conference, most attention was given to the question of financing. Two points were immediately evident. First, the Russian government lacks funds to launch such an expensive construction program and is dependent on outside aid.[36] Second, in order to meet the standards of international nuclear stations, it is likely that foreign technology, and therefore hard currency, will also be required. Reshetnikov noted that in order to complete the three units at Kursk, Kalinin and Balakovo, "we will need 33 billion rubles this year [1993]."[37] Some of the costs of the future units, it was noted, are to be met by the conversion of defense facilities. Moreover, given the rate of inflation in 1993, nominal costs increased considerably, and will continue to do so in 1994–95.

The goal is to raise capacity at Russian nuclear power stations from 20,000 MW to 37,000 MW by the year 2010. There is little to distinguish the new program from the Soviet plan for the Russian Republic, with the exception of some uncertainty about the Rostov station and the decision to build nuclear power plants in remote regions of the country. The new Russian plan provides for small stations catering only to the local communities, so transmission problems would be minimized.

Nuclear Power in Belarus

Lacking natural resources, Belarus is heavily dependent upon Russia for energy. The question of energy requirements was addressed in the spring of 1993 by three leading energy specialists of the republic.[38] They noted that all fuel-energy resources of Belarus (the small oil supplies in the south, natural gas, peat and firewood, and forestry byproducts) covered only about 12 per cent of energy needs; the remainder were being imported. Almost 25 per cent of Belarusian electricity needs were being supplied by Russia and Lithuania, from the Smolensk and Ignalina nuclear power plants.[39] Most of the local thermal-electric stations are approaching the end of their lifespans and will soon need to be taken out of service. As in Ukraine, many Belarusians associate economic independence with national survival; they resist the notion of relying on imports to fulfill basic economic needs. Such thinking may also reflect the autarkic values of the current and former Communists who continue to dominate Belarusian politics.

The three energy experts also identified two ways to resolve energy problems: either to increase energy production in the republic or to import power from outside. They challenged the "mistaken impression" that energy difficulties could be resolved through simple conservation techniques such as switching off televisions and lights. What is required, in their view, is a total reconstruction of industry, agriculture and communal services at a cost of billions of rubles and decades of time. However, the need for energy is immediate.[40]

Recently, much attention has been focused on alternative energy sources – solar, wind, small-scale hydro power and livestock waste. Belarus is not in a position to benefit substantially from any of these sources. At best, they could provide 10–15 per cent of total needs.[41] In this context, Russian oil remains crucial. Reductions in Russian oil output, should they lead to reduced oil available for export, will therefore create problems for Belarus.

Even coal and shale are not promising alternatives. Domestic coal is of a low calorific value and has high ash content. Coal-based thermal-electric stations are currently one of the biggest environmental hazards in the European part of the former USSR. It is estimated that one station, with a capacity of 1,000 MW, releases into the atmosphere annually about 100,000 tons of sulfurous acid, 20,000 tons of nitric acid and forms over 750,000 tons of ash.[42] A 1993 study conducted by several research institutes in Minsk has shown that thermal-electric stations in heavily populated areas have caused significant health damage in industrialized regions, with a particularly adverse effect among children.[43] Furthermore, coal output in both Russia and Ukraine has declined considerably over the past decade, and prices for imported coal have already risen steeply.

In conclusion, the energy experts posed a grim future involving energy cutbacks on a broad scale. For example, measures might include a reduction in the volume of cargo and passenger transport,[44] a flexible schedule for each working day, closure of some plants on days of heavy energy demand, and a reduction of the temperature of hot water in apartments. All these measures are short-term solutions, and some had already been adopted by late 1993. At the same time, the total debt of Belarus incurred for import of oil, gas and electricity (mostly owed to Russia) was 140 billion rubles by the end of 1993.[45]

Faced with these problems, Belarusian authorities are seriously considering the nuclear power option, despite the devastating effects imposed on the country by the Chernobyl accident. By the spring of 1992, it was reported that Belarus had decided to construct two nuclear power stations, probably based on French technology.[46] In December 1993, Vladimir Zablotskii, Deputy Chairman of the Committee for Scientific and Technical Progress, affiliated with the Supreme Soviet, held discussions with Russian and Canadian experts in Moscow on the question of building a nuclear power station in Belarus, using a modern design and based on natural uranium and heavy water.[47]

However, two Green Party spokespersons have maintained that the actual number of nuclear power stations being considered in Belarus is not one or two, but seven or eight. The Greens oppose the plan. They point out that intensive energy use occurs in the chemical and metallurgical industries, which are for the most part unprofitable. If energy intensiveness were reduced by 50 per cent, to West European levels, then Belarus would need some 25–30 billion kilowatt-hours annually, a figure that was generated internally in 1978.[48] Such a solution does not, however, take into account the problems of importing raw materials, such as coal for thermal power stations. Further, the Belarusian Greens were lacking in both power and influence in 1993.

Ukraine's Nuclear Power Program

Ukraine still has five stations in operation,[49] with a total capacity in 1993 of 15,880 MW. Two issues loomed in 1993: the status of the Chernobyl station, and the 1990 moratorium on the building of new reactors. In late 1992, President Leonid Kravchuk stated that Ukraine could not survive without nuclear energy. The country had begun to solicit the aid of the IAEA for the preparation and training of qualified Ukrainian personnel for the safe operation of Ukrainian nuclear power plants.[50]

In October 1993, the Ukrainian parliament lifted the moratorium on the construction of new reactors and resolved to keep the Chernobyl station in operation. This decision predictably horrified some of those who had taken part in the anti-nuclear movement.[51] It has frequently been pointed out that Ukraine's nuclear power plants have been particularly accident-prone since independence, possibly a result of the departure of some experienced Russian personnel. Wages for employees at the stations are very low when compared to workers in other energy industries such as coal mining.[52]

Which of Ukraine's stations are likely to bring new reactors on line in the immediate future? Three VVER-1000 reactors (Zaporozh'ye-6, Khmel'nitskii-2 and Rovno-4) were very close to completion at the time of the moratorium. The first could be brought into service by the middle of 1994, while the Khmel'nitskii and Rovno stations could be on line by mid-1995. They could make a significant impact on the Ukrainian economy: in 1992, the station at Zaporozh'ye alone (with five reactors operational) produced 31.5 billion kilowatt-hours of electricity, or 13.3 per cent of total output in Ukraine.[53] Ukraine could also add capacity at the South Ukraine station, which combines a nuclear power plant with a hydro-electric station.[54]

Ukraine's decision to return to the nuclear power program followed directly that of Russia. Perhaps, however, the Ukrainians had fewer options. The Ukrainian economy experienced a near total collapse in 1992–93. Both the reforming Prime Minister, Leonid Kuchma, and the Deputy Premier with responsibility for economic reform, Viktor Pynzenyk, resigned during the course of 1993, while by October, Kravchuk, who assumed responsibilities for the premiership in addition to those of the presidency, declared in a sober address that "monetarism had failed" (some cynical observers maintained that it had not yet been tried). With hyperinflation and an increasingly worthless currency, Ukraine ran into debt with its energy-exporting partners and was obliged to search desperately for other options. This helps to explain why Ukraine entered into an agreement with Iran in 1992 for the construction of a pipeline, 4,500 kilometers in length, to import oil and gas from Iran, starting in the mid-1990s.[55] In this way it hoped to circumvent some of its problems with energy imports from Russia.

Armenia and Lithuania

Turning to the other two republics that have used or currently use nuclear energy, both are at least considering the nuclear alternative for the future. Armenia is in such a desperate energy crisis that it has begun to sink shafts into coal mines not used since the 1940s.[56] A pipeline carrying gas into Armenia from Georgia was blown up during civil strife early in 1993 and this led to serious problems in Armenia. In this context, the government has decided to restart its Metsamor station, located in a zone of high seismic activity.[57] Moreover, the Armenian nuclear power plant needs a regular supply of electric power in order to control the uranium fuel and radioactive deposits at the decommissioned nuclear power station. Without such a supply, authorities fear a "catastrophe on a regional scale."[58] Early in 1993 the country was reported to be receiving only a few hours of electrical power per day.[59]

In Lithuania both the previous Sajudis government (which earlier, as a political movement, had criticized nuclear energy) and the present communist government have continued to rely on the Ignalina station for about 40 per cent of electricity needs.[60] At 1,500 MW, it is the largest capacity RBMK. The station is regarded with particular concern in neighboring Belarus, which has already experienced some radiation leakage from the plant onto its territory.[61]

Some Concluding Remarks

Less than seven years after the Chernobyl disaster, Russian nuclear authorities proposed a bold yet flawed program to meet increased energy needs in the Federation. Later in 1993, Ukraine followed suit, while both Belarus and Armenia gave strong indications that they were also considering the nuclear power option as a means out of an energy impasse. These developments demonstrate the resilience of the group of nuclear authorities and proponents, a pro-nuclear constituency similar to that of the Soviet period. The Russian program seems particularly illogical in a country that has the largest coal reserves in the world and ranks among the world leaders in terms of the size of its oil and gas deposits. At present, it has become financially difficult for Russia to develop any industry that requires imported technology or high-level state investment. This has left the oil industry at a standstill. At the same time, the nuclear industry will require extensive aid if its goals are to be met.

The renewed nuclear commitments of post-Soviet governments are an indirect result of the diluted international response to Chernobyl. Many observers argue that researchers have not always investigated with sufficient thoroughness or impartiality the extent of the health and radiation impact on the most affected sections of the population.[62] One difficulty here is that the scientific expertise rests largely in the hands of those who have long supported nuclear energy. In response to Chernobyl, Soviet nuclear authorities first kept silent, then classified the pertinent information, then blamed the hapless operators who conducted the fatal safety experiment. International attention was not initially focused primarily on the danger of operating RBMK reactors. Only in the early 1990s did the world finally recognize the imperative need for investing money to make former Soviet reactors more reliable.

Concern over the safety of reactors in the former Soviet Union and Eastern Europe has surfaced regularly in the West and Far East. At a July 1992 summit, the Group of Seven (G-7) countries proposed an assistance program to improve the safety of such reactors and estimated the minimum cost at $700 million. To date, however, neither a plan nor much funding has materialized. A breakthrough of sorts occurred in late January 1993, when France and Germany pledged $110 million over three years.[63] The G-7 countries, however, had not envisaged an *expansion* of these countries' nuclear energy program. One Western expert, concerned about Russia's decision to launch a "questionable program," has suggested that a series of measures should be taken, including emergency assistance for the most dangerous reactors, a halt to the purchase of Russian and Ukrainian nuclear electricity by West European countries, and commercial investment in the natural energy resources of the USSR.[64]

Many Russians have become frustrated with the lack of substantial and timely Western aid in overcoming the problems of transition to a market economy. For them, domestically produced nuclear power is a possible and realistic solution to energy requirements. Anti-nuclear environmental movements are in decline, and the nuclear lobby has resurfaced, emboldened with policies as ambitious in scope as any in the past. While some in the international community may fear the consequences of this path, their criticisms are likely to remain ineffectual unless they can offer concrete support for economically viable alternatives.[65]

Notes

An earlier version of this paper was published in *Post-Soviet Geography*, 34 (March 1993). The author wishes to thank Andrew Bond for helpful comments on the original.

1. *Demokratychna Ukraina*, March 31, 1992; *Pravda Ukrainy*, December 30, 1992. The source for the figures was the then Ukrainian Prime Minister, Leonid D. Kuchma.

2. Interview with Stanislav Shushkevich, Chairman of the Belarusian Supreme Soviet, Minsk, Belarus, April 15, 1992.

3. V.A. Legasov, "Atomnaya energetika i nauchno-tekhnicheskii progress," in A.M. Petrosyants, ed., *Atomnaya nauka i tekhnika SSSR* (Moscow, 1987), 13.

4. *Ibid.*, 22.

5. USSR Committee for State Security (KGB), "Construction Flaws in the Chernobyl Nuclear Power Plant," Document No. 346-A, Moscow, February 21, 1979. This document was among those on display at the Library of Congress in 1992. It confirms some of the remarks made about these defects and published posthumously by Valerii Legasov, First Deputy Director of the Kurchatov Institute of Atomic Energy. See David R. Marples,

Ukraine Under Perestroika: Ecology, Economics and the Workers' Revolt (London and Basingstoke: The Macmillan Press, 1991). A "positive void coefficient" means essentially that the reactor becomes unstable at low power.

6. Legasov, "Atomnaya energetika," 16. For a comment on the fast breeder type of reactor, see Judith Thornton, "Chernobyl and Soviet Energy," *Problems of Communism*, 35 (November-December 1986), 13–14.

7. In fact, proximity of heat consumers to sites of power generation is necessary to ensure the economic feasibility of the stations. For background, see *Soviet Geography*, 29 (April 1988), 452–53.

8. V.L. Losev, M.V. Sigal and G.E. Soldatov, "Nuclear District Heating in CMEA Countries," *IAEA Bulletin*, 3 (1989), 48.

9. The distance of existing ATETs stations from the urban centers they supply varies. The author has personally seen only the one near Minsk, which was under construction quite close to the Minsk-2 international airport, approximately 40 kilometers outside the city. The distance in theory depends upon the size of the respective cities. With an electrical output of 4,000 MW, the distance must be at least 25 kilometers for cities of 100,000 to 500,000 population. If the population is over 2 million, the distance must be over 100 kilometers, in theory. Had the Minsk station been brought into service, this would shortly have led to problems as the Minsk population is likely to surpass 2 million by the turn of the century. *Ibid.*, 48.

10. *Pravda*, March 9, 1986; David R. Marples, *Chernobyl and Nuclear Power in the USSR* (London: The Macmillan Press, 1987).

11. Vyacheslav S. Romanov, "Nuclear Power and Public Opinion," *IAEA Bulletin*, 2 (1990), 20.

12. *Ibid.*

13. See, for example, Zhores Medvedev, *The Legacy of Chernobyl* (New York: W.W. Norton, 1990); David R. Marples, *The Social Impact of the Chernobyl Disaster* (London: The Macmillan Press, 1988); and David R. Marples, "Chernobyl: Five Years Later," *Soviet Geography*, 32, 5 (1991), 291–313.

14. V.G. Asmolov, et al., "The Chernobyl Accident: One Year Later," *Atomnaya energiya*, 64, 1 (January 1988), 3.

15. Unit 3 at Chernobyl lost cooling water after a pump shut down. *Soviet Geography*, 32 (April 1991), 289.

16. *Ibid.*

17. *Ibid.*

18. *Soviet Geography*, 31 (April 1990), 311.

19. Marples, *Ukraine Under Perestroika*, 116.

20. The result was his book: Yurii Shcherbak, *Chernobyl: A Documentary Story* (London: The Macmillan Press, 1988). The account was originally published in *Yunost'* (Moscow), 6 and 7 (1987).

21. *Izvestiya*, August 3, 1990.

22. British Broadcasting Corporation, *Summary of World Broadcasts: Soviet Union* (SU/WO263), January 8, 1993, A14.

23. *Interfax Petroleum Report*, January 8–15, 1993, 12.

24. Of the three, an increasingly dominant role has been played by natural gas, which by 1985 had outpaced coal as the main fuel used in central thermal-electric power

stations, accounting in 1987 for 48 per cent of the total fuel balance (compared to 33 per cent for coal, and 17.4 per cent for oil). This situation is of particular significance for Ukraine, which possesses only coal in adequate supplies. *Soviet Geography*, 31 (March 1990), 228 and 32 (April 1991), 276.

25. In the early post-Soviet period, the Vorkuta region was notable for its labor unrest. In December 1992 workers at a coal mine remained on strike despite the fact that it had been declared illegal. The miners were afraid that they faced unemployment as the result of privatization efforts. *Izvestiya*, January 13, 1993.

26. *Izvestiya*, January 12, 1993.

27. Information of the Russian Ministry of Energy, cited in *RFE/RL Daily Report*, July 14, 1993.

28. At the time of writing the official figures for oil output in 1993 were not available.

29. Romanov, "Nuclear Power and Public Opinion," 20.

30. *Washington Post*, January 13, 1993, A15-6; British Broadcasting Corporation, *Summary of World Broadcasts: Soviet Union* (SU/WO263), January 8, 1993, A11; *Stroitel'naya gazeta*, March 17, 1993.

31. "Press Conference by the Atomic Energy Ministry of the Russian Federation," *Federal News Service* (Washington, D.C.), January 21, 1993.

32. *Ibid.*

33. *Ibid.*

34. Kostroma originally was selected as a site for the new RBMK station. Subsequently the design was to be changed to that of a VVER, which suggests that construction had not yet begun.

35. Such plans are based on an expectation of an abundant supply of uranium over the next 15 years. See the financial section of *Izvestiya*, January 14, 1993, viii.

36. This was acknowledged at the January 1993 press conference by officials of the Atomic Energy Ministry.

37. Press conference by Russian Ministry of Atomic Energy, January 21, 1993.

38. The three experts are Aleksandr Mikhalevich, Director of the Institute for Problems of Energetics, Academy of Sciences, Republic of Belarus; Fedor Molochko, Director of the Belarusian Thermal Energy Institute; and Andrei Stavrov, Director of the Republican Scientific-Educational and Information Center for Problems of Radiation Safety, Energetics and Radio-ecological Education, Administration Department, Council of Ministers, Republic of Belarus.

39. The scientists did not elaborate on these stations, but it is of no small significance to the energy equation that both these stations are graphite-moderated, i.e., of the same design as Chernobyl. Ignalina is a RBMK-1500, and Smolensk represents the most modern version of the RBMK-1000, the third, and last, generation of such plants. All three stations are located on the Belarusian border.

40. *Narodnaya hazeta*, March 31, 1993, 1.

41. *Ibid.*

42. *Ibid.*

43. Department of Health, Minsk City Council, the Institute of Radiation Medicine, Ministry of Health, Republic of Belarus, and the Endo-Ecological Center, *Mediko-ekologicheskii monitoring zdorov'ya detei i podrostkov goroda Minska, oktyabr' 1992-mai 1993 g.* (Minsk, 1993).

44. Public transport in Minsk appears to be at the minimal level, i.e., buses and trains are grossly overcrowded and the system is heavily overused. One can anticipate therefore a significant rise in the price for usage of such transport from the current (almost negligible) 5 rubles per ride. A further reduction in volume would cause serious transportation problems for many citizens.

45. *Minsk Economic News*, December 1993, 7.

46. Interview with Stanislav Shushkevich, Chairman of the Supreme Soviet of Belarus, Minsk, Belarus, April 15, 1992. Shushkevich had just returned from Paris where he had reportedly discussed this question with French nuclear experts.

47. *Minsk Economic News*, December 1993, 7.

48. *Zvyazda*, April 21, 1993. The Green Party in Belarus is believed to be small. Based in Minsk, it publishes a newspaper called *Ekologiya Minska*.

49. These are Chernobyl, Rovno, Khmel'nitskii, Zaporozh'ye, and South Ukraine. All except Chernobyl are VVER-1000s.

50. *Robitnycha hazeta*, December 22, 1992.

51. *Vecherniy Kyiv*, October 21, 1993.

52. For example, on June 28, 1993, Zaporozh'ye-3 was shut down because of a sudden rise in pressure. Earlier in the same month, radioactive water had seeped through a wall and contaminated an open area in the same complex. *RFE/RL Daily Report*, June 28, 1993.

53. *Pravda Ukrainy*, April 24, 1993, 2.

54. The South Ukraine station is part of a vast energy complex which includes two hydro-electric stations. The moratorium stalled not only the fourth reactor unit at South Ukraine (Mykolaiv Oblast), but also work on the hydro-electric stations. See *Robitnycha hazeta*, December 18, 1992, 3.

55. *Radio Ukraina*, September 7, 1992.

56. *Izvestiya*, January 14, 1993.

57. *Rossiiskaya gazeta*, January 21, 1993; DJ Peterson, *Troubled Lands: The Legacy of Soviet Environmental Destruction* (Boulder, Colo.: The Westview Press, 1993), 246–47.

58. *Nezavisimaya gazeta*, January 29, 1993.

59. *Pravda*, January 30, 1993. William C. Potter notes that in March 1993, the Armenian parliament revoked its own decree which stipulated that only a national referendum could result in the opening of the nuclear plant. The Armenian government hoped that the station could be in operation by January 1994, using western loans to finance its operation. William C. Potter, *Nuclear Profiles of the Soviet Successor States* (Monterey, California: Program for Nonproliferation Studies, 1993), 3–4.

60. For information on the Ignalina station, see Juris Dreifelds' chapter in this volume.

61. David R. Marples, "The Response to Health Care in Belarus," *Post-Soviet Geography*, 35 (February 1994).

62. See, for example, the "Statement by the Chairman of the BSSR [Belarus] Committee on the Consequences of the Chernobyl Accident," in The International Chernobyl Project, Proceedings of an International Conference, *Assessment of Radiological Consequences and Evaluation of Protective Measures* (Vienna: IAEA, 1991), 45.

63. Justin Burke, "Russia Pushes Expansion of Nuclear Power," *The Christian Science Monitor*, February 2, 1993.

64. *Ibid.*

65. Energy questions, in any case, are generally overshadowed by political events, particularly in Russia. At the time of writing, international opinion was focused almost entirely on two events: the relative success of Vladimir Zhirinovskii's ineptly named Liberal-Democratic Party in the December 1993 parliamentary elections and President Clinton's accord on nuclear weapons with Russia and Ukraine.

5

Energy and the Environment in Eastern Europe

John M. Kramer

Eastern Europe is completely reliant upon an energy producing sector that is totally hostile to the environment.

–*Rzeczpospolita* (Warsaw), 20 October, 1990.

Eastern Europe has pursued an energy policy enormously deleterious to the environment. This policy comprised an integral component of the Stalinist model of economic development that the USSR imposed on Eastern Europe after World War II. It stressed the forced draft development of energy intensive industries, including steel, chemicals, and mining.[1] Consequently, the economies of the East European countries traditionally expended between 30 per cent and 50 per cent more energy than their counterparts in Western Europe to produce the same unit of national income.[2] It is a truism that, all things being equal, higher energy consumption equals higher pollution levels. Further, Eastern Europe consumes the wrong *kinds* of energy to promote environmental quality. Low grade soft coal of high sulfur, ash and cinder content predominates in the production of primary energy in all countries of the region except in Poland, where hard coal predominates.

Therefore, any decisive improvement in the environment will occur only if Eastern Europe reduces its now prodigious consumption of energy in general and of low grade coal in particular. To assess the prospects for these conditions to emerge requires an analysis of the present and likely future status of the principal forms of primary energy consumed in the region.

Primary Energy Resources

Coal

Communist ideologues traditionally glorified coal miners and their industry as constituting one of the pillars of the new socialist society. In contrast, critics saw coal as a backward, inefficient, highly polluting fuel consumed abundantly only in less developed societies.[3] At least through the mid-1970s, coal appeared to be experiencing the fate its detractors desired. Whereas in 1965 it comprised 79 per cent of primary energy consumed in Eastern Europe, by 1977 the comparable figure was 57 per cent.[4]

Prospects for coal revived with the twin oil "shocks" of 1973 and, especially, 1979 which substantially drove up both world market prices (WMPs) and the Soviet price for oil. All of the East European states, except Hungary, planned increases in the production of coal between 1976 and 1980. Yet numerous factors – escalating costs, declining labor productivity, a shrinking work force, and the long lead time needed to renovate existing mines and to construct new ones – largely frustrated these plans. In 1985, production of hard and soft coals was only 8.5 per cent and 27 per cent, respectively, greater than comparable output in 1975.

The national economic plans for 1986-1990, with the typical exception of Romania's formulated under the megalomaniac regime of Nicolae Ceausescu, reflected a sober assessment of the prospects for coal. Most states planned minimal or no increases, and Czechoslovakia became the first East European state to plan an absolute decrease, in production of coal.

Environmental considerations played an important, albeit probably not decisive, role in Czechoslovakia's landmark decision to plan a lower level of coal output. The deleterious ecological consequences of Czechoslovakia's heavy reliance upon coal had become so manifest by the mid-1980s that they even compelled the communist regime of Gustav Husak, hitherto unknown for its sensitivity to environmental protection, to promulgate a comprehensive program to this end that included, *inter alia*, a substantial diminution in the consumption of coal.[5]

The post-communist government of Czechoslovakia reaffirmed the commitment to reduce reliance upon coal. In 1990, it adopted a program to begin closing coal-burning power plants, especially in the intensively polluted region of northern Bohemia.[6] To date, the government has taken off-line coal-fired power units in northern Bohemia with a generating capacity of 650 megawatts (MW) and plans to close similar units with a capacity of 850 MW by 1995. The results of a recent public opinion poll conducted in the Czech Republic indicate that the public overwhelmingly supports such initiatives: 79 per cent of the sample responded that the use of coal as a source of energy should be either limited or abandoned.[7]

Coal will play a diminishing, albeit important, role in most future East European energy balances. In 1990, coal still constituted approximately 57 per cent of the primary energy consumed in the region, a level of consumption equivalent to that in 1977. Production of hard coal has peaked in the region and only Romania continues to maintain its current production of soft coals.

Overall, the production of all types of coal in Eastern Europe declined by approximately 20 per cent between 1980 and 1991.[8]

How decisively the East European states introduce market economies where prices reflect marginal costs will profoundly affect prospects for coal mining. Both the communist and post-communist governments of Eastern Europe have heavily subsidized the coal industry. The elimination of such subsidies as part of the transition to a market economy inevitably will result in the closure of numerous highly inefficient and economically unprofitable collieries throughout the region. This trend already is apparent in several countries.[9] A substantial improvement in the quality of the environment requires that all East European governments vigorously pursue a similar policy.

Oil

Oil has been a mixed blessing for the environment in Eastern Europe. It has improved environmental quality, especially in the 1970s, when it replaced more heavily polluting solid fuels in primary energy consumption. Yet, oil presents no panacea for the environment. Gasoline-powered motor vehicles, those ubiquitous polluters of the urban landscape, stand as the quintessential symbol of this circumstance. Even cursory observation reveals how motor vehicles have degraded the environment of such cities as Budapest, Prague, and Warsaw.

Communist Eastern Europe, except for Romania, relied upon importation from the USSR for most of its crude oil. Eastern Europe paid for most of this oil in barter trade with "soft" goods.[10] The traditional Soviet–East European oil relationship remained essentially unchanged until the "energy shock" of 1990 when the USSR substantially slashed oil exports to Eastern Europe and demanded that future oil supplies be paid for in hard currency at WMPs.[11]

A complex of economic and political factors led to the "energy shock." Most fundamentally, the substantial decline in domestic petroleum production forced the USSR to reassess the opportunity costs of its oil exports to Eastern Europe. In 1990, oil extraction in the USSR declined to 570 million metric tons (MMT) compared to 607 MMT in 1989 and approximated the level of extraction attained in 1978. This trend has continued in post-communist Russia. In 1991, Russia extracted approximately 461 MMT of oil while in 1992 the respective figure was 395 MMT.[12]

These developments existed against the backdrop of declining WMPs for oil that severely crimped hard currency earnings for both the USSR and Russia. In 1989, the USSR earned only $10.5 billion from exports of oil and petroleum products to the West compared to respective earnings of $23.6 billion in 1983. In 1992, Russia itself barely earned $10 billion from oil exports to the international market.[13] It is both a truism and an understatement that these circumstances made the traditional terms of trade with Eastern Europe even less economically attractive than previously. Finally, the demise of communist regimes in Eastern Europe eliminated the traditional political rationale for countenancing economic losses in energy trade. This rationale, a Soviet source candidly admitted, entailed using energy exports to help Eastern Europe "build socialism Stalinist-style."[14]

Yet Eastern Europe has largely avoided the most dire predictions about the devastating impact of the "energy shock."[15] A confluence of factors helps explain this circumstance.

First, Eastern Europe was lucky that "worse case" scenarios about skyrocketing WMPs for oil devised during the Gulf war against Iraq did not materialize. Then, analysts were predicting that the benchmark price for crude likely would hover well over $30 per barrel in the 1990s whereas the respective price in actuality has been around $20 per barrel in recent years.[16]

Second, Eastern Europe was more successful than many anticipated in obtaining preferential terms of trade for oil with the USSR and its successor states. The enduring political and economic crises in the USSR, and perhaps depressed prices for oil on the international market, made barter trade with Eastern Europe attractive in Soviet eyes. By mid-1991 a Polish source claimed that barter was again "the name of the game" in Soviet–East European trade.[17] Post-communist Russia has also proved willing to engage in barter trade. Thus, the 1993 trade protocol concluded between Russia and the Czech Republic includes among "the most important goods" to be exchanged, seven MMT of Russian oil for Czech foodstuffs, pharmaceuticals, and industrial commodities.[18]

The crumbling of centralized political authority also permitted Eastern Europe to conclude barter deals for oil directly with political subunits within Russia. In 1992, Hungary concluded the largest such deal when Tatarstan agreed to ship 1.5 MMT of crude oil annually through 1998 in exchange for a wide variety of Hungarian commodities.[19] Hungary exports upwards of $500 million worth of goods annually to the Russian Federation republics of Tatarstan and Bashkortostan, primarily in exchange for oil.[20]

Third, Western aid proved helpful in mitigating the effects of more costly oil. The International Monetary Fund (IMF) has targeted part of its loans to Eastern Europe specifically to this end. For example, the IMF granted Bulgaria a special credit to import 1.1 MMT of crude oil in 1991.[21] Similarly, the European Economic Community (EC) agreed to extend upwards of $400 million to Romania to finance importation of energy during the winter of 1991–92.[22] Finally, if there is a "silver lining" in the economic malaise gripping Eastern Europe, it is that consumption of energy is considerably less than it would be in booming economic times. "Large plants which devour energy declare bankruptcy one after another," comments a Hungarian source, reflecting this circumstance.[23]

That the "energy shock" has not proved as deleterious to the political and economic welfare of Eastern Europe as some observers had predicted should not obscure the dramatically changed circumstances it has created for the region since 1990. Most obviously, all East European states now devote a proportionately greater share of their national wealth to acquire oil in volumes that are substantially less than the respective volumes acquired before 1990. This is especially true when they purchase oil on the international market which typically requires payment in hard currency. Poland has resorted to such purchases far more than other East European states. In 1992, Poland already was importing approximately two-thirds of its oil from suppliers outside the former Soviet Union.[24] The Czech Republic may soon follow Poland's path. It is currently finalizing plans to import upwards of 10 MMT of crude annually by building a new pipeline linking northern Bohemia with existing pipelines in Ingolstadt, Germany.[25]

Then, too, Eastern Europe is now subject to the vicissitudes of the international energy market wherein political turmoil and economic dislocation can vitiate seemingly secure sources of supply. The closure of the Adria pipeline due to war in the former Yugoslavia across whose territory it traverses represents the most obvious, and costly, example of this circumstance. The pipeline's closure has effectively precluded East European states such as the Czech Republic and Hungary from receiving any of the oil for which they contracted with suppliers in the Middle East.[26]

The oil relationship with Russia exhibits similar uncertainty. For example, Bulgaria and Russia concluded a trade protocol for 1992 envisioning the supply of five MMT of Russian crude to Bulgaria in barter trade. In May 1992, a Bulgarian source reported that to date "not a single drop" of the Russian crude contracted for had reached Bulgaria.[27] Vladimir Dlouhy, the Czech Republic Minister of Industry and Trade, reports that Russia has resisted providing his state with sought-after "guarantees" for the "long-term coverage of Czech demands" for oil.[28] Indeed, Russia is not legally obligated to supply the Czech Republic with the seven MMT of crude oil specified in the aforementioned 1993 trade protocol between the two states. The protocol states that the lists of agreed upon goods for trade contained therein represent only targets "and cannot be considered binding for the conclusion of contracts."[29]

The ethnic strife now tearing apart much of the former Soviet Union injects a new variable into the Russian–East European oil (and overall energy) relationship. East Europeans worry especially about the possibility of economic warfare erupting between Ukraine and Russia, which could disrupt the flow of oil through the Druzhba pipeline which traverses the former's territory. Ukrainian authorities already have threatened to reduce the flow of oil through Druzhba if Russia does not pay pipeline transit fees now in arrears.[30]

Fluidity, uncertainty, and confusion characterize the "new world" of energy upon which Eastern Europe has embarked since the energy shock of 1990.

Natural Gas

East Europeans typically see natural gas as an "environmentally friendly" fuel that will increasingly displace more heavily polluting solid and liquid fuels in primary energy consumption. Eastern Europe possesses limited indigenous capacities to meet these plans.[31] Only in Romania and Hungary does natural gas play more than a negligible role in primary energy production. Between 1980 and 1989, indigenous production of natural gas declined in every country of the region.[32] Financial and technical assistance from the West could somewhat alter these trends.[33]

Realistically, however, importation must account for any dramatic increase in consumption. The USSR traditionally was the principal exporter of natural gas to Eastern Europe which receives most of this gas as repayment for its participation in joint projects to exploit Soviet gas fields and construct associated pipeline facilities to bring the gas to both domestic and foreign markets.

Natural gas has been the star performer of the Soviet and, subsequently, Russian energy industry since the 1980s.[34] Production of natural gas increased by over 80 per cent between 1980 and 1989. Output increased by two per cent in 1990 compared to 1989, while extraction of crude oil declined by six per cent in this period. This performance led to new commitments for export. For example, in 1992 Russia delivered upwards of 22 per cent more gas to Poland than previously agreed upon in return for foodstuffs.[35] Then in August 1993, in what Polish Prime Minister Hanna Suchocka called an "investment of the century," Poland and Russia initialled an agreement to construct a natural gas pipeline with an annual throughput of 67 billion m^3 across their territories (and that of Belarus) to markets in Western Europe. The proposed pipeline, to be constructed between 1994 and 2000, would provide Poland annually with 14 billion m^3 of gas purchased on preferential terms as repayment for its investment in the project, variously estimated at between $3 and $4 billion. The gas received each year in repayment would be close to 50 per cent greater than the volume of gas now consumed in Poland annually.[36] Finally, both the Soviet and Russian governments have negotiated agreements to make above-plan deliveries of natural gas to repay outstanding debts with selected East European states. To this end, the USSR agreed to supply Czechoslovakia with over 16 billion m^3 of natural gas, an amount that exceeds by approximately three billion m^3 the total volume of gas that Czechoslovakia imported in 1989. Subsequently, Russia made a "provisional agreement" to pay off with natural gas "more than" $1 billion of its $5 billion debt to Czechoslovakia.[37] The successor states of Czechoslovakia have agreed on a ratio of 2:1 favoring the Czech Republic over Slovakia in dividing up this gas.[38]

Yet the East European–Russian gas relationship remains troubled. For one thing, Russia has proposed, so far unsuccessfully, "delaying repayment" in gas for work East European states did as part of the joint projects to exploit gas reserves in the Soviet Union. The professed aim of the delay would be to free gas for export to Western Europe, as Russia desperately seeks ways to earn more hard currency from one of its few tradeable commodities on international markets.[39] This proposal should be assessed against the backdrop in recent years of substantially declining rates of increase in the extraction of natural gas in Russia.[40] Further, it remains unclear what terms of trade East European states can negotiate with Russia for gas deliveries after the latter has repaid its debt to the former for their work on the joint projects. East European states had been hoping for preferential terms in acquiring this gas, but a Russian source categorically asserts that once Russia repays its gas debt subsequent gas deliveries to Eastern Europe "will be made at world prices exclusively."[41] Finally, the breakup of the Soviet Union and the ensuing acrimonious relations between Russia and Ukraine have led to disruptions in the supply of Russian gas to the Czech Republic, Poland, and Slovakia. Ukraine, exploiting the fact that all gas export lines from Russia traverse its territory, has siphoned off gas intended for export to Eastern and Western Europe. This is in retaliation for Russia's cuts in deliveries to Ukraine, instituted due to Ukraine's failure to repay debt.[42] Russia now proposes to build a new gas export pipeline via Belarus and Poland, thereby bypassing Ukraine.

Eastern Europe has responded to such developments by seeking additional sources of natural gas. Iran, which under the Shah began shipping gas to communist Europe in the 1960s, is one potential supplier. Members of the Central European Initiative (Austria, Croatia, the Czech Republic, Hungary, Italy, Poland, Slovakia, and Slovenia) are discussing the possibility of building a new pipeline to bring Iranian natural gas to Central and Western Europe via Turkey and Greece. Romania has also expressed interest in this project.[43] However, the potential for disruptions in supply attendant upon political instability along the proposed pipeline route has caused reservations about this project.[44] These deals are still pending, although Iran has indicated its willingness to export three billion m^3 of gas annually to both Bulgaria and Czechoslovakia on a long term basis in return for goods.[45]

Norway, Britain, and Algeria represent other potential sources of supply. Poland has expressed keen interest in importing gas – upwards of three to five billion m^3 annually – from Norway to reduce its reliance upon coal.[46] Similarly, Norway had proposed exporting natural gas to Czechoslovakia in part to mitigate the latter's environmental pollution. The two countries subsequently established a "bilateral forum" to deal with issues of energy and environment.[47] These bilateral arrangements could become part of a broader project involving members of the Central European Initiative in the construction of a pipeline to bring gas supplies from Norway.[48] Polish sources estimate that this project would cost "billions of dollars."[49] Hungary and Poland are contemplating importing natural gas from Algeria, although the cost of doing so may prove prohibitive. Hungary could receive approximately four billion m^3 of gas annually from Algeria as early as 1996 via a proposed pipeline linking Hungary with Austria. Reportedly, Hungary and Austria have agreed to most of the conditions necessary to construct the estimated $80 million pipeline which is to be funded in part with a $45 million loan from the World Bank.[50]

Thus, natural gas will probably play a much more prominent role in East European energy balances. This circumstance would manifestly benefit the environment. Yet natural gas will not cure all the ills energy inflicts on the environment. For one thing, its increased utilization does nothing to mitigate the effects of that ubiquitous polluter of the environment – the gasoline powered motor vehicle.

Nuclear Power

Nuclear power received its start in Eastern Europe on January 17, 1955 when the Soviet Union announced that it would cooperate with its allies in the "peaceful development of atomic science, technology, and national economy."[51] Shortly thereafter, the Soviet Union concluded agreements with all East European states to promote this end. The USSR often reneged on these agreements for a complex of reasons, including a reluctance to permit members of the "fraternal socialist commonwealth" to develop independent nuclear capacities. Nevertheless, by the mid-1980s Bulgaria, Czechoslovakia, East Germany, and Hungary had opened nuclear power stations (NPS) with Soviet-designed equipment manufactured either by the USSR or Czechoslovakia (see Table 5.1). Romania constituted the exception to this pattern. In 1977, Romania concluded an agreement with Canada to supply it with five Canadian-designed and Canadian-built reactors for a NPS at Cernavoda. Romania thus became the first (and, to date, only) East European state to base its nuclear program mostly on Western technology.

A country-by-country survey suggests that the atom faces an uncertain future in Eastern Europe. Bulgaria through this century will not increase its existing nuclear capacities beyond making the 1,000 MW sixth block at the Kozloduy NPS fully operational. The status of the four 440 MW blocks at Kozloduy, all of which have been periodically shut down for extensive renovation, is more problematic. Officially, Bulgaria has made clear that Western aid is essential to modernize these nuclear capacities and/or to provide alternative supplies of energy to compensate for the closure of obsolete reactors.[52] To date, Western aid, principally from the EC in the form of $13 million to modernize the oldest reactors at Kozloduy and $8 million to purchase electricity abroad, is far below estimated requisite monies to meet these ends. To compensate for the loss of power capacities if Kozloduy's oldest reactors do not again become fully operational, Bulgaria is considering building a new 1,000 MW reactor at Kozlo-

TABLE 5.1 Eastern Europe: Installed Nuclear Capacity, 1992

	Installed Reactors	*Capacity (megawatts)*	*Production (per cent[a])*
Bulgaria			40
Kozloduy	5	2,760	
Czechoslovakia			25
Jaslovske Bohunice	4	1,760	
Dukovany	4	1,760	
Hungary			48
Paks	4	1,760	

[a]Electricity produced as a percentage of national production.

Source: Official statistics of the respective countries.

duy and even reviewing the possibility of restarting construction at the Belene NPS which had been abandoned in 1990 under the pressure of public opinion.[53]

The status of nuclear power has proved equally contentious in the Czech and Slovak Republics. Before the break-up of Czechoslovakia, the specific point of contention was whether to bring on stream two 1,000 MW reactors now under construction at the Temelin NPS in southern Bohemia. In May 1992, the Czech Prime Minister asserted that the future of Temelin is "more open than ever before" and did not rule out halting its construction. He argued that the likely demand for power in Czechoslovakia in this century made Temelin superfluous.[54] However, in March 1993 the present Czech government headed by Prime Minister Vaclav Klaus decided to complete construction of the two reactors at Temelin. In announcing his decision, Klaus singled out the key role that Temelin would play in improving environmental quality by permitting the closure of coal-fired power plants in northern Bohemia. According to Klaus, the closure of these plants would reduce emissions of sulfur dioxide annually in northern Bohemia by 23 per cent and throughout the Czech Republic by 10 per cent.[55] President Vaclav Havel was decidedly less upbeat in defending the Temelin decision but also did not support abandoning the project. Havel called Temelin a "relic" of the communist era, as the decision to begin construction of the plant had been made in 1986. He went on to argue both that it would be too expensive to abandon the project now that it was approaching completion and that the government would ensure that the plant conforms to "all international safety standards" in its operation.[56]

Similar controversy surrounds nuclear facilities in Slovakia under construction at Mochovce and operating at Jaslovske Bohunice. In August 1993, the government adopted an "Energy Concept to the Year 2005" that envisaged making operational four nuclear blocks at Mochovce and continuing to operate two blocks at Jaslovske Bohunice at least through this century.[57] Yet it remains uncertain if Slovakia can even obtain the estimated DM 1.3 billion in financing to bring the first two reactors on stream at Mochovce. The Slovak Minister of Economics admitted that negotiations with a consortium of Western banks to borrow this amount are "causing us a lot of headaches" and he "would rather not even think about" what would happen at Mochovce if the negotiations are not eventually successful.[58] The uncertain status of the Mochovce NPS casts doubt on whether Slovakia can fulfill its pledge to shut down the two reactors at Jaslovske Bohunice which critics (both domestic and foreign) have repeatedly assailed as outdated and unsafe. Previously, officials had predicated the closure of these reactors upon making operational three reactors at Mochovce as well as completing construction at the highly controversial Gabcikovo hydro-electric power project on the Danube River.[59]

Hungary likely will retain the nuclear status quo, although a high-ranking official indicated that the government has "not completely rejected" the idea of a new NPS at some (unspecified) future date.[60] Predicting the future status of the atom in Romania is risky, given the tortuous saga of the Cernavoda NPS. The first reactor at Cernavoda was originally scheduled to become operational in 1985 and the entire project was to have been completed by 1990. In reality, no reactor has yet been made operational at Cernavoda. Romania now projects that the first reactor at the plant will become operational in 1994 and, "if financial resources are found," a second reactor at the plant could be brought on stream by 1998.[61] Poland, which in 1990 officially abandoned construction of its first NPS to be located at Zarnowiecz, is the only East European country devoid of prospects for exploiting the atom commercially by the year 2000. Official policy projects that only in the next century will Poland begin to rely to a "limited" degree on nuclear power with 6,000 MW of installed nuclear capacity by 2010.[62]

Conclusion: The Case for Energy Conservation

The preceding analysis makes clear that Eastern Europe can no longer pursue its traditional strategy of extensive growth based upon seemingly inexhaustible supplies of cheap fuels and power from the USSR and indigenous resources. East European states today simply do not possess the financial resources (particularly in hard currency), to continue expending between 30 per cent and 50 per cent more energy than their counterparts in Western Europe to produce a similar unit of national income. The imperative to conserve energy becomes obvious under these circumstances. Concomitantly, the realization of this imperative constitutes the *sine qua non* to mitigate substantially environmental degradation in Eastern Europe.

Most fundamentally, an effective program of energy conservation requires the establishment of a market economy in which wholesale and retail energy prices reflect marginal costs. As a Western source accurately (but untactfully) explains, efforts to conserve energy must "start with non-crazy prices" for these resources.[63] For several reasons – the Marxist law of value which considers natural resources "free goods," a desire to encourage the production of energy-intensive commodities, and a concern to avoid political unrest among the population – communist regimes traditionally attached prices to energy resources that were too low to encourage their conservation.

Political and economic conditions exist in post-communist Eastern Europe that both facilitate and hinder the development of an effective program of energy conservation. Conditions facilitating this end include a strong public consensus in most countries regarding the need for such a program, the rise of post-communist political elites committed (with varying degrees of enthusiasm) to democracy and marketization, and the willingness of international lending institutions such as the IMF and the World Bank to make loans to Eastern Europe contingent upon the latter's enactment of market-based economic reforms. These institutions have also targeted loans specifically to promote energy conservation through industrial restructuring and technological modernization. Such aid is especially needed given the limited financial resources available to East European states themselves to invest in these ends.[64]

All regimes in post-communist Eastern Europe have enacted measures, including increases in wholesale and retail prices for fuels, to conserve energy. For example, Bulgaria adjusts its fuel prices bi-monthly to reflect changes in market conditions.[65] Even more encouraging are proposals in the Czech Republic and Poland to establish a largely free market in energy where prices reflect supply and demand.[66] Market-determined prices for gasoline already prevail in these latter countries and in Hungary. Such measures undoubtedly have contributed to the approximate 14 per cent reduction in primary energy consumption Eastern Europe experienced between 1987 and 1990.[67] Yet some Western analysts have overstated the impact of these measures.[68] East European sources themselves make clear that idle industrial capacities, especially in energy-intensive industries, have played a much greater role in fostering this circumstance.[69]

Ironically, by giving citizens meaningful input into public policy, the establishment of democratic polities in Eastern Europe could hinder the pursuit of energy conservation. To argue, as we have, that there exists a strong public consensus favoring energy conservation does not mean, *ipso facto*, that citizens will willingly shoulder the inevitable economic dislocations that accompany marketization and energy price reform. For example, a Gallup poll survey of public opinion in Hungary found that an overwhelming majority supported the goal of energy conservation but only 38 per cent of the sample felt that "families and households should conserve energy."[70] A threatened political backlash has already forced East European regimes on several occasions to postpone or modify proposed plans for increases in energy prices.[71]

Hence, *homo economicus* and *homo politicus* in post-communist Eastern Europe may increasingly diverge over the imperative of energy conservation, the former arguing strongly for decisive measures to this end and the latter advocating caution to placate constituencies unable or unwilling to shoulder the economic burdens it entails. The outcome of their conflict will have profound consequences for the quality of the environment in Eastern Europe.

Abbreviations Used in the Notes

FBIS	Foreign Broadcast Information Service
FBIS-*EEU*	*East Europe Daily Report*
FBIS-*SOV*	*Soviet Union Daily Report*
FBIS-*USR*	*Central Eurasia Report*
JPRS	Joint Publications Research Service
JPRS-*EER*	*East Europe Report*
JPRS-*TEN*	*Environmental Issues*
RFE/RL	Radio Free Europe/Radio Liberty Research Institute

Notes

1. "Eastern Europe" herein includes the following countries: Bulgaria, Czechoslovakia (also referred to as the Czech Republic or Slovakia where appropriate), Hungary, Poland, Romania. For a comprehensive treatment of energy policies in Eastern Europe, see John M. Kramer, *The Energy Gap in Eastern Europe* (Lexington, Mass.: D.C. Heath, 1990).

2. *New Times* (Moscow), January 12, 1987, 32.

3. For a typical exposition of this position, see *Zycie gospodarcze* (Warsaw), May 20, 1990, in JPRS-*EER*, August 14, 1990, 37.

4. Unless otherwise indicated, all materials on policies towards coal in the 1970s and 1980s are drawn from Kramer, *The Energy Gap in Eastern Europe*, 70–83.

5. For details of the program, see *Hospodarske noviny* (Prague), 34, 1986, in JPRS-*EER*, December 10, 1986, 35.

6. All materials on this program are drawn from *Ceskoslovenska Tiskova Kancelar* (Prague), February 25, 1993 in JPRS-*TEN*, March 19, 1993, 17.

7. *Lidove noviny* (Prague), April 7, 1993 in JPRS-*TEN*, April 20, 1993, 14.

8. Computed from data in Directorate of Intelligence, *Handbook of International Economic Statistics 1992* (Washington, D.C.: Government Printing Office, 1992), 133, 134 (Tables 44, 45).

9. For examples of these trends, see: for Hungary, *Figyelo* (Budapest), June 4, 1992 in JPRS-*EER*, June 26, 1992, 20; for Poland, *Polska zbrojna* (Warsaw), May 4, 1992 in JPRS-*EER*, June 22, 1992, 19; for Bulgaria, *Bulgarsko Telegrafna Agentsiia*, April 12, 1993 in FBIS-*EEU*, April 15, 1993, 10.

10. For a detailed discussion of the Soviet–East European oil relationship, see John M. Kramer, "Soviet-CEMA Energy Ties," *Problems of Communism* (July-August, 1985), 32–47.

11. Unless otherwise noted, all materials on the "energy shock" are drawn from John M. Kramer, "Eastern Europe and the 'Energy Shock' of 1990–91," *Problems of Communism* (May-June, 1991), 85–96.

12. Data on oil production in Russia in 1991 and 1992 are from *Moscow News*, 4, January 21, 1993, 6.

13. *Rossiiskaya gazeta* (Moscow), February 3, 1993.

14. *Trud* (Moscow), March 12, 1990.

15. For examples of these dire predictions, see Kramer, "Eastern Europe and the 'Energy Shock' of 1990–1991," 95–96.

16. For example, a representative analysis advanced in September 1990 argued that the WMP for oil likely will be "settling in for an extended time" at more than $30 per barrel. *The Washington Post*, September 20, 1990, E1.

17. *Gazeta wyborcza* (Warsaw), September 10, 1991, in FBIS-*EEU*, September 24, 1991, 19.

18. The text of the protocol is reprinted in *Hospodarske noviny*, September 16, 1993, in FBIS-*EEU*, September 23, 1993, 8–9.

19. *Magyar Tavirati Irada*, May 11, 1993, in FBIS-*EEU*, May 12, 1993, 16.

20. According to data supplied by Lajos Berenyi, Deputy State Secretary in the Hungarian Ministry of International Economic Relations, as reported by *Magyar Tavirati Irada*, April 2, 1993, in FBIS-*EEU*, April 5, 1993, 31.

21. *Duma* (Sofia), October 25, 1991, in FBIS-*EEU*, October 30, 1991, 11.

22. *Romanian Press Service* (Bucharest), September 12, 1991, in FBIS-*EEU*, September 13, 1991, 27.

23. *Mai Nap* (Budapest), July 19, 1991, in FBIS-*EEU*, August 14, 1991, 13. Officials identified this circumstance as the "main reason" Hungary imported 16 per cent less crude oil in 1991 than in 1990. *Magyar Tavirati Irada*, January 8, 1992, in FBIS-*EEU*, January 9, 1992, 23.

24. *Rzeczpospolita* (Warsaw), June 13–14, 1992 in JPRS-*EER*, July 28, 1992, 19.

25. Details of the proposed project are provided by *Ceskoslovenska Tiskova Kancelar*, May 26, 1993, in FBIS-*EEU*, June 1, 1993, 13.

26. The pipeline's closure has especially affected Hungary. Prior to its closure, Adria was supplying Hungary with approximately 40 per cent of its total volume of imported crude oil. Hungarian officials recently have suggested that the United Nations mediate efforts to reopen the pipeline. RFE/RL Research Institute, *News Briefs*, June 7–11, 1993, 15.

27. *Bulgarsko Telegrafna Agentsiia*, February 20, 1992, in FBIS-*EEU*, February 21, 1992, 3; *Trud* (Sofia), May 1, 1992, quoted in RFE/RL Research Institute, *Research Report*, May 15, 1992, p. 13.

28. The quotation is from the report on Dlouhy's remarks carried by *Ceskoslovenska Tiskova Kancelar*, April 8, 1993 in FBIS-*EEU*, April 14, 1993, 12.

29. *Hospodarske noviny*, September 16, 1993 in FBIS-*EEU*, September 23, 1993, 8–9.

30. Radio Ukraine World Service, June 2, 1992, in FBIS-*SOV*, June 3, 1992, 46.

31. For data on reserves of natural gas, see *Petroleum Economist* (August 1988), 257.

32. Data on production of natural gas are from Directorate of Intelligence, *Handbook of International Economic Statistics 1992*, 132 (Table 43).

33. For example, the World Bank and the European Investment Bank have jointly loaned Poland $310 million to help double its output of natural gas by the year 2000. *Gazeta wyborcza*, September 13, 1990, in FBIS-*EEU*, September 20, 1990, 24. As part of the loan agreement, Poland pledged to begin pricing domestic gas at prevailing WMPs. *Polska zbrojna* (Warsaw), May 4, 1992, in JPRS-*EER*, June 22, 1992, 19.

34. Data on production of natural gas are from *Ekonomika i zhizn'* (Moscow), 5 (January 1991); *Ekonomika i zhizn'*, 30 (July 1991).

35. Calculated from data supplied by *Polska Agencja Prasowa*, August 6, 1992 in FBIS-*EEU*, August 6, 1992, 14.

36. Suchocka's comments are reported by *Polska Agencja Prasowa*, August 19, 1993 in FBIS-*EEU*, August 20, 1993, 22. Further details on the proposed project are provided by *Polska Agencja Prasowa*, July 28, 1993 in FBIS-*EEU*, July 29, 1993, 22. The latter source provides an estimate of $3 billion for Poland's contribution to the project whereas a respective estimate of $4 billion is provided by *Moscow News*, 36, September 3, 1993, 4.

37. Materials on Czechoslovakia are from *TASS*, August 2, 1991, in FBIS-*SOV*, August 5, 1991, 26; *Ceskoslovenska Tiskova Kancelar*, March 5, 1992, in FBIS-*EEU*, March 6, 1992, 6. For details of similar agreements with Bulgaria and Hungary, see, respectively, *Demokratsiia* (Sofia), July 11, 1991, in FBIS-*EEU*, July 17, 1991, 6; RFE/RL Research Institute, *Report on Eastern Europe*, June 28, 1991, 53.

38. *Ceskoslovenska Tiskova Kancelar*, March 23, 1993 in FBIS-*EEU*, March 29, 1993, 5.

39. For a discussion of the Russian proposal, see *Rossiiskie vesti* (Moscow), December 17, 1992 in FBIS-*USR*, December 25, 1992, 72.

40. In 1991 extraction of natural gas increased by barely 0.5 per cent over the amount extracted in 1990. Directorate of Intelligence, *Handbook of International Economic Statistics 1992*, 132 (Table 43).

41. *Kommersant'* (Moscow), July 17, 1993, 3.

42. For a discussion of how Ukraine's actions have affected Eastern Europe, see *INTERFAX*, October 21, 1992 in FBIS-*SOV*, October 22, 1992, 17.

43. *Ceskoslovenska Tiskova Kancelar*, March 11, 1991, in FBIS-*EEU*, March 14, 1991, 12 provides information on the project. For comments expressing Romania's interest in participating therein, see *Romanian Press Service*, October 7, 1991, in FBIS-*EEU*, October 8, 1991, 34.

44. For a Polish report to this effect, see *Rzeczpospolita*, January 22, 1992, in JPRS-*EER*, February 25, 1992, 32.

45. *Ceskoslovenska Tiskova Kancelar*, June 20, 1991, in FBIS-*EEU*, June 26, 1991, 10; *Duma*, March 14, 1991, in FBIS-*EEU*, March 25, 1991, 10.

46. For details of the discussions with Norway and with Britain to the same end, see *Rzeczpospolita*, January 22, 1992, in JPRS-*EER*, February 25, 1992, 31–32.

47. RFE/RL Research Institute, *Report on Eastern Europe*, May 31, 1991, 31.

48. *Hospodarske noviny*, September 25, 1990, in FBIS-*EEU*, October 30, 1990, 20.

49. *Rzeczpospolita*, January 22, 1992, in JPRS-*EER*, February 25, 1992, 32.

50. For details of these developments, see *Nepszabadsag* (Budapest), August 26, 1993 in FBIS-*EEU*, September 15, 1993, 34; *Magyar Tavirati Irada*, July 3, 1992, in FBIS-*EEU*, July 6, 1992, 21. A Polish source argues that Poland will not import natural gas from Algeria in this century, in part because of the considerable financial investments that must be marshalled to this end. *Rzeczpospolita*, January 22, 1992 in JPRS-*EER*, February 25, 1992, 32.

51. *Pravda* (Moscow), January 18, 1955. Unless otherwise noted, this analysis of the development of nuclear power from its inception to the present in Eastern Europe is drawn from John M. Kramer, "Chernobyl and Eastern Europe," *Problems of Communism* (November-December 1986), 44–56.

52. For an extended discussion of these issues – and the numerous other controversies surrounding Kozloduy – see George Stein, "Kozloduy: A Nuclear Time Bomb?" RFE/RL Research Institute, *Report on Eastern Europe*, November 15, 1991, 4–10.

53. For commentary on the possibility of restarting construction at the Belene NPS, see *Bulgarsko Telegrafna Agentsiia*, January 20, 1993 in FBIS-*EEU*, January 21, 1993, 15.

54. *Ceskoslovenska Tiskova Kancelar*, May 27, 1992 in FBIS-*EEU*, June 2, 1992, 18.

55. See, for example, Klaus' remarks as reported in *Cesky denik* (Prague), February 19, 1993 in FBIS-*EEU*, February 25, 1993, 15.

56. Havel's remarks were reported by *Oesterreich Eins Radio Network* (Vienna), March 15, 1993 in JPRS-*TEN*, March 25, 1993, 27.

57. For a discussion of the provisions of the "Energy Concept," including those relating to the status of nuclear power, see *Hospodarske noviny*, August 23, 1993 in FBIS-*EEU*, August 26, 1993, 9.

58. From an interview with J. Kubecka, Minister of Economics, as published in *Narodna obroda* (Bratislava), July 1, 1993 in FBIS-*EEU*, July 8, 1993, 17.

59. See the remarks to that effect by President Michal Kovac as carried by *Rozhlasova Stanica Slovenska Network* (Bratislava), July 14, 1993 in FBIS-*EEU*, July 15, 1993, 16. For more on the Gabcikovo-Nagymaros dam controversy, see the chapter in this volume by Barbara Jancar-Webster.

60. As reported in *Kurier* (Vienna), August 2, 1990.

61. *Romanian Press Service*, January 28, 1993 in FBIS-*EEU*, January 29, 1993, 21.

62. *Polska Agencja Prasowa*, September 4, 1990.

63. *The Economist*, August 15, 1992, 16.

64. For a cogent argument stressing this point, see *Uj Magyarorzag* (Budapest), May 26, 1992 in JPRS-*EER*, July 13, 1992, 24.

65. *Bulgarsko Telegrafna Agentsiia*, April 12, 1993 in FBIS-*EEU*, April 14, 1993, 6.

66. On plans in the Czech Republic to effectuate a "substantial deregulation" of energy prices by 1995, see the interview with Vladimir Dlouhy, Minister of Industry and Trade as published in *Lidove noviny* (Prague), January 29, 1992 in FBIS-*EEU*, January 31, 1992, 18. Details of similar initiatives to this end in Poland are reported in *Gazeta przemyslowa i handlowa* (Warsaw), 20, 1992 in JPRS-*EER*, July 30, 1992, 30.

67. Calculated from data in Directorate of Intelligence, *Handbook of International Economic Statistics 1992*, 123 (Table 32).

68. For example, Anders Aslund, who attributes reduced demand for energy in the region primarily to technological modernization and the rationalization of consumption. *Svenska Dagbladet* (Stockholm), January 31, 1992, 48.

69. For recent commentaries making this argument, see, for example, *Cesky denik*, February 19, 1993 in FBIS-*EEU*, February 25, 1993, 14; *Polska Agencja Prasowa*, August 13, 1993 in FBIS-*EEU*, August 16, 1993, 20.

70. The results of the poll are reported in *Nepszabadsag*, April 10, 1991, in JPRS-*EER*, June 25, 1991, 29.

71. For examples of such actions, see: for Czechoslovakia, *Ceskoslovenska Tiskova Kancelar*, August 19, 1991, in FBIS-*EEU*, August 22, 1991, 9; for Hungary, RFE/RL Research Institute, *Report on Eastern Europe*, May 31, 1991, 32; for Poland, *Zycie gospodarcze*, May 20, 1990, in JPRS-*EER*, August 14, 1990, 38. To this same end, a Bulgarian source warns that governments must be careful to enact energy conservation measures, including increases in prices, "without triggering an extremely adverse social reaction." *Delovi svyat* (Sofia), July 22, 1991, in JPRS-*EER*, September 11, 1991, 16.

PART THREE

National and Regional Dimensions of Environmental Quality

6

Building Bureaucratic Capacity in Russia: Federal and Regional Responses to the Post-Soviet Environmental Challenge

DJ Peterson

Revelations of glasnost over the past five years have brought to light the staggering extent of environmental degradation in the newly independent states of the former Soviet Union.[1] While democratization of the political process in Russia has led government officials to acknowledge earnestly the gravity of the situation, they have made little progress toward resolving their environmental problems. One obstacle has been the lack of effective governmental institutions for environmental protection.

This chapter examines how governmental institutions engaged in environmental protection and resource management are evolving and discharging their duties under the new political and economic conditions of post-Soviet Russia. The first section provides an overview of federation-wide developments. Following this is an examination of regional and local trends, given the importance of decentralization of governmental functions, an increase in regional political autonomy, and the varied pace of change across Russia. Here we explore the challenges of building environmental protection institutions at the regional and local levels, and highlight several important factors that affect the capacity of these organizations to pursue their goals of environmental protection and resource management. On this basis, the concluding section of the chapter presents a new conceptual framework for approaching the broader question of the redevelopment of the state, institutions, and governance in post-Soviet Russia.

Institutions for Environmental Protection at the Federal Level

After several years of discussion of the issue, the Russian government in 1988 organized the first federal agency devoted solely to environmental protection, the Ministry for the Protection of the Environment and Natural Resources (*Ministerstvo okhrany okruzhayushchei sredy i prirodnykh resursov* – commonly abbreviated as *Minpriroda* in Russian).[2] Minpriroda sets the standards for and oversees a network of committees (*komitety*) located in the capital of each of the federation's 82 main administrative regions or provinces.[3] While actual jurisdictions are fluid and open to debate, the federal ministry claims responsibility for long-range policy planning; the elaboration of federation-wide rules and regulations (governing, for instance, pollution emissions and the use of natural resources); the management of plant and animal resources (including endangered species), and nature reserves; and the administration of international agreements on the protection of nature. The regional committees are responsible for carrying out the instructions of the center, including the collection of information on environmental quality; issuing permits for (or participating in the licensing of) uses of land, mineral, water, and air resources; monitoring compliance with these permits; and enforcement. In cities and districts (*raiony*), the regional environmental authorities, in conjunction with the local governmental authority (*administratsiya*) have set up local committees to help with the monitoring and enforcement functions.

In contrast to the system of environmental protection in the United States, the Russian system on paper appears more unified, despite the fact that the country nominally is a federation. All legislation and regulations concerning the environment and natural resources are to be implemented federation-wide. Local agencies answer to the regional committees which implement the federal regulations and report to the ministry in Moscow. Given the federal system of the United States, the Environmental Protection Agency (EPA) relies on a network of ten regional affiliates, while states and localities maintain their own independent bureaucracies. Many responsibilities, such as water pollution and radioactive waste management, are not managed by the federal government, but are left to the states. The more unified nature of the Russian system reflects historical trends and the impact of the executive authority of the CPSU and Soviet government which created the system in 1988, while the EPA was created in an environment which discouraged the concentration of power in Washington.[4]

Like the EPA, Minpriroda was intended to supersede the hodgepodge of departments, state committees, and ministries that formerly shared responsibility for environmental policy. Nevertheless, many important functions regarding natural resource management initially remained outside Minpriroda's jurisdiction, hampering its ability to carry out some of the functions mentioned above; its representatives view this as a weakness of their organization. To take an example, a prolonged turf battle raged between the environment ministry and *Gidromet*, the hydrometeorological service, over control of ambient air quality monitoring and data analysis.[5] This perceived fragmentation and the ensuing power struggles tended to undermine the environment ministry's status as the government's preeminent environmental protection authority.

The Yeltsin administration attempted to remedy the problem of fragmentation of the environmental protection apparatus as part of its greater reorganization and simplification of the Russian government's structure after the collapse of the Soviet government in 1991. Eleven different agencies – four from the Russian government and seven from the rump Soviet government – were subordinated as committees in a "bloc" under Minpriroda. These committees included: Geodesy and Cartography, Water Resources, Geology and Mineral Resources, Forestry, and Hydrometeorology. Many of these agencies had poor environmental records, and this move by the Yeltsin administration to combine the functions of monitoring, planning, resource development, and enforcement was hailed by environmentalists as a significant advance that would help Minpriroda meet its mandate. The only apparent result of this move, however, was the near paralysis of Minpriroda, as the newly-subordinated departments fought to regain their autonomy. To the chagrin of the new environment minister, Viktor Danilov-Danilyan, most of the committees quickly managed to reassert their bureaucratic independence from his superministry, and "ruined this logical principle" of unified management.[6]

While the creation of Minpriroda was, in itself, a welcomed measure, the subsequent barrage of governmental shake-ups (including the demise of the Soviet Union), interagency power struggles, center-periphery conflicts, economic reforms, and legislative initiatives has resulted in a policy dominated by institution-building and sorting out bureaucratic processes rather than by solving pressing environmental problems.

What's Happening Around Russia?

Western observers traditionally have considered politics in Russia and the former Soviet Union to be highly centralized and uniform across the region. Despite the tendencies for outsiders to continue to focus on Moscow, the nature of government in the periphery has changed dramatically.

In 1988, the Gorbachev regime initiated a political reform campaign calling for significant decentralization of administrative authority over broad issue areas, including environmental protection, land-use management, and public works. Decentralization was pushed further in Russia with the adoption of the July 1991 law on local self rule, the 1992 law on regional (krai and oblast) administration, as well as other legislation such as the 1992 environmental law. In addition to *de jure* decentralization, one of the most important trends of the recent reform period has been *de facto* decentralization. Given the broad types of legislation adopted by busy deputies in Moscow, decision-makers at the regional and local levels have been left to fill in the blanks as they see appropriate. While power struggles rage in Moscow, a power vacuum has allowed regional and local political entrepreneurs to take the initiative to push ahead with or retard reforms, particularly in the economic sphere.[7] Rising ethnic and regional awareness and assertiveness have limited the ability of Moscow to control developments in republics such as Karelia, Tatarstan, and Sakha (formerly Yakutia).

Political leaders and environmentalists alike expect that the decentraliza-tion and democratization of the policy process will result in greater responsibility and accountability for the management of natural resources. It is assumed that local control over natural resources tends to foster a spirit of stewardship. The Soviet government never seriously considered the interests of the republics and their communities, argued Vyacheslav Vashanov, an environmental official from the Russian Federation; rather, "all-union interests," such as boosting state power, prevailed.[8]

A devolution of authority does not guarantee that environmentally sound policies will follow, however. Officials in the Republic of Tuva, one of the poorest and least developed regions of the Russian Federation, flagrantly violated federal laws and regulations by turning over a section of the autonomous republic's only nature preserve to a local collective farm for reindeer grazing.[9] A devolution of funding and resource allocation also may not bring about the desired results. In 1992, the Russian government cut all central budget funding to the local environmental protection committees. The regional governments were expected to cover the shortfall, partly from environmental fees and fines deposited in local environmental funds, but as Minpriroda chair Danilov-Danilyan predicted: "The potential implications of such a decision are very clear ... local agencies would be completely dependent on the oblast administrations, which would be able to do whatever they wanted with them." In fact, many regional governments attempted to undermine environmental regulation and cut funding. The environment minister went on to point out that many oblast administrations were selling rights to log forest land in order to make a quick ruble, "something they have no right to do."[10] For 1993, the entire system was returned to centralized, albeit insufficient, financing.

The trend towards increased regional autonomy and assertiveness also has invited new conflicts among local interests as well as between the center and the periphery. Jurisdictional battles surrounding control of natural resources have flared as regional and local officials take advantage of the uncertainty in Moscow and of poorly defined laws and property rights in order to usurp executive authority for themselves. In October 1991, for example, the Krasnoyarsk Krai parliament passed a resolution calling on the Russian government to grant their region the status of a republic within the Federation. Deputies objected to the fact that their territory, which is roughly the size of Argentina, had no right of ownership of its vast natural resources and, thus, no ability to capture the wealth of its industry or to shape the path of its future development. "Colonial policies towards Siberia continue to this very day," asserted V. Novikov, chair of the territorial soviet.[11]

Thus, when leaving the metropoles and traveling in the periphery, a foreign observer becomes sharply aware of the divergence of regional politics and how little outside analysts know about important developments there. While the parameters of environmental protection are set by the parliament and Minpriroda in Moscow and are intended to be applied consistently and uniformly across the federation, outcomes are shaped predominantly by the actions of officials in the periphery and vary significantly from region to region. In this light, discussion of environmental institutions as they exist on paper or appear from Moscow is wholly inadequate for understanding the state of environmental affairs across the entire federation, a territory which covers the area of the United States and Canada combined.

The Challenge of Building a Capable Bureaucracy

The regional branches of Minpriroda – the oblast, krai and republican environmental committees – are the most important units in Russia's environmental protection system in terms of the implementation and oversight of federal environmental policy. Local (city and rural district) environmental committees together with their superior regional committee are responsible for monitoring, inspection, and enforcement of regulations.

As new entities, the first and most important environmental challenge has been to build a capable and effective nation-wide bureaucracy to implement policy, and this requires a competent, motivated staff that is politically autonomous from the interests they seek to regulate.[12] Unfortunately, environmental regulators and managers have been criticized for lacking all three of these qualities.

Competence. Sharp criticism of the ability of governmental officials to address Russia's natural resource problems comes from all corners: the media, environmentalists, and international lending institutions. For example, non-governmental environmental activists repeatedly criticize environmental protection agencies for the fact that the bulk of their functionaries were hired from other state committees and ministries which were forced to reduce their staffs because of budget and operational cutbacks. Many environmental officials came from agencies with dubious environmental histories, such as *Gidromet* and the Soviet ministries responsible for fisheries, and land reclamation and water resources. In many cases, environmentalists allege that some agencies used this game of bureaucratic musical chairs as an opportunity to rid themselves of incompetent or unproductive staff. Critics also charge that leadership positions in environmental protection organs, particularly at the regional and local levels, have been filled with former Communist Party *apparatchiki* (full-time paid party officials) who obtained their jobs through patronage connections rather than by their environmental qualifications.

An underlying assumption of these arguments is that because these officials served in governmental institutions during the Soviet era, a period of marked environmental degradation, their poor past performance dictates that they cannot adequately perform their duties in the post-Soviet transition period. While critics focus on the questionable pedigrees of environmental officials, they overlook the most important question: the actual performance of these incumbents in the present era.[13] Examining the record reveals that while officials lack formal training and experience in many aspects of contemporary environmental management, they are qualified and able to make progress in practical ways.

Governments in Russia do lack an adequate pool of qualified experts available and willing to work in the environmental field. This shortage of capable specialists increases as one moves down the hierarchy to local offices and is most acute in smaller, more remote, and poorly-funded offices, such as those in parts of Siberia and the Far East. Even though offices in rural regions are responsible for very important functions such as land-use management, staff members often lack professional training or experience in any aspect of nature protection and often serve only as paper shufflers, compiling data that flow into the office and reporting it to superiors above.

One reason for the shortage of qualified personnel is the fact that the Soviet higher education system produced few people capable of fulfilling the full range of tasks necessary for a contemporary environmental official. Because of the educational biases of the Soviet regime, Russia is heavy on technical experts (such as biologists, chemists, and engineers) and short on administrative and organizational talent (regional planners, lawyers, public policy experts, and economists). The technical specialists themselves are often trained in particularly narrow fields. Russia has large numbers of compressor engineers, hydraulics engineers, and pump engineers, but few broadly trained civil engineers who can tackle the wide-ranging needs of a small environmental protection office. Thus, most of the skilled professionals employed by environmental offices are trained in technical fields. In contrast to the large number of lawyers and non-technical specialists employed in the administrative echelons of the U.S. environmental protection bureaucracy, most of the leadership of the regional and local environmental committees in Russia are engineers. (Tomsk is an exception in that it employs a lawyer in a senior position at the oblast environmental committee.)

The emphasis on narrow technical specialties has come at the cost of training experts in interdisciplinary problem analysis, particularly in the areas of economics, public policy, and law. Thus, environmental officials are handicapped when it comes to complex tasks such as elaborating comprehensive land-use policies, evaluating the environmental and economic impact of development, prioritizing environmental problems, designing effective policies, and writing workable regulations. A pervasive culture of professional and institutional parochialism has compounded problems by inhibiting the development of comprehensive and multi-disciplinary efforts to manage such tasks. The end result is that Russian environmental specialists are relatively good at tackling discrete technological problems such as environmental monitoring and data analysis or designing a waste-water treatment plant; they are not very good at handling complex practical problems such as policy development and analysis.

The undeveloped state of the Russian labor and housing markets combined with residence restrictions imposed by the internal passport system impede the process of searching for and attracting qualified personnel. In almost all cases, an environmental agency must draw from the local pool of available candidates. One obvious source of available managerial and technical skill are functionaries of the old Soviet-era Communist Party. Indeed, in smaller cities with limited opportunities for career advancement in industry, the CPSU often attracted the best qualified managers.[14] As one observer of the Yaroslavl' political scene contended: "The heads of the executive departments are almost all old *nomenklatura*. They know how to get things done."[15] Petr Poletaev, a deputy in the now defunct union-wide environmental agency argued: "There are many scientists in the *apparat*."[16]

Local industries provide a second source of environmental expertise. The role of industry cannot be underestimated, because development in many areas of Russia – especially Siberia and the Far East – was managed not by regional and local governments, but by the relevant industrial branch ministry. In St. Petersburg, for example, many environmental inspectors come from the pulp and paper sector.[17]

A third source of available talent has been other governmental agencies: Rostov Oblast boasts a well-developed air pollution monitoring system because Rostov-on-Don happened to be the location of the air quality authority responsible for all of southern Russia prior to 1988. Another important source of personnel has been local divisions of the former Ministry of Reclamation and Water Resources. As environmentalists rightfully point out, this agency had a dubious history as designer and builder of the dams, canals, diversion and irrigation projects that have created many of Russia's water resource problems today. On the other hand, the local inspectors and engineers from the water resources agency, which probably did not have a major role in shaping water resources policy under the Soviet regime, are the most knowledgeable. Moreover, many environmental committees, such as the Krasnoyarsk Krai environmental authority, have been able to take over laboratories and monitoring stations of the water resources ministry, making theirs one of the best equipped in Siberia.

A cursory survey of regional environmental protection committees in Russia reveals that those with some of the best staffed and equipped offices, and thereby more active and effective environmental bureaucracies, occur in regions which were the sites of large water projects and large water resources agencies: Krasnoyarsk, Volgograd, Krasnodar, Kostroma, and Vologda (a variation on the argument of the theory of hydraulic despotism).

Motivation. Environmental officials also have been criticized for not being motivated in their work. Since many employees came from other agencies with poor environmental histories or from the Communist Party *apparat*, critics assert that their interest does not lie in protecting the environment. Alexei Yablokov, Boris Yeltsin's advisor on health and the environment and a respected environmentalist, complained that the environmental protection agency lacks environmental *entuziasty*, or zealots.[18]

Like the issue of competence discussed above, these criticisms appear to be inspired by populist anger over the fact that former communist officials continue to occupy positions of power and authority, similar to anger over the perceived phenomenon of "*nomenklatura* privatization" in the business sector.[19] An appropriate assessment must be based on outcomes rather than perceived intent. To this point, there is little evidence that past institutional affiliation serves as a good predictor of one's present interests in Russia today.

Bunce and Csanadi rightly argue that the fluidity of society and absence of durable political and economic structures in post-communist states have prevented the consolidation of well-defined interests.[20] Many regions run by ex-communists, for example, have pushed ahead with economic reform.[21] Civil servants appear loyal to the institutions in which they presently work, adding credence to Graham Allison's classic assertion: "Positions define what players both may and must do," or "Where you stand depends on where you sit."[22] In the northern Russian town of Cherepovets, for example, V.I. Samburskii had worked for twenty years at the giant Cherepovets steel mill, rising to a position as head of a production unit. The town's mayor and the head of the Vologda Oblast environmental committee asked Samburskii to lead the city's environmental committee. Rather than see his new position as a conflict of interest, Samburskii argued that his prior experience and inside knowledge gave him an advantage when it came to negotiating norms and assessing the environmental protection efforts of plant management.[23]

When asked about the motivation of their employees, regional environmental administrators respond that a position in the civil service in the present reform era is not highly remunerative, a point especially true of jobs in the environmental bureaucracy. Therefore, those who accept such positions often make a financial sacrifice with little reward of professional prestige; and this may represent an act of commitment. A visit to the Kemerovo Oblast environmental office found the entire staff (except the chair) out at a farm in the country harvesting carrots to supplement their winter food supply. Vasilii Bakunin, the chair of the Chelyabinsk Oblast environmental committee, contended that his employees came on their own will and took pay cuts to do so, a sign of their allegiance to the agency and a "belief in the rectitude of their work."[24] On the other hand, lower wages, combined with the upheavals and uncertainties plaguing the system, tempt many talented employees to leave local environmental agencies to take jobs in the private sector, and many offices, such as the one in Kemerovo Oblast, have been plagued by high employee turnover.[25]

In some cases, environmental regulators may stand to receive considerable material gain from office holding. For example, Sergei Pomogaev, of the Delta environmental group in St. Petersburg, contends that environmental inspectors often take bribes to overlook a problem.[26] Given the prevalence of corrupt practices in post-Soviet Russia, such an allegation is not surprising. There is no clear evidence, however, of the widespread capture of regulatory agencies through corruption.

The personality of an administrator also can shape outcomes. The fluid nature of politics and policy-making and the resulting high levels of uncertainty during the transition leave the regulatory process open to idiosyncratic influences. In the West, bureaucrats are guided (some would say constrained) by stable and well-defined rules, procedures, principles, institutions, and interests. The weakness of these constraints in Russia has resulted in enhanced power and influence of the individual.[27] Thus, an administrator who is highly motivated, resourceful, innovative, and a good manager can make a big improvement in the performance of his or her agency.

Autonomy. A third important component of bureaucratic capacity is the ability to act autonomously. One of the most important factors affecting institutional autonomy is access to adequate funding. Efforts to cut governmental spending at all levels have minimized the funding available for environmental protection, a trend made worse by the high rate of inflation. As a result, regional and local agencies suffer from under-staffing and a heavy workload for inspectors conducting audits of polluters. For example, 64 inspectors are responsible for overseeing the activities of 1,200 enterprises in the heavily-industrialized and polluted Kemerovo Oblast. This, combined with a lack of adequate laboratory equipment, means that the environmental protection system in Russia (including fee arrangements) often is dependent on honest self-reporting by the polluters themselves. Not surprisingly, environmental activists often charge that industries engage in massive cover-ups and that enforcement agents go along.[28] Environmental officials counter that they are doing their best given the resources available.

Government officials also have attempted to circumscribe the legal authority of environmental regulators. Under the Soviet system, most enterprises of major economic or military significance were vertically subordinated to their Moscow-based all-union ministry. They rarely had to answer to any governmental authority at the local, regional, or even Russian Federation level. In the post-Soviet era, the situation has changed dramatically: branch ministries no longer exist and enterprises face a rash of new rules, regulations and demands imposed by local and regional governments. In 1991, the Chelyabinsk Metallurgical Factory, the largest enterprise and the major polluter in this Urals city, attempted to avoid paying air pollution fines by securing special legislation from the regional soviet, which granted the factory more lenient air emissions standards. (The firm's director was a good friend of the assembly's chair.) The environmental agency successfully challenged the measure in inter-governmental arbitration, but Chelyabinsk Metallurgical then appealed to the local courts and had the new law upheld. The environmental agency then appealed to the Russian Supreme Court, where it expects to obtain a favorable decision. On the other hand, an environmental official in Krasnoyarsk Krai claimed that her committee was "sufficiently independent" and that regional authorities never had tried to influence her committee's decisions.[29]

While industry in market economies generally is perceived to be opposed to governmental regulation or able to capture regulatory authorities, this is not necessarily the case in Russia. As mentioned above, interests remain poorly defined in a transitional economic and political system where the incentive structure is changing rapidly. In part, this is due to the fact that property rights are ill-defined or vaguely established. In addition, many enterprises continue to operate under the notorious soft budget constraint and do not follow standard profit-maximizing behavior.[30]

For the most part, industrial managers do not appear to engage in widespread cover-ups of environmental damage resulting from enterprise activity; on the contrary, they frequently acknowledge negative impacts on the environment and, in spite of economic stringencies, continue to look for ways to improve the situation, particularly when conditions are adversely affecting public health. In interviews, coal mining executives consistently stressed the catastrophic nature of environmental problems caused by their mining operations, although a preliminary analysis by international experts did not substantiate such dire claims.[31] The Norilsk Mining and Metallurgical Combine, for example, has invested considerable funds in environmental protection, and its specialists enjoy esteem in the Russian regulatory community.[32] Accordingly, many managers speak of working with regulators in a partnership to find solutions to environmental problems rather than oppose them. Whether relations between regulators and industry will become more conflictive as property rights and liabilities become more defined, remains to be seen.

As in the case of Chelyabinsk Metallurgical, the courts can play an important role in establishing the capability of environmental protection agencies to enforce their policies. During its first years of operation, the Cherepovets environmental authority frequently had to take enterprises to court to prove its case; in most instances its position was upheld. In turn, the number of suits instigated by the agency in recent years has fallen as potential defendants realize their unfavorable position. Unfortunately, the court system is not uniformly reliable. In the Soviet era, judges were appointed for their credentials as good communists, not as authoritative and impartial jurists. Moreover, environmental matters were one of the lowest judicial priorities of the Soviet era, and few magistrates and lawyers have experience in the field. Since Russia functions under a civil law system based on strict application of statutes, judges frequently abstain from hearing cases related to the environment because of the absence of applicable or appropriate codes.

Environmental officials have attempted to establish their authority and autonomy by building an independent base of support among the public at large. Environmental officials frequently stress the positive role of non-governmental environmental organizations, especially in the area of consciousness-raising and agenda-setting. One common tactic to build public support is to publish an environmental newspaper. Sometimes these publications have been joint ventures: the Kurgan Oblast committee joined with the local branch of the All-Russian Society for the Protection of Nature to publish *Ekologicheskaya gazeta* (Ecological Newspaper). By regularly publicizing the extent of environmental degradation, officials hope to build public support for remediation. The Chelyabinsk regional environmental agency also has used video presentations in innovative ways to further their public relations efforts. After Moscow agreed to shut down the antiquated and dirty Karabash copper smelter for extensive capital renovation in 1990, the oblast environmental committee made a video to document the plant's final day of operation and highlight the impending improvements in environmental quality, thus establishing the agency as a credible enforcer of regulations.[33] When the committee wanted to stop illegal construction of country homes in a sensitive watershed, the agency sent a film crew to the site and made a compelling film stating its case. The film was shown to the regional parliament, after which deputies voted to take measures to stop construction.[34]

Emerging Trends in Environmental Protection in the Periphery

Political uncertainty and the pressures of economic transformation have resulted in an opportunistic, short-term, get-rich-quick or "frontier" mentality which threatens nature in the post-Soviet era. Environmentalists fret that the weak environmental institutions created under the Soviet regime are completely inadequate and overwhelmed by the new challenges of this era. There are, however, some positive signs.

Where all major planning and development projects were once managed by Moscow-based bureaucrats and institutes, the trend towards increased autonomy for industry and local governments means local environmental committees are forced to handle more matters on their own, especially in the area of land-use planning and natural resource management. Before 1992, no organization outside of Moscow worked on land reform issues. Now, as a result of new legislation, local governments have been given responsibility for land management.[35] With the privatization of economic activity, regional and local organs will carry considerable responsibility for the allocation of property rights, implementation and enforcement of licenses, and the setting of prices and development quotas.[36] These arrangements bring new challenges and will invite new conflicts among various local interests as well as between the center and the periphery. While authorities in the periphery in the past often turned to Moscow for assistance in resolving conflicts in their districts, they will be less able or likely to use this tactic in the future. As pointed out above, many local authorities openly contravene rules from Moscow, particularly when it comes to the management of local natural resources.

As Russian political commentators frequently point out, Russia lacks a law-based civil society. Transactions in the political market, therefore, are not governed by established rules, principles, or even expectations. How each region attempts to meet its environmental challenges depends, in part, on the nature of the local political environment. Therefore, considerable regional variation is emerging. Some regions, such as Nizhnii Novgorod and St. Petersburg, are moving rapidly forward with privatization programs while other regions, Tatarstan and Ulyanovsk for example, cling to practices characteristic of the Soviet past.[37] In the case of environmental affairs, we are also beginning to see variations in bureaucratic capacity and regulatory approaches among different geographical and administrative regions.

Broadly speaking, some regions seem to work, while others do not. Within a federation-wide system that is standardized and uniform on paper, some regional agencies appear demoralized, severely handicapped, and ineffectual, while others exude a motivated, self-assured, "can do" attitude and are making headway. The Moscow city committee, for example, shows little evidence of assertive regulatory activity. In Chelyabinsk and Vologda, on the other hand, environmental agencies have developed strategic plans, and are pursuing their mandate with zeal and optimism despite objective constraints. As Yurii Bazanov, the head of the Vologda Oblast environmental agency, modestly pointed out, they are accomplishing enough to "prevent a worsening of the situation."[38] This has profound implications for environmental security in Russia in the coming years.

The polluter-pays system has become a central element of the government's strategy to reduce environmental degradation and to provide revenues to support non-budgetary environmental protection programs.[39] According to this system, which was implemented federation-wide in 1991, the collection of permit fees and pollution fines is a function of the local and regional committees. But as the environment minister noted at a meeting of regional environmental officials:

> There are oblasts and republics in the structure of Russia where they collect far more than half of payments for environmental pollution than in principle can be collected. But there [also] are places where not even a kopek is collected and, accordingly, nothing is transferred to the budget or to ecology funds. And these places, from an ecologist's point of view, are far from favorable.[40]

Backing up this point, officials from the Moscow Oblast committee have pointed out that 60 per cent of enterprises in the capital do not have pollution permits (on which to base payments) and those that do almost never pay their environmental fines or fees. Only managers who are "good citizens" or "fools" pay fines.[41] Compliance has been somewhat better in Chelyabinsk. Conversely, officials in Krasnoyarsk and Cherepovets claim almost no problems collecting polluter-pays revenue.

What factors have led some environmental agencies to be more effective than others? One major factor is leadership; the impact of the individual cannot be underestimated in this period characterized by institutional fluidity and an uncertain environment. A second related factor is the existence of a well-defined plan of action. Third is an agency's strategy for asserting its authority. Some regional authorities have taken aggressive stances: Krasnoyarsk took the unusual step of obtaining direct access to enterprises' bank accounts to ensure their collection efforts. A common tactic is to go after the largest polluters. Thus, authorities in Chelyabinsk targeted Karabash Copper as one of their first challenges. The Irkutsk Oblast environmental committee repeatedly has battled with the Bratsk Aluminum Plant, one of Russia's largest aluminum smelters and a major exporter. When asked why the agency had chosen to go after such a powerful concern when targeting smaller, less well-connected enterprises may have been easier to handle, a regional official pointed out that they wanted "to set a precedent."[42]

While the presence of large, monopolistic industries in a region can be an obstacle to enforcement, many regulators see big industries as prime targets from which they potentially can extract huge fines. For regulators in Irkutsk, this was another rationale for going after Bratsk Aluminum. In 1989, the Irkutsk committee had extracted a large fine from the smelter, a share of which went into a local environmental fund managed by the regional authorities. With the demise of the old centralized command-administrative system and the rise of federal budget deficits, local governmental administrators have lost a large share of their revenue from the center while demands for local governmental expenditures have increased.[43] To help cover this gap, many local governments are implementing alternative tax schemes; environmental and natural resource fees are one potential source of revenue.

Because most industrial enterprises do not meet existing environmental regulations, which are formally very strict, potential conflicts exist between governmental regulators and enterprise managers. The local political culture also appears to affect the nature of these relations. In some regions, particularly in the south and Siberia, politics are more polemical and conflictive. In Irkutsk Oblast, a pharmaceutical firm refused to accept the strong demands of environmental regulators and continued to operate without the proper license. Some regions are caught in gridlock. Political conflicts in Moscow pit the mayor's office, the city council, district councils, the environmental committee, and environmental activists against one another. In northern regions like Kostroma and Vologda, officials like to point out that local politics are managed in a more corporatist fashion. All parties involved – government, industry, labor, and the general public – appear cognizant of the problems they face and are committed to solving them cooperatively. "There are no sharp confrontations here," asserted Eduard Parakhonskii, special assistant to the mayor of Cherepovets.[44]

Time appears to be on the side of the regulators. With time and experience, local and regional environmental committees have been able to assemble their staffs and get them up to speed. Many committee heads contend that, despite its shortcomings, the 1992 environmental law has bolstered their position. People criticize the law without trying to make it work, says Vologda's Bazanov. Instead, agencies need to work with it for a few years to see how it should be perfected.[45] Given their heavy workload, environmental officials have little time to assess programs: "We are learning on the run," proclaims the head of Kemerovo's agency.[46]

Despite challenges by polluters, cases tested in arbitration and the courts increasingly have upheld the authority of the regulators, setting valuable precedents which will hold in the future. Moreover, industrial managers are discovering that these new regulators probably are not going to disappear soon. Through repeated interactions and the increasing possibility of punishment, defection on the part of managers becomes a less viable operating strategy.[47] Committees which have enjoyed greater stability in cadres, such as Cherepovets and Vologda (the founding chairs are still in office), have an advantage over others. In contrast, new actors have yet to establish their authority and staying power. The local authority in Achinsk (part of Krasnoyarsk Krai) has taken several years to get its act together, and as a result, local industries still do not consider them to have "the last word" on environmental matters.[48]

Conclusion: The Implications for Governance in Russia

For decades, Western scholars characterized the USSR as the epitome of the strong, unitary state with its centralized command economy, mobilized bureaucracy, and monolithic Communist Party. For example, Samuel Huntington described the Soviet Union (along with the United States and Great Britain) as having "strong, adaptable, coherent political institutions" as well as "effective bureaucracies."[49] Musing over the collapse of the USSR, Alexander Dallin queried:

> What we are really puzzling over is how as thoroughly controlled, as tightly disciplined, as rigidly programmed, and as heavily indoctrinated a system as the Soviet Union managed to fall apart, unravel so easily and so completely, and in the process prompt in its citizenry an utter scorn for authority, and disregard for laws and regulations.[50]

With the demise of the Soviet regime and the emergence of centrifugal forces threatening the integrity of the region's new states, area specialists find themselves poorly equipped to follow and comprehend rapidly-evolving developments across the region. Beyond the borders of Moscow and St. Petersburg, scholars rarely have probed to examine the character of regional and local governmental institutions and to assess how effective they are at negotiating the rigorous challenges of the post-Soviet era. In 1953, Merle Fainsod published his landmark book on Soviet politics, *How Russia is Ruled*. In the 1990s, we ask: Is Russia ruled? An examination of one aspect of state activity, natural resources management, can provide some answers.

Alexander Dallin attributes the collapse of the Soviet system to, among other causes, a "loosening of control," weakening of ideology, and the rise of corruption. One important factor Dallin omitted was that the Soviet regime was overwhelmed not only by demands from a politically mobilized citizenry (in a conventional Huntingtonian fashion), but also by the managerial challenges posed by economic and political transition and sustained development in the contemporary world. Leninist ideology and the suppression of political demands during the Soviet era created strong incentives for the public *not* to participate in essential government decision-making. The Soviet political system also stunted the development of local and regional policy-making structures, as they were designed only to carry out orders from above with minimal external input into the process. As illustrated in the case of natural resource management, regional and local governments largely failed to develop bureaucratic capacity in planning, policy-making, and policy analysis, focusing instead on ritualized monitoring and enforcement of regulations handed down by central organs.[51]

Models of the political process in Western nations depict well-developed and robust interest groups, states, and organizational processes. Conversely, Russian governmental structures, and arenas of decision-making in general, continue to suffer from underdevelopment, while the demands placed on them mount in quantity and complexity. Generally speaking, day-to-day government in Russia is run through bureaucratic organizations which are formally structured and fairly uniform across the federation, and officials assume their positions in a serious manner and pay attention to standardized procedure, leaving aside the phenomenon of corruption. Yet, when more essential issues present themselves, this patina of formal arrangements does not suffice: politics and policy-making tend to be dominated by individual actors, to be subject to idiosyncratic influences, and to resemble *ad hoc* responses to the problem of the moment. In sum, government in Russia, like its nascent economic markets, could be characterized as being thin.

Bureaucratic style and effectiveness vary significantly across Russia and give rise to substantial regional differences in outcomes. This variance arises from how individual actors fill in this formal skeleton of rules, roles and structure. As mentioned above, the personalities of key actors play an important role. Another factor may be historical legacy. Douglass North argues that while formal rules and institutions may be changed quickly, informal constraints are much more glacial in character; they tend to embody only gradual modifications of past arrangements, leading to a situation of path dependence.[52] In his detailed comparison of regional governments in Italy, Putnam reaches back one thousand years into the past to conclude that medieval traditions play a significant role in determining whether contemporary politics tend towards centralized autocracy or democratic civic community.[53] The historic roots of authority patterns in contemporary Russia require further research. For example, gridlock in Moscow may result from the legacy of communist culture, while in the Russian North authority patterns inherited from the Soviet period may be less deeply rooted and have a less enduring influence. Alternatively, it is possible that better environmental protection agencies resulted from the presence of big water projects in the Soviet era.[54] Understanding variations in political and institutional traditions, in turn, could improve our comprehension of emerging trends in environmental protection and natural resource management.

Regardless of the starting point, global experience suggests that the proper management and coordination of reforms affecting natural resource management require a robust, capable, and adaptable government bureaucracy, insulated from conflicting demands of the domestic and international political environment.[55] The experiences of the developing and newly industrializing countries teach that the growth of independent and effective state structures does not arise automatically with the reform imperative. Rather, political leaders deliberately must promote the development of bureaucratic capacity in order to implement reform programs, to foresee imminent problems and to respond with the appropriate corrective action.[56]

As political uncertainty continues to preoccupy Moscow and as federal environmental laws remain broad and unspecific, local and regional actors will be relatively free to shape environmental protection efforts. The process of establishing bureaucratic structures will be political, and outcomes will be shaped by the interests and relative power of the participants in the process. We should not expect these structures to be wholly coherent, their positions entirely independent, or their programs completely effective.[57] Despite these obstacles, the breakdown of the Soviet system created the first opportunity to effect real measures of environmental protection and to pursue wise resource management in Russia. With luck, skill, and persistence, these efforts will prevent a return to the destructive legacy of the past.

Notes

Work on this chapter was made possible by a generous fellowship from the University of California's Institute on Global Conflict and Cooperation.

1. For the latest overviews of the state of the environment and environmental affairs in Russia and the former Soviet Union, see DJ Peterson, *Troubled Lands: The Legacy of Soviet Environmental Destruction* (Boulder, Colo.: Westview Press, 1993); Murray Feshbach and Alfred Friendly Jr., *Ecocide in the USSR. Health and Nature under Siege* (New York: Basic Books, 1992); Philip R. Pryde, *Environmental Management in the Soviet Union* (New York: Cambridge University Press, 1991).

2. Although the ministry has undergone several organizational shake-ups and name changes in its short history, the institution has changed little in substance and therefore will be referred to throughout as Minpriroda.

3. In this paper, the term "regional" government is used to describe the most important administrative subdivisions in the Russian Federation, of which there are essentially three types – region (*oblast*), territory (*krai*), and republic (*respublika*) – each with varying levels of autonomy. Within these levels, the *raion* is a district-level administrative subdivision.

4. Terry Moe, "The Politics of Bureaucratic Structure," in John E. Chubb and Paul E. Peterson, eds., *Can the Government Govern?* (Washington D.C.: The Brookings Institution, 1989).

5. The fact that the functions of air and water quality monitoring, policy setting, and enforcement were separated bureaucratically is not necessarily problematic. However, in the Russian institutional culture of bureaucratic parochialism and restricted access to information, this division arguably undermined the ability of the new environment ministry to carry out its functions.

6. *Kuranty*, March 12, 1992, 4. Some critics of the ministry, such as Yeltsin advisor Alexei Yablokov, were not dissatisfied with the change.

7. Philip Hanson, "Local Power and Market Reform in Russia," typescript, September 1992.

8. Presentation at a conference on Democratic Federalism and Environmental Crisis in the Republics of the Former Soviet Union, Moscow, August 1991.

9. *Izvestiya*, May 8, 1991, 8.

10. *Kuranty*, March 12, 1992, 4.

11. *Izvestiya*, February 25, 1992, 2. See also *Izvestiya*, November 22, 1991, 2. For more on natural resource issues in Siberia, see Andrew R. Bond, ed., "Panel on Siberia: Economic and Territorial Issues," *Soviet Geography*, 32, 6 (June 1991), 363–432.

12. Barbara Geddes, "Building 'State' Autonomy in Brazil, 1930-1964," *Comparative Politics*, 22, 2 (January 1990), 217–35.

13. This point is drawn from an analysis of industrial managers in reform-era Poland. See Janusz M. Dabrowski, Michal Federowicz, and Anthony Levitas, "Stabilization and State Enterprise Adjustment: The Political Economy of State Firms after Five Months of Fiscal Discipline, Poland 1990," Harvard University Minda de Gunzburg Center for European Studies, Program on Central and Eastern Europe, Working Paper Series No. 6, n.d.

14. See, for example, Mary McAuley, "Politics, Economics, and Elite Realignment in Russia: A Regional Perspective," *Soviet Economy*, 8, 1 (1992), 46–88.

15. Jeffrey W. Hahn, "Local Politics and Political Power in Russia: The Case of Yaroslavl'," *Soviet Economy*, 7, 4 (1991), 322–41.

16. Petr I. Poletaev, "Vosstanovit' garmoniyu prirody i cheloveka," *Zdorov'ye*, 6 (1989), 1. The experience of the environmental agency is not unique within the governing structures of the Russian Federation. During the March 1993 political power struggle between President Boris Yeltsin and Supreme Soviet Chair Ruslan Khasbulatov, the latter contended that the President had inherited the entire staff of the CPSU Central Committee (*RFE/RL Daily Report*, March 24, 1993). A reliance on an ideological opponent has a precedent in Soviet history: shortly after the October Revolution in 1917, the Bolshevik government was forced to call back many of the deposed imperial government's bureaucrats whom the new regime had summarily fired. The revolutionaries could not manage the government.

17. Olga V. Snopkovskaya, chief of environmental inspection, Leningrad Oblast Environmental Protection Committee, personal communication, St. Petersburg, February 1993.

18. Vladislav Larin, "Opasnoe neponimanie," *Energiya: ekonomika, tekhnika, ekologiya*, 4 (1990).

19. Dabrowski, et al., "Stabilization and State Enterprise Adjustment."

20. Valerie Bunce and Maria Csanadi, "Uncertainty in the Transition: Post Communism in Hungary," *East European Politics and Societies*, 7, 2 (1993).

21. Mary Cline, "The Micromanagement of Reform: Regional Responses to Privatization in the Russian Federation," typescript, March 1993.

22. Graham T. Allison, "Conceptual Models and the Cuban Missile Crisis," *American Political Science Review*, 58 (September 1969), 689–718.

23. Interview with V.I. Samburskii, Cherepovets, February 1993.

24. Interview with Vasilii Bakunin, Chelyabinsk, August 1992.

25. In Almaty, for example, a local enterprise Eko-eksp (short for *ekologicheskaya ekspertiza*, or environmental study) has been able to draw many environmental professionals away from the government to conduct environmental impact studies for local businesses. The pay at Eko-eksp is two to five times higher than a government job. Interview with Rafael and Hamida Yernazarov, staff members, Kazakh Ecological Fund, Los Angeles, April 1992.

26. Peterson, *Troubled Lands*, 70-71.

27. Bunce and Csanadi, "Uncertainty in the Transition."

28. Peterson, *Troubled Lands*, 70-71.

29. Anna Yerashchova, Chief Specialist, Department of Scientific and Technical Information, Krasnoyarsk Krai Committee for Environmental Protection, personal communication, Krasnoyarsk, August 1992.

30. Barry W. Ickes and Randi Ryterman, "The Interenterprise Arrears Crisis in Russia," *Post-Soviet Affairs*, 8, 4 (1992).

31. This analysis was part of a coal sector restructuring study conducted by the World Bank in Autumn 1993, in which this author took part.

32. DJ Peterson, "Norilsk in the Nineties," *RFE/RL Research Report*, 2, 5 (29 January 1993).

33. When the U.S. Environmental Protection Agency was created in 1970, Administrator William Ruckelshaus similarly turned to the media to establish his new agency's credibility. Alfred Marcus, "Environmental Protection Agency," in James Q. Wilson, ed., *The Politics of Regulation* (New York: Basic Books, 1980).

34. On the other hand, many environmental officials chafe when they see their autonomy infringed by what they perceive as overly zealous and amateurish environmental groups. While they accept the principle of environmental activism, such officials prefer the public to leave the solution of environmental problems to "the experts."

35. Yurii Bazanov, Chair, Vologda Oblast Environmental Protection Committee, personal communication, Vologda, February 1993.

36. Yelena Nikitina, "New Challenges for Russia's Natural Resources Management," *CIS Environmental Watch*, 3 (1992), 22–25. See also *Zelenyi mir*, 35-36 (1992).

37. Cline, "The Micromanagement of Reform."

38. Bazanov, personal communication, Vologda, February 1993.

39. For more on the polluter pays system, see Peterson, *Troubled Lands*, 171-74.

40. *Zelenyi mir*, 35-36 (1992).

41. Nataliya Zelentsova, Scientific-Technical Department, Moscow Oblast Committee for Environmental Protection, personal communication, Moscow, July 1992.

42. Larisa I. Dedova, Department Chief, Irkutsk Oblast Committee for Environmental Protection, personal communication, Irkutsk, August 1992.

43. Daniel Berkowitz and Beth Mitchnek, "Fiscal Decentralization in the Soviet Economy," *Comparative Economic Studies*, 34, 2 (Summer 1992), 1–18.

44. Eduard Parakhonskii, mayor's assistant for environmental planning, personal communication, Cherepovets, February 1993.

45. Bazanov, personal communication, Vologda, February 1993.

46. Ol'ga Pavlovna Andrakhanova, Chair, Kemerovo Oblast Environmental Protection Committee, personal communication, Kemerovo, September 1993.

47. Robert Axelrod, *The Evolution of Cooperation* (New York: Basic Books, 1984).

48. Yerashchova, personal communication, Krasnoyarsk, August 1992.

49. Samuel P. Huntington, *Political Order in Changing Societies* (New Haven: Yale University Press, 1968).

50. Alexander Dallin, "Causes of the Collapse of the USSR," *Post-Soviet Affairs*, 8, 4 (1992), 279–302.

51. This problem is not limited to Russia. Critics in the United States have decried the emphasis on regulatory enforcement over long-range environmental planning by the EPA.

52. Douglass C. North, *Institutions, Institutional Change, and Economic Performance* (New York: Cambridge University Press, 1990).

53. Robert D. Putnam, *Making Democracy Work: Civic Traditions in Modern Italy* (Princeton: Princeton University Press, 1993).

54. In explaining the stellar economic performance of the Asian newly industrializing countries, Thomas M. Callaghy links their effective governmental bureaucracies, particularly those of South Korea and Taiwan, to the legacy of Japanese colonial rule. See "Toward State Capability and Embedded Liberalism in the Third World: Lessons for Adjustment," in Joan M. Nelson, ed., *Fragile Coalitions: The Politics of Economic Adjustment* (New Brunswick, NJ: Transaction Books, 1989).

55. See, for example, Stephen Haggard, *Pathways from the Periphery: Politics in the Newly Industrializing Countries* (Ithaca: Cornell University Press, 1990); Joan M. Nelson, "The Politics of Long-Haul Economic Reform," in Joan M. Nelson, ed., *Fragile Coalitions;* Thomas J. Biersteker, "Reducing the Role of the State in the Economy: A Conceptual Exploration of IMF and World Bank Prescriptions," *International Studies Quarterly*, 34 (1990), 477–92; Russell Mardon, "The State and Effective Control of Foreign Capital," *World Politics*, 43, 1 (October 1990), 111–38.

56. Callaghy, "Toward State Capability and Embedded Liberalism."

57. Moe, "The Politics of Bureaucratic Structure."

7

Citizen Participation and the Environment in Russia

Lisa Van Buren

The extent of environmental problems in the post-communist region and the associated social and health costs may seem overwhelming, but growing awareness of these difficulties may also encourage a search for solutions. An environmental threat of this magnitude requires that these solutions come from people in all walks of life and not only from politicians and scientists. Sometimes only collectively and over time do these efforts add up to visible results. It may be that the current period of crises will open opportunities for people to work together in new and constructive ways in the former Soviet Union.

This chapter examines the effects of the collapse of the Soviet Union on citizen-based environmental movements in Russia. What new strategies are helping citizens to cope with currently chaotic and difficult political and economic conditions? How might legal mechanisms prove useful in empowering citizen activism?

Background on the Environmental Movement

A Russian doctor of philosophical sciences, Oleg Nikolaevich Yanitskii, once referred to the environmental movement in the Soviet Union as "the most radical of all civic initiatives," in the sense that these initiatives "are for the most part oriented to changing the system of values."[1] The environmental movement also has been called "newborn"[2] under the regime of Mikhail Gorbachev, but it is not without a history. While the mass form of the eco-movement is indeed new, historically there exists a long tradition of environmental initiatives with extensive networks and, in particular, a close connection to independent science. A number of Western scholars have written about the history of the environmental movement in the former Soviet Union.[3] In this chapter, only some of the important influences on the movement since the beginning of perestroika will be mentioned.

Mikhail Gorbachev's policy of glasnost opened up the arena for public debate and allowed greater public expression in the form of petitions, letter-writing campaigns, demonstrations, meetings, and media accounts. This greater political openness made possible the formation of informal environmental groups in addition to the formal Communist Party-sanctioned organizations. Besides glasnost, two other factors increased popular activism under Gorbachev. The nuclear accident at Chernobyl in 1986 demonstrated the government's incompetence and fallibility and the seriousness of environmental threats. Citizen participation was also empowered by the connection of environmental concerns to nationalist movements and the struggle for greater national autonomy from the Soviet government. Environmental degradation became a symbol of the consequences of Soviet domination and provided a rallying cause for people, particularly those from the non-Russian republics.[4]

Under Gorbachev's rule, the few routine or legalized mechanisms that linked citizens to decision-makers, in either industry or government, were largely ineffective. Exerting direct social or political pressure, when it was possible, remained the only means to achieve a response. To their credit, informal groups in some cases were successful at getting decision-makers to respond to environmental problems, such as the postponement or cancellation of environmentally harmful projects and economic activities. In some cases, however, government cancellation of such projects was based on financial rather than environmental considerations.

With the collapse of the Soviet Union and the emergence of independent states, the political motivation for citizen activism has diminished. The politicized nature of the environmental movement along nationalist and ethnic lines changed when the Communist Party fell. As power devolved to lower levels of government, people found themselves having to weigh the economic costs of environmental protection, since assertive action against polluting enterprises might lead to job loss or production declines. Nevertheless, the downfall of the Communist Party has in no way led to the demise of the eco-movement. Severe environmental conditions, pervasive anti-ecological attitudes, and a power structure with interests that resemble those under Soviet rule have led citizen activists to continue to confront environmental issues in political terms.[5]

Instability Under Yeltsin

Plagued by an unstable system of markets, legal regimes, and political decision-making, Russia has limited social resources to address environmental difficulties. It can be argued that the condition of the currently weakened system of governance and distribution in Russia will itself be further incapacitated by the growing severity of environmental problems.[6] The vicious spiral of the economic and political maelstrom is having a profound effect on the ability of citizens to make their ecosystem habitable. Unfortunately, conflict and even violent conflict may be the result of insufferable living conditions.

Fortunately, Russians have not yet come to the point at which violent confrontation seems to be the only option. Some citizens continue to seek non-violent means of achieving better living environments, while others take no action at all, either due to ignorance or apathy about conditions. Some feel that environmental problems are not the first priority, while others may see that action is futile. Those citizens who continue to be actively involved in environmental problems at the grassroots are encountering a wide variety of difficulties, some new and some old. In terms of financing, governmental support has not been forthcoming. Support from the Russian private sector, including wealthy individuals or public organizations, continues to be the mainstay of existing groups. However, that support has dwindled as economic conditions have worsened.

As a result of worsening economic conditions, citizen activists have been seeking new and creative sources of assistance. There is a growing pipeline of aid from foreign sources, specifically foreign non-profit organizations and wealthy individuals. Some of these organizations include the MacArthur Foundation, Kettering Foundation, Soros Foundation, ISAR, Greenpeace International, and Natural Resources Defense Council (NRDC).

In addition, it has become clear to some activists that alliances must be made with those who now have funds in Russia, including commercial sources such as industry and various businesses. For instance, oil and gas companies in Russia, although traditionally considered the bane of the environment, may find it in their interest to support activists in order to avoid potential conflict. However, cooperation with economic interests may also limit the ability of environmental activists to make demands that counter those interests. Some activists point out that the few environmental funds now in existence in Russia are created by economic interests that seek to portray an image of environmental concern while heavily influencing how those funds are used.[7]

Another source of financing for environmental activists is to engage in their own commercial ventures. This includes providing environmental consulting, setting up companies that sell "green" products such as clean water or water filters, engaging in the trading of goods solely for the purpose of raising money for environmental projects, or helping businesses to obtain environmental equipment and farmers to obtain better agricultural implements or chemical substances. This is the case, for instance, with an organization called Green Movement. It is one of the few environmental groups in St. Petersburg that is able to make some profit because it is trying to combine environmental activism with trade and business arrangements.[8] Many activists use their workplace as a base for environmental activities because of access to office supplies, telephones, computers, and possibly fax machines.

The future of the environmental movement may depend on the ability to generate funding. Consulting is one activity that may become increasingly profitable in a country desperately in need of environmentally-related information.[9] As economic priorities continue to be the main focus not only of governmental policy but also of the average Russian citizen, people must find ways to survive in an environment which encourages negligence of the law and promotes a survival-of-the-craftiest mentality. Citizen activists may also be tempted to seek short-term profits over longer-term investment needed to improve environmental conditions. Unfortunately, the economic hardships faced daily by Russians due to rapid inflation and, for many, stagnating wages and looming unemployment, create a situation of fear and stress not conducive to environmental activism.

Economic realities also mean that those projects previously canceled, in part due to popular opinion, are now being reconsidered. A power-generating station scheduled to be constructed north of Moscow was canceled following a petition drive that garnered over 400,000 signatures. Now, due to economic circumstances, the project has become an issue again. The construction of additional nuclear power plants has surfaced as an issue following the promulgation of a decree in December of 1992 "On the Construction of Atomic Stations in 1992–1995." Some environmental activists believe that the head of the Russian Federation Ministry for the Protection of the Environment and Natural Resources (*Minpriroda*), Viktor Danilov-Danilyan, has bowed to economic pressures and now supports the construction of additional reactors at existing nuclear power plants.[10]

Psychologically, it takes a dedicated individual to maintain environmental activism in Russia. The period of perestroika and the fall of the communist regime held out the possibility for reform in the system and in particular for changes in the values that led to environmental destruction; but now there is a sense of disillusionment. Fewer citizens actively participate in environmental organizations and those who do often find themselves isolated in rural areas or with only a core group of people in large cities.

Disillusionment also extended to the previous parliament which was elected in 1989. Many deputies were voted into office on environmental platforms that were subsequently abandoned. These officials are now viewed mostly as opportunists, despite a few deputies who have persisted in raising environmental issues. Hope that government is a venue for change has decreased dramatically because of continuing political conflict and the lack of results, in spite of numerous pieces of environmental legislation and the creation of an environmental ministry.

The decline of the Communist Party's hold on information has not helped citizens to improve environmental conditions much either. An increase in newspaper, journal, and television coverage has perhaps made more people aware of environmental problems, but that knowledge has not necessarily been translated into tangible results.[11] Despite a decrease in government censorship, the state of education and media coverage about environmental matters remains inadequate. Danilov-Danilyan sharply criticized the press coverage of the UNCED Conference in Rio de Janeiro as being "extremely weak, incompetent and tendentious." He also noted that in the first nine months of 1992 his Ministry received over 15,000 letters from citizens, an average of one in ten written collectively; however, in his view, the volume of questions and demands put forth in these letters "testifies to a lack of information for the public about the factual ecological conditions in the regions."[12]

A lack of public information on environmental issues is not just a media problem, however. Although Soviet citizens may have grown up hearing the environmental slogans, there are many spheres where environmental education is insufficient. In response to mounting citizen concern, training in environmental education and management is now growing in Russia. Many universities have opened up departments of ecology, and the number of courses related to the environment is expanding. Ecological issues have mostly been addressed in scientific and technical fields in the past, but they are now becoming more important in areas such as law and policy studies. There are now opportunities for people to specialize in the previously non-existent sub-field of environmental law.

Environmental groups are also continuing to improve their knowledge base. To date, many groups and individuals lack a variety of experiences and skills needed to strengthen their initiatives.[13] Learning how to interact constructively with advocates of diverse interests, to create dialogue, to negotiate, and to carry out decisions is important for many activists. Although many environmentally-active citizens have scientific backgrounds, few have adequate experience in carrying out environmental impact assessments, for example. There also needs to be a system for standardization of information between groups, in order to make environmental findings and statistics more informative and useful.

Fortunately, shortages of office supplies are not the problem they were in the recent past. However, the expense of obtaining equipment and supplies, distributing information, photocopying, and communication has made it more difficult to carry out activities. Shortages of money and time are growing problems as people are still plagued with difficult shopping conditions and decreasing incomes.

New Strategies

Environmental activists are learning new strategies, such as tapping new sources of funds, using computer networks, developing negotiating and communication skills, and applying recent environmental legislation to aid their cause. The Russian environmental movement is becoming increasingly able to affect government policy, despite hardships. The movement will grow as a result of worsening environmental conditions, but also as it matures and finds new tactics to address its concerns.

As mentioned previously, there is growing support from foreign sources. The global economic recession has been a hindrance to receiving foreign support but, nonetheless, more international contacts are improving the availability of information and the ability to influence decisions. Representatives of donor organizations such as the MacArthur Foundation are also hoping that governmental officials will see the importance of their efforts. The Director of the Foundation in Russia has said that Russian leaders need to realize "the importance of having good and strong grant-making institutions here," and to "realize the benefit to their people of having support for good people here ... then there is a possibility for NGOs to act as a lobbying group for change."[14] Unfortunately, such foreign sources provide only a small portion of the necessary funding, and clearly the onus of developing grant-making institutions and creating a solid foundation for lobbying rests largely on the citizens themselves.

One of the most promising developments for citizen activists is the improvement in telecommunications linkages, particularly in the form of computer-generated electronic mail. E-mail circumvents official censorship and provides users with a system that is rapid and relatively less expensive and more reliable than direct telephone calls, faxes, letters, or telexes. Activism in Russia has traditionally been plagued by inadequate and outdated telecommunications networks. People who have access to the necessary electronic equipment and phone lines are still relatively few in number and are found mostly in large cities. However, the growing number of system users is already opening up global communication to a degree that was previously unknown and thus empowering citizen efforts. Working together with ISAR and the SEU, an organization based in the United States called The Sacred Earth Network (SEN) has enabled numerous individuals and groups in Russia, and other former Soviet republics, to communicate by providing the necessary tools, technical support, and encouragement. For example, updates on the environmental problems of the Udeghe (or Udegeitsy), an indigenous group living in relatively remote regions in the Far East, became internationally known in minutes through the use of an e-mail system set up by a visiting SEN delegation.[15]

In terms of new strategies, it was mentioned earlier that financial difficulties are prompting people to seek new alliances. In general, alliances are important not just for financial purposes but also for improving the power base of the Russian environmental movement. The movement lost momentum politically as well as economically with the collapse of the Soviet empire. The task of finding common ground with religious organizations, trade unions, governmental officials and scientists has become more difficult and perhaps more important than ever due to changes in Russia's political and economic environment. Protection of the environment is an issue that affects people personally, no matter what their creed or occupation; this is particularly the case due to health implications. An example of a citizen-based effort to bring people of diverse backgrounds together, including industry representatives, governmental officials and local farmers is a project called the "Regulation of Boundary Environmental Problems between Estonia and Russia in the Peipsi-Pihkva Lakes Watershed." The project involves 15 to 20 institutions from Estonia, Russia and the United States, with limited funding provided by the International Research and Exchanges Board (IREX) in the United States and Central European University in Hungary. Although environmental activism has often been characterized by confrontation, current conditions are prompting many activists to seek problems where common concern can be found and where cooperative results can more readily be achieved.[16]

Finally, there now exists greater potential for legal mechanisms to empower citizen activism. The Russian parliament adopted a Law on Environmental Protection in December of 1991, which gave Russian citizens unprecedented rights. One of the most noteworthy statements, found in article 91, establishes that "citizens have a right to [file lawsuits] in court, demanding termination of environmentally harmful activities which are damaging the health and property of citizens, the economy, and the environment." The document also enumerates a list of rights in articles 11 and 12 whereby citizens can be compensated for environmentally-related health damage, can demand that projects be canceled by administrative means or by court order, and can even "raise the issue of prosecution of guilty officials and private citizens."[17]

Furthermore, the law states that "public environmental assessments conducted by scientific collectives or public associations at their own initiative may become legally binding." However, actual consideration of such assessments still requires approval by the "appropriate state environmental assessment organs." Such a requirement may thus work to limit public initiatives.[18]

In theory, the law empowers citizens to an extent not found in environmental legislation in North America. The law does not demand that citizens must prove a causal relationship between health problems and environmental damage. In addition, the legal system is financially accessible to most people because court fees remain relatively unaffected by inflationary pressures. However, what appears possible in law bears little resemblance to what is actually happening.

The courts in Russia maintain a very conservative stance and are slow to change in accordance with legislation. Incompetence is widespread in the courts and generally in the government bureaucracy with regard to environmental legislation.[19] For the law to be effectively utilized by environmental proponents, court officials and government bureaucrats must be educated about its provisions. A lack of knowledge is not surprising considering the veritable onslaught of legislation promulgated by the Russian government, the difficulty of obtaining legal information, and the past undervaluation of environmental legislation. Lawyers and judges are not only poorly trained in environmental legislation, they are also not highly regarded within Russia. In addition, Communist Party rule did not further development of a legal culture. A political consciousness has yet to be established which encourages belief in and respect for the law.

Despite these difficulties, the law holds out the possibility of empowering citizens. Now that a legal framework has been established for people to seek compensation or demand environmental protection, a few well-informed citizens are testing the application of the law. In November 1992, a Russian non-profit environmental organization, the SEU, attempted to take an oil consortium to court on the basis of the new Russian environmental protection law. This first attempt was unsuccessful because the agreement the oil consortium had with the Russian government had been concluded prior to the environmental legislation and was therefore considered exempt. An article in the newspaper *Izvestiya* reported that the court refused to hear SEU's case against the government on the basis that SEU did not have "the right to file complaints in the Arbitration Court in defense of the interests of state and society."[20]

A few other cases brought by citizen groups are still pending. At the writing of this chapter, the Udeghe are continuing a legal battle to stop the Korean firm, Hyundai, from clear-cutting virgin forests on their land. The Udeghe are challenging the local government, not under the environmental protection law, but under administrative law, since the local government allegedly did not consult the indigenous peoples on the decision, as the law requires.[21] There are also two lawsuits being argued against local officials by a NGO organization in St. Petersburg (the Russian International Center for Environmental Law); the cases involve alleged violations of the Helsinki Convention on the Protection of the Baltic Sea and illegal dumping of raw sludge.[22] Other lawsuits have been filed, particularly in Moscow; some, to date, have not been granted court proceedings.

The success of a few cases could have a major impact on the future of the Russian environmental movement. People are more likely to be interested in the law and feel increased political efficacy if even a few significant successes are achieved. However, currently chaotic conditions and limited knowledge of the law in Russia do not make legal mechanisms a very effective means of change.

It should be noted that all of the cases mentioned above have some foreign support in the form of information gathering and coordination, consultation, or provision of material resources. A number of the lawyers involved in filing these suits also have had educational experiences abroad. Although foreign assistance can play a major role in publicizing and sustaining legal mechanisms, it seems likely that it will be some time before Russian laws become enforceable legal instruments. Not only economic and political stability are important. It will take time to change the legacy of social disregard for the court system.

Conclusion

At a time when the existing environmental infrastructure and governmental institutions are failing to meet adequately the environmental security threat within Russia, citizens have not given up hope for change. Many citizens foresee increasingly severe environmental threats but feel incapable of stopping them. People are seeing the effects of pollution on their children now and are desperate to ensure the basic necessities for health – clean air, water, and food. Nevertheless, intelligent and skilled Russians are applying their know-how to environmental problems, and it seems that their concern is bound to have an increasingly strong influence on the course of events.

The collapse of the Soviet Union has created increasingly difficult conditions for those citizens making efforts to improve environmental quality. Russia, like all the other former communist countries, must contend with economic and political instability that affects the viability of a citizen-based environmental movement. More than ever, activists are under pressure to find means of support and to compete with other very demanding economic and social priorities. As a result of such conditions, however, some citizens are turning to new strategies. Groups are seeking funding from foreign grant-making institutions, and compromise with industry and government officials has become more important. Networks through telecommunications systems are developing, and access to information is improving. A handful of knowledgeable citizens are also turning to newly adopted environmental legislation in order to bolster the environmental movement.

Chances are high that health conditions will worsen and that conflict over environmental issues will increase. Support for citizen-based activism is crucial if Russia is to make government and industry more accountable and to help democratic institutions take hold. The growth of citizen participation should not be seen in terms of abetting future conflict between citizens and those in power, but as helping to ensure that people can survive in increasingly hostile living conditions.

Notes

The research for this paper was conducted partly over the summer of 1992 and most recently on a trip to Russia during January and February of 1993. Interviews were carried out with citizen activists mainly in St. Petersburg and Moscow. The major environmental groups contacted were the Socio-Ecological Union (SEU), the Russian International Center for Environmental Law (RICEL), Del'ta, and Green Movement (formerly the Bureau for Ecological Projects). Data were also collected from individuals in the Russian Ministry of Environmental Protection, at St. Petersburg State University's Department of Ecology, and from Americans working with the Citizens Exchange Council, the Natural Resources Defense Council (NRDC) and ISAR (formerly the Institute for Soviet-American Relations).

1. O.N. Yanitskii, "The Environmental Movement," *The Soviet Review*, 32, 1 (January-February 1991), 51.

2. Tatyana Zaharchenko, "The Environmental Movement and Ecological Law in the Soviet Union: The Process of Transformation," *Ecological Law Quarterly*, 17 (1990), 455–75.

3. For more reading on the history of environmental activism, see Barbara Jancar-Webster, *Environmental Management in the Soviet Union and Yugoslavia: Structure and Regulation in Federal Communist States* (Durham, N.C.: Duke University Press, 1987); Charles E. Ziegler, *Environmental Policy in the USSR* (Amherst, Mass.: University of Massachusetts Press, 1987); and Douglas R. Wiener, *Models of Nature: Ecology, Conservation, and Cultural Revolution in Soviet Russia* (Bloomington, Ind.: Indiana University Press, 1986).

4. See the contributions by James Critchlow and Juris Dreifelds in this volume.

5. DJ Peterson discusses this in *Troubled Lands: The Legacy of Soviet Environmental Destruction* (Boulder, Col.: Westview Press, 1993), 193–234.

6. Thomas F. Homer-Dixon, Jeffrey H. Boutwell and George W. Rathjens, "Environmental Change and Violent Conflict," *Scientific American*, 268, 2 (February 1993), 38–45.

7. Interview with Vladimir Zamoiskii, member of SEU, Moscow, February 1993.

8. Interview with Yu.S. Shevchuk of the Green Movement, St. Petersburg, February 1993.

9. In an interview with Vladimir Trifonov, an employee of the Russian Ministry of the Environment, it was mentioned that many of the brightest minds had left the Ministry for more lucrative consulting jobs.

10. Nanette van der Laan, "Ecology Focus of Planned Program," *The Moscow Times*, January 29, 1993, 3, and V. Zamoiskii interview.

11. A number of Russian activists interviewed complained that the problem was not the lack of information. Rather, even with information about problems, they have been unable to sway decision-makers.

12. Viktor Danilov-Danilyan, *Zelenyi Mir*, 42–44 (1992).

13. Interview with Mary Shea, Citizen Exchange Council, New York, January 1993.

14. Carey Scott, "MacArthur's Agent for Aid," *The Moscow Times*, February 17, 1993, 9.

15. Davis Chapman, "Former Soviet Union Environmental Telecommunications Project Update," *The Sacred Earth Network Newsletter*, 4 (Summer 1992), 7.

16. Interview with Gulya Ishkuzina, formerly a teacher from St. Petersburg University's Department of Ecology and currently working for RICEL, St. Petersburg, February 1993.

17. "RSFSR Law on Protection of the Environment," *Rossiiskaya gazeta*, March 3, 1992, 3–6, in *Federal Broadcast Information Service* (FBIS-URS-92-049), April 28, 1992, 3–34. For more on the law and its relevance to citizen participation see the contribution by DJ Peterson in this volume.

18. *Ibid.*

19. Interview with Konstantin Ryabchikin, RICEL, St. Petersburg, February 1993.

20. Alexei Portanskii, "The Complaint Against the Government Has Been Dismissed, and the Road to the Oil Has Been Cleared," *Izvestiya*, November 25, 1992, 2.

21. Interview with Kristen Suokko, NRDC, Washington, D.C., March 1993.

22. T. Artemova, "To Turn One Million Complaints into One Million Lawsuits," *The Neva Times*, November 17, 1992.

8

Central Asia: How to Pick Up the Pieces?

James Critchlow

In the years immediately prior to breakup of the USSR, environmental activists in Central Asia quite rightly blamed Moscow for their region's ecological plight. They held the center responsible for the economic imbalance that made the region ecologically vulnerable. The center's refusal to provide capital investments for local manufacturing industry relegated the region to the status of agricultural producer and raw-materials base. Pollution of the soil, water and atmosphere had been caused by activities decreed by the center, such as ruthless expansion of cotton growing, nuclear testing, and construction of "dirty" plants for primary processing of raw materials. The environmental movement, which in the Gorbachev period acquired a deeply nationalistic coloration, adhered to an implicit belief that relaxation of Moscow's grip would provide relief from environmental problems.

Today, in the aftermath of the Soviet breakup, the environmental reality in Central Asia is complex, with a few hopeful signs and a heavy burden of unsolved problems. The governments of the new states are now free to address environmental concerns on their territory without outside interference, but in achieving independence they have been confronted with sudden new challenges. They must find the means to assert political legitimacy and maintain social stability without discipline imposed from the outside. Perhaps the greatest challenge of all is how to meet the growing economic needs of their populations. These insistent questions divert governmental attention and resources away from environmental priorities. In addition, a major external threat to the Central Asian environment is the resumption, in October 1993, of Chinese nuclear testing at Lop Nor, Xinjiang Province, across the former Sino-Soviet border.

On the positive side, collapse of Soviet rule has expanded possibilities for a more searching investigation and identification of environmental problems, as well as for outside assistance in dealing with them. International organizations (for example, the World Bank, the United Nations Environmental Program, and the World Meteorological Organization), foreign ones (for example, the U.S. Agency for International Development and the U.S. Environmental Protection Agency) and a host of non-governmental organizations (NGOs), have become an active presence. Others, like NATO, have plans to become involved. At the same time, activities of local entrepreneurs and foreign business interests seeking to exploit resources present potential new sources of environmental degradation. The London-based weekly *Nefte Compass* has listed 29 foreign petroleum ventures in the Central Asian republics, a listing that does not include U.S. firms.[1]

Aftermath of the Soviet Collapse

Few, if any, of Central Asia's environmental activists could have anticipated the suddenness and totality of the collapse of Soviet power. In voicing environmental grievances on behalf of their region, they were calling on the center not only to modify harmful environmental policies but also to provide future redress for past harm. That was, for example, the idea behind support for a colossal scheme of water diversion from the Siberian rivers to the Central Asian plains to forestall the approaching death of the Aral Sea.

Now, *pace* the Commonwealth of Independent States (CIS), Moscow is to all intents and purposes out of the environmental picture in the region. The web of old ties between republics created and orchestrated under rigid central control has fallen by the wayside, to be replaced in a few instances by *ad hoc* bilateral arrangements for hard-currency or barter transactions. Moscow is still a presence, of course, if only because of its might and continuing importance as a trading partner. There is a vestigial CIS presence in such manifestations as the officer corps of the new Uzbek armed forces, 80 per cent of whose members are said to be native Russian-speakers, or deployment of the Russian 201st Motorized Rifle Division to help keep the peace in Tajikistan, apparently with the enthusiastic concurrence of the other Central Asian governments fearful of unrest.

With the passage of time since the Soviet breakup, the newly independent states have begun to be more dispassionately aware of their genuine mutual interests, as opposed to synthetic "friendship of the peoples." This has given new impetus to CIS cooperation on a voluntary basis. But the CIS has hardly emerged as the replacement for the Soviet state that some Western observers rather naively expected it to be.

With the dissolution of the USSR, the Russian government announced its readiness to shoulder certain international obligations of the defunct Union. Little has been said, however, of restitution to the former Soviet republics for damage caused by the policies of the old government. In any case, even were the Russian government to overcome the paralysis of its political process and summon the will to assist other republics with environmental problems, the magnitude of its own domestic difficulties casts doubt on its ability to render meaningful practical assistance.

Thus, in coping with the environmental heritage of arbitrary Soviet actions, the Central Asian republics are essentially left to their own devices.[2] This has created an entirely new playing field.

Since independence, the nationalistic fervor has gone out of environmental movements, reflecting a drastic change in the politics of ecology. If prior to the Soviet collapse environmental complaints were part of a panoply of ethnic grievances (including such other matters as cultural Russification or mistreatment of native recruits conscripted into the Soviet military) that is no longer the case. The external enemy has essentially vanished, and while retrospective attacks on Soviet actions continue to appear in public media, that has become increasingly like beating a dead horse. Attention to environmental questions as a means to whip up anti-Soviet outrage has subsided.

Meanwhile, the problems remain largely unabated. The Aral Sea continues to dwindle, now before the eyes of the world, with as yet untold environmental consequences. (See section below on "The Aral Sea: A Case Study of Environmental Inertia.") Throughout the region, there are pockets of soil, water and atmospheric pollution. In the zone of nuclear testing in Kazakhstan there is a continuing legacy of environmental pollution and dire health consequences for populations exposed to decades of radioactivity. Little has happened to remedy a situation where, in all of the republics, unsafe drinking water has jeopardized human life. In their book *Ecocide in the USSR*, Murray Feshbach and Alfred Friendly, Jr. detailed other aspects of Central Asia's environmental heritage from the late Soviet period:

- The large, succulent melons for which the Central Asian oases are justly famous were reported to contain two to four times the legal limit of nitrates.[3]
- In Uzbekistan and Tajikistan, it was reported that "between 44 and 48 per cent of the townships lacked sewer systems."[4]
- The incidence of cholera, presumably from contaminated drinking water, was three times the Soviet average in Uzbekistan and thirteen times the average in Tajikistan.[5]
- Air pollution of both those republics from the Tursunzada Aluminum Plant was a recurring problem.[6]

• In one locality of Kazakhstan, children were found to have beryllium levels as high as 400 per cent over the legal limit.[7]
• In both Kazakhstan and Uzbekistan, inhabitants are threatened by radioactive dumps.[8]
• As the result of such conditions, and of inferior medical care, military recruits from all five of the Central Asian republics were found by Soviet Army doctors to have severe health problems.[9]

Since independence, the response of individual Central Asian governments to environmental challenges has been conditioned by domestic political factors. The evolution of the republics has been far from uniform. Uzbekistan, the most populous, has emerged under the leadership of an authoritarian president, Islam Karimov, who relies on a one-party system (with himself as party head) in efforts to impose strict controls on political life, including freedom of association and the press. Turkmenistan has followed a similar course under its president, Saparmurad Niyazov. Both men are the former Communist Party chiefs of their republics. In both republics, there is a cult of personality of the supreme leader: public activity outside the officially sanctioned framework is discouraged, and reports of human-rights violations are frequent. This atmosphere is hardly conducive to independent initiatives to deal with environmental questions, but it has not completely stifled environmental activism. Paradoxically, the clamp-down on political activity has been accompanied by a degree of economic liberalization, introducing the possibility of new environmental abuses, while depriving citizens of the means to combat them in organized fashion. In Tajikistan, civil war has created a volatile situation, but – due in large part to Russian military intervention – forces representing the old communist system seem to have prevailed.

Kazakhstan and Kyrgyzstan, on the other hand, have pursued a more open course of political development. In Kazakhstan, whose geographic area dwarfs the other Central Asian republics, President Nursultan Nazarbaev, although also a holdover Communist Party chief from the Soviet era, has behaved differently from his opposite numbers in Uzbekistan and Turkmenistan. He has refused, for instance, to head the renamed Communist Party and has endorsed pluralism. Kyrgyzstan's president, Askar Askaev, an academic who replaced the former Communist Party leader of the republic in the perestroika period, is reputedly the most liberal of the Central Asian leaders. In December 1992 he actively supported the holding of a human-rights conference in his capital of Bishkek (which did not prevent Uzbekistan security agents from kidnapping a prominent Uzbek human-rights activist and returning him forcibly to Uzbekistan). Given the legacy of the past and concerns about present and future instabilities – particularly the perceived threat of ethnic conflict between European and indigenous groups – neither republic is a model democracy in the

Western sense. Still, in the post-Soviet period both have achieved a healthy measure of pluralism, as reflected in the media and in the somewhat limited rights of political parties and public organizations to act independently.

At the same time, all of the Central Asian states continue to be administered by bureaucratic institutions which at the grassroots have changed little since Soviet times. They are plagued by clannish and other factional networks which work at variance with civic equity, and are in some cases blatantly corrupt. Still, in even the most retrograde republics there is relatively greater freedom of association compared with the days of Soviet rule, at least for those who are not working openly against the governments. This has opened the way for limited growth of non-governmental green movements, and for some ties with foreign environmentalists.

Facing the Environment

The new national governments, which now bear sovereign responsibility for dealing with problems on their territory, are not anxious to direct public attention to continuing policy failures. They are more apt to portray environmental activism (and other reform movements) as an impediment to citizens' economic well-being. When forced to make a show of action on environmental problems, they prefer to cast about for outside help in finding solutions. Indeed, there is a tendency in the newly independent states, on the part of both governments and the public, to believe that such help will be forthcoming, even where the premises for that belief are flimsy. (Part of the enthusiasm for external assistance may stem from the expectation in some quarters that it will offer new opportunities for corrupt enrichment.)

Still, sensitivity to environmental questions continues to be reflected in various ways at the official level. The new constitution of Uzbekistan adopted in December 1992 refers to treatment of the environment in four of its 127 articles; for example, Article Four states that "citizens are obligated to behave protectively toward the surrounding natural environment."[10] The Uzbek government includes a Minister for Protection of Nature (whose recent incumbent was a former Communist Party oblast first secretary) and a Committee of the Supreme Council for Ecology and Rational Use of Natural Resources.[11] Officials have also made a show of regional and international cooperation. In March 1993, an intergovernmental agreement on solving the problems of the Aral basin was signed in Kzyl Orda, Kazakhstan, and in May of that year Tashkent was the locus of the Third International Ecology Conference devoted to implementation of that agreement and other matters. Participants from other CIS states (except Ukraine, Turkmenistan and Moldova) were greeted by Uzbekistan's First Deputy Prime Minister, with United Nations representatives in attendance.[12]

Within their own borders, some of the Central Asian governments have set up purportedly "non-governmental" organizations to deal with ecological problems. An example is Uzbekistan's "Ecosan Ecology and Health Assembly." This organization dispatches railroad trains around the republic with the stated purpose of rendering health and ecological assistance to the population. In May 1993, under the slogan "Ecosan for a Healthy Generation," one such five-car train visited two regions (*vilayatlar*) of the republic, carrying officials of the health and defense ministries and representatives of "Ozbeksavda," a retail trading organization. A newspaper report said that some thirty senior health workers and eight "professors" had treated needy patients along the way and that medicated beverages and food, as well as clothing and school supplies, had been distributed.[13]

Organizations like Ecosan are dismissed by one reporter in these words:

> Most of these new entities are encouraged to seek foreign donations and all of them, though they parade as non-governmental organizations, are directly connected to the government. ... Though they may put some money toward worthwhile projects, they are widely observed to take care of their own, serve as political machines, accost foreigners, and even be available as petty cash funds for the government. Yet, it is precisely these types of organization that will likely receive [foreign] assistance.[14]

In Kazakhstan and Kyrgyzstan, where environmental activism is most advanced, truly grassroots green movements are nonetheless clinging to a precarious existence in the face of formidable legal and organizational difficulties.

In Kazakhstan, the "International Fund for Salvation of the Aral Sea" and the "Elimai Ecological Fund" are said to be official organizations posing as non-governmental ones. On the other hand, grassroots Greens have succeeded in setting up a political party, headed by Mels Eleusizov. The party is an outgrowth of a movement that began in 1987 with the formation of a group in Almaty (then called Alma-Ata) called "Initiative" and another in Pavlodar (northern Kazakhstan) called "Ecology and Public Opinion." The following year popular indignation over pollution of a nearby village by Almaty's sewage led to establishment of a Green Front in that city. In 1989, Greens won seats in local and regional councils. That same year Kazakhstan's largest and most influential environmental organization, Nevada-Semipalatinsk, was established to protest nuclear testing, presided over by two writers, Olzhas Suleimenov (who publishes in Russian) and Mustafa Shakhanov (who publishes in Kazakh). Ironically, 1991, the year of the Soviet breakup, was a difficult one for the Greens: internal feuding led to fragmentation of some of their groups and formation of new ones, including Tabighat (Nature), Green Salvation and Ecofund. The government promulgated a new law on registration of public groups that has reportedly kept some groups from achieving legal status right to the present day. Kazakhstan's environmental organizations are also handicapped by the difficulty of establishing media for dissemination of information in local areas.[15] A pressing challenge to Kazakhstan's green movement came in 1993 with resumption of nuclear testing across the Chinese border at Lop Nor in Xinjiang Province. According to a report from Kazakhstan:

> China's test last week consolidated the fears of people here and firmly placed the issue on everyone's Top Ten list. The government of Kazakhstan is audibly concerned about the test site and the large exile Uighur community in Central Asia is latching on to the issue as ethnic Kazakhs did to the Semipalatinsk issue, especially since the new director of Nevada-Semipalatinsk is an ethnic Uighur and the grandson of the last President of Eastern Turkestan.[16]

Kyrgyzstan's Greens stem from "a conservation movement in Bishkek" that has been "active for more than a decade." The movement's concerns include radiation hazards (not only from Chinese nuclear testing but from indigenous production of uranium and other radioactive ores), wilderness protection, and preventing excessive growth of tourist facilities. Ekolog, registered in 1988 as the first official green group in the country, collected information on pollution-related illnesses and, in 1990, organized a campaign against conditions at a factory in Bishkek. The campaign seems to have been only a partial success, but helped to raise citizens' awareness. However, Ekolog has been weakened by the departure of many Russian members from Kyrgyzstan in the wake of independence. The Kyrgyz branch of the Lop Nor movement, which opposes Chinese nuclear testing, is "largely made up of Uighur people from the Lop Nor region." The organization seeks to increase Kyrgyz awareness of the dangers of the tests, but has been inhibited by pressure on Kyrgyzstan from Chinese officials, who have wielded financial assistance as a lever. A third group, registered in July 1993 as the "Kyrgyzstan Environmental Movement," concentrates on environmental issues, especially those relating to protection of Lake Issyk-Kul.[17]

In the other three Central Asian republics, conditions for grassroots environmental organizations are less favorable. Still, a listing of environmental groups "doing important work" has one such group (complete with electronic-mail address) in each of the three republics as well as one in Nukus, capital of the "autonomous" republic of Karakalpakistan located on the territory of Uzbekistan. (Karakalpakistan has suffered more than any other territorial unit from the Aral Sea tragedy.)

Despite a range of obstacles, the best hope of progress in dealing with the Central Asian environmental crisis lies in partnerships between foreign and indigenous NGOs (where the latter are truly non-governmental voluntary movements). Such partnerships can be beneficial in fulfilling the following functions:

1. On-site monitoring of trouble-spots;
2. Publicity of problems and of official failures to take remedial action (in foreign media where local media are closed to such information);
3. Establishment of communication networks for pooling of information;
4. Advice to foreign governmental and international organizations on priorities and effective ways of administering aid;
5. Oversight of environmental programs to increase their likelihood of being effectively conceived, efficiently administered, and untainted by corruption.

One Western NGO that has helped to demonstrate opportunities for environmental action in Central Asia is the Washington-based ISAR, a "small, non-partisan, non-profit organization" that "has been working in the field of Soviet-American relations since 1983."[18] In addition to offices in Russia and Ukraine, it has one in Almaty from which "in-country representatives" fan out through Central Asia. For example, a representative reported his observations of pollution and other problems during a recent trip to Northern Kazakhstan.[19] ISAR provides small grants to environmental NGOs in Central Asia (and other CIS republics) and concentrates on facilitating communication among them by helping to set up an "environmental electronic mail network." It brings environmental activists from the CIS, including Central Asia, to six-week fellowships with U.S. environmental groups. Among its publications, *Surviving Together* (quarterly) and *Ecostan News* are rich sources of information on regional environmental problems.

The Aral Sea: A Case Study of Environmental Inertia

The Aral Sea has by now attracted worldwide attention as the most outwardly visible evidence of environmental abuse in Central Asia. The tragedy of the Aral is important in itself, but the sea's plight is also important as a weathervane of environmental action in the region. In the long run, what happens to the Aral will be significant in determining whether effective remedies can be found and implemented on other environmental fronts.

The Aral lies between two republics, Uzbekistan and Kazakhstan, and near a third, Turkmenistan. All three republics are directly affected by the changes that have occurred in the sea. Its tributary rivers, the Amu-Darya (Oxus) and Syr-Darya (Jaxartes), reach it via the territory of Uzbekistan, and it is there that most of its problems have been caused – and continue to be caused.

The Aral Sea was once the world's largest inland body of water, greater in area than Lake Michigan. A rare American visitor in 1873, the diplomat and scholar Eugene Schuyler, was impressed by its natural beauty and wildlife:

> The charm lay in the sky, light blue with fleecy clouds, and a sun which lighted up the clear, very clear, shallow pools of water and shore and sea with silver and pearly hues. While gulls soared and dipped into the bay, hovering even over our heads; while further away the water was covered with flocks of ducks and other water-fowl. ... The water looked so clear and pure that I scooped up a cup of it and drank it. In taste it was slightly brackish, but not strongly saline.[20]

Today, wildlife has been eliminated in the littoral region. The sea's formerly flourishing fish industry, which once produced a tenth of the entire Soviet catch, has been destroyed, its ships rusting at their moorings. Trapping of muskrats for their pelts, also once a lively local occupation, is no longer possible as the animals have disappeared. U.S. Vice-President Al Gore, who visited the region as a senator, has described the experience of standing on a hot steel deck in the desert:

> side of the ship, there was nothing but hot dry sand – as far as I could see in all directions. The other ships of the fleet were also at rest in the sand, scattered in the dunes that stretched all the way to the horizon.[21]

The sea has divided into two parts, the "Big" and "Little" Aral, and its total area has declined from 66,900 square kilometers in 1960 to 33,800 square kilometers in 1991, as the mean level (for the Big Aral) dropped from 53.4 to 37.3 meters.[22] It is predicted that, if this trend remains unchecked, the total area will decline a further 50 per cent by the year 2000.[23] The salinity of the Aral is now 30 parts per thousand, five times the level in Schuyler's day, and is expected to reach 65 to 70 by the year 2000.[24]

The tragedy of the Aral Sea stems from ruthless expansion of cotton-growing in the Aral Basin, particularly important since the 1960s. In Soviet days the region contributed 95 per cent of the national cotton crop. Moscow's frenzy to increase cotton crops led to diversion of land from other crops and to massive deforestation to provide still more acreage. To spur the Central Asian *dihqans* (peasants) to ever greater efforts in the fields, propagandists used the rallying cry of *aq altin*! (white gold).

Cotton is an extremely water-intensive crop. Yet during its growing season in Central Asia there is little or no rainfall, necessitating development of an extensive irrigation system. To obtain water for irrigation, it has been diverted from the Aral tributaries into a network of sloppily-built, porous irrigation canals from which liquid seeps into the surrounding area; in Turkmenistan's capital of Ashgabat below the terminus of the Kara Kum canal, pumps are kept going day and night to prevent flooding by water previously destined for the desiccated Aral Sea. At the same time, the tributaries and canals, which feed into drinking-water sources, are polluted by irrigation run-off containing the residue of chemical fertilizers, herbicides and pesticides which were applied recklessly in an effort to improve cotton-yields.[25]

Wind erosion from the increasingly broad expanse of the former sea bed has deposited salty sand in locations thousands of miles away, even as far as the Arctic Circle, threatening damage to arable land. Reduction of the sea's moderating effect has caused climatic change, leading to hotter summers, colder winters, and a shorter growing season which has affected cotton crops. But the most dramatic impact of ecological change in the region has been on human health. Mothers have been warned not to nurse their infants for fear that toxic chemicals in their systems will poison them; as it is, infant mortality in some districts has been reported at greater than 100 per thousand, meaning that at least one child in ten dies before reaching the age of one year. Diseases of the stomach, intestines and liver are endemic.[26] It is reported that in Karakalpakistan the rate of esophageal cancer was seven times the Soviet average.[27]

Local environmentalists in Uzbekistan had hoped that the divorce from Moscow would do miracles for their republic; they have reason to feel disappointed. In the case of the Aral, abuse of water resources continues, and effective remedial actions to provide water for the sea from other sources have not been undertaken.

In independent Uzbekistan, cotton is still king. Even though the crop is no longer confiscated by Moscow under a delivery quota set by the dread *goszakaz* (state order), the Uzbek government has found that cotton remains, at least in the near term, the key to effective functioning of the national economy. The country is increasingly burdened by high population growth that every year creates a half-million new mouths to be fed and a like number of new bodies to be housed. Cotton, either for cash or barter, is still *aq altin*, the main instrument for obtaining all of the commodities, especially manufactured goods, which the Uzbek economy is unable to provide. In a republic where the "administrative-command system" continues to hold sway despite much talk of transition to a market economy, the *goszakaz* has been replaced by the Uzbek government's own state plan. The importance of cotton is reflected in a decree issued by Uzbek President Karimov requiring that all cotton exports above a certain limit receive his personal approval.

Apparently plans to conserve water by levying a usage fee have been abandoned in Uzbekistan. To be sure, there has been some cutback in the extreme cotton targets set (and never reached, except on paper) in the latter

Brezhnev years: in 1992 the cotton harvest was just over 4 million tons, down about 20 per cent from 1990, the last full year of Soviet rule, and down about 27 per cent from the estimated Brezhnev-era peak in 1980. Karimov has decreed a modest reallocation of land for private use by peasants and others to grow food, but water-intensive cotton is still the backbone of the economy. Symptomatic of the continuing priority for cotton is the fact that students are still drafted from their classes to help with the harvest – a practice decried in the Soviet period by Uzbek nationalists who saw it as brutal exploitation by Moscow.

Lack of access to safe drinking water and contamination of plant and wildlife remain major problems in Uzbekistan. As for the Aral, it is doubtful that any of the measures taken since independence, either by Uzbekistan or the Central Asian republics jointly, will reduce its continuing decline, to say nothing of helping to restore it to its former size.

Although Uzbekistan is the main cause of the Aral crisis, its government prefers to sit back and rely on the hope of regional or international intervention to save the day. Gone are the days when the press of Uzbekistan carried bold headlines about "The Agony of the Aral" and heartrending verse by leading poets about the sea's impending demise. The media of the republic, still controlled about as tightly by censorship as in the Soviet period, are now much more restrained. A "Committee to Save the Aral" founded in the late Soviet period still exists, headed by the prominent Uzbek writer Pirmat Shermuhamedov, but little has been heard about it recently.

That is not to say that the Aral is being passed over in total silence. The problems are too great, and the emotion over them that was allowed to build in the late Soviet period too intense. The country's leading cultural weekly has carried a thoughtful article by a native geographer on the need for expanded training of specialists in ecological matters; toward the end of his article he was able to mention in passing that such persons are needed to overcome problems of the Aral littoral.[28] The same newspaper carried a review, with jacket photograph of "The Aral Catastrophe," of a book published in Moscow.[29]

Despite Uzbekistan's responsibility for the Aral problem and the fact that the brunt of the consequences are being borne by its population (especially in Karakalpakistan) President Karimov has effectively distanced his government from primary responsibility for a solution. He makes it clear that he is counting on regional or outside leadership. In December 1992 he visited the heart of the disaster zone in Karakalpakistan to take part in observance of the sixtieth anniversary of its capital, Nukus, a city that is the product of Stalinist urbanization. On this occasion Karimov could hardly ignore the Aral question, but he dealt with it rather evasively, without committing his own government to independent action. Here are some excerpts:

> I want to touch on a problem that disturbs us all: the ecological situation in Karakalpakistan, the health of the people, the fate of our only sea, the Aral. ... You know that many decrees have been adopted about the Aral but much has stayed only on paper. The problem is that our destiny was controlled by others. Now the time has come to take a serious approach to the task. ... The fate (of the Aral) is inseparably linked with that of the independent states of Turkestan as a whole. ... Therefore, Uzbekistan, Kazakhstan, Turkmenistan, Kyrgyzstan, and Tajikistan must create a single powerful international organization to solve the problems.[30]

What are the prospects for regional action to help the Aral? It was reported that at a summit conclave of Central Asian states held in January 1993, a fund was established to help deal with the Aral, with a "recommended" contribution of one per cent of national income by participatory states.[31] This step was preceded by various agreements among the states on the Aral question, all couched in high-sounding terms but containing few concrete goals or commitments. Despite such moves, the Aral crisis does not appear to be a major domestic priority for any of the Central Asian governments. As Eric Sievers has suggested:

> Not only are the governments of Central Asia holdovers from the Soviet era, they are also inappropriate spokespersons and representatives of the people of the Aral region. None of the national capitals are within 500 kilometers of the sea ...[32]

In any case, hopes appear to remain fixed on foreign countries for a solution to the Aral crisis. During a meeting of February 17, 1993 with some visiting Central Asian university rectors at Harvard, the present author was assured by both the Uzbek and Kazakh representatives that the principal responsibility for dealing with the Aral now rests with an "international organization." Neither could identify the organization in question, but expressed a belief that it is based in the United States.

In fact, various foreign entities have shown interest in becoming involved with this or that aspect of the Aral crisis. One of the most prominent is the World Bank, which has sent representatives to visit the region and prepared a report on a "proposed framework of activities" for dealing with the crisis. The report calls for "identifying and preparing projects" to alleviate conditions of the sea and surrounding area. It is most outspoken in calling for "urgent action" to deal with human suffering in the Aral littoral, describing the situation there as "too desperate to ignore or delay."[33] In September 1992, the United Nations Environmental Program held a conference in Geneva on "The Development of an Action Plan for the Aral Sea" which was based on its international team's "diagnostic study" of the crisis. The study was scathing in its assessment of local responsibility for the sea's condition, and called for formulation of short-, mid- and long-term actions, which it warned "will require considerable funds and the introduction of modern technology and methodology."[34] Other organizations which have shown an interest in the Aral are the Japan-based Global Infrastructure Foundation, whose representatives have also visited the Aral basin; the Aral Sea Information Committee in San Francisco, which concentrates on bringing Central Asian representatives to the United States for orientation and training; and the United States Agency for International Development.

While the various activities of these groups may be taken to be a good beginning, action on the Aral is still at the talking stage. What appears to be lacking is high-level governmental leadership to assure a coordinated unitary approach to the problem and, especially, its root causes. In their 1992 paper, Glantz, Rubinstein and Zonn concluded:

> Perhaps, when the Aral Sea level drops to below 34 meters and the Big Aral is on the verge of further dividing into two, more serious assessment of the true value of maintaining a healthy Aral Sea, healthy rivers such as the Amu-Darya and the Syr-Darya, and a healthy human population, will override the tendency of policy-makers to pursue short-term economic benefits at the expense of long-term economic and ecological stability.[35]

The Aral challenge is a test of whether the international community will be able to summon the determination to devise and implement an effective solution, and whether local jurisdictions will cooperate constructively with efforts to achieve a solution, or interfere by pursuing interests that have nothing to do with the problem at hand.

Conclusion

People – many of them children – are dying every day in Central Asia as the result of environmental deterioration. This should be of concern to the whole world not only on humanitarian grounds but because it affects stability: it may be recalled that the bloody violence which in 1989 and 1990 swept the Ferghana Valley at the nexus of three of the countries was attributed in part to dissatisfaction with pollution and struggle for scarce water resources.

Joan DeBardeleben is one of those who have argued for a "global" strategy to deal with environmental deterioration: as she puts it, "pollution and environmental damage respect no political boundaries."[36] Al Gore, writing for an American audience, has called for a "global Marshall Plan."[37] But Central Asia is remote, and dramatic pictures of events in Bosnia or Somalia or other more accessible parts of the world leave little room for coverage of its problems in newspapers and television broadcasts.

Notes

Acknowledgements: Among those who have contributed material for preparation of this paper, I am especially grateful to Professor Gregory Gleason of the University of New Mexico; Dr. Michael Glantz of the National Center for Atmospheric Research in Boulder, Colorado; and Eric Sievers and Kate Watters of ISAR.

1. *Nefte Compass*, October 7, 1993, 9-12.

2. The Central Asian states are by no means alone in having to bear these problems. For example, post-Soviet Ukraine is also suffering from grave environmental damage. See "The Environment: Pollution Plagues Large Areas of Ukraine," *The Ukrainian Weekly*, February 7, 1993, 1. On the Baltic states, see the contribution in this volume by Juris Dreifelds.

3. Murray Feshbach and Alfred Friendly, Jr., *Ecocide in the USSR: Health and Nature Under Siege* (New York: Basic Books, 1992), 61.

4. *Ibid.*, 5–6.

5. *Ibid.*, 124.

6. *Ibid.*, 108–09.

7. *Ibid.*, 177.

8. *Ibid.*, 178; see also James Critchlow, *Nationalism in Uzbekistan: A Soviet Republic's Road to Sovereignty* (Boulder, Colo.: Westview Press, 1991), 92–95.

9. Feshbach and Friendly, *Ecocide in the USSR*, 163–65.

10. *Pravda Vostoka*, November 21, 1992, 2,3.

11. According to a RFE/RL Research Institute listing provided by electronic mail, October 28, 1992.

12. *Ozbekistan avazi*, May 28, 1993, 1.

13. *Ozbekistan avazi*, May 19, 1993, 1.

14. Eric Sievers (compiler), *Ecostan News: Ecological News from Central Asia*, 1,1 (September 1, 1993), 6.

15. Information in this paragraph is based mainly on Sergei Kuratov, "The Kazakhstan Green Movement," *Surviving Together* (Fall 1993), 20–21. Kuratov is a member of Green Salvation. Eleusizov was identified for me as president of the Green Party by Reef Altoma, a Harvard graduate student who has done extensive fieldwork in Kazakhstan. Information about Suleimenov and Shakhanov comes from my own sources, including a meeting with the latter.

16. Electronic mail communication received October 14, 1993 from Eric Sievers of ISAR's Almaty office. Since the Uighurs are indigenous to Xinjiang Province, their kin are especially vulnerable to the Chinese tests. According to the 1989 Soviet census, the last taken, there were 263,000 Uighurs on the territory of the USSR, most of them in the Central Asian republics.

17. Information for this paragraph is, in entirety, from Lynn Richards, "The Greens of Kyrgyzstan," *Surviving Together* (Fall 1993), 21, except that the information on reaction to the Chinese tests was sent to the author from Almaty via electronic mail by Eric Sievers, ISAR field representative, on October 13, 1993.

18. Telephone interview with Kate Watters, ISAR Environmental Programs Director, Washington, D.C., September 29, 1993.

19. *Surviving Together* (Fall 1993), 17–19.

20. Eugene Schuyler, *Turkistan*, Vol. I (New York: Scribner's, 1876), 26–27. Schuyler includes in his report a Russian scientist's analysis of the Aral water, which then contained about six parts per thousand of salt (sodium chloride).

21. Al Gore, *Earth in the Balance: Ecology and the Human Spirit* (New York: Plume, 1993), 19. Jim Rupert, a reporter for the *Washington Post*, has informed me (telephone conversation, February 22, 1993) that the Aral "ship cemetery" is now disappearing, as a nearby fish cannery recycles the metal to make tins for fish now being brought by rail and truck from the Baltic region.

22. Michael Glantz, Alvin Z. Rubinstein, and Igor Zonn, "Tragedy in the Aral Sea Basin: Looking Back to Plan Ahead?" in Hafeez Malik, ed., *Central Asia: Its Strategic Importance and Future Prospects* (New York: St. Martin's Press, 1994), 159–89. The present author glimpsed the "Little" Aral in September 1991 through the window of an airliner en route from Moscow to Chimkent; from that height it looked exactly like a mud puddle sitting in a basin of salt.

23. *Ibid.*, 15.

24. *Ibid.*, 15. Glantz uses figures from Philip P. Micklin, *The Water Management Crisis in Central Asia* (Pittsburgh: Pittsburgh Center for Russian and East European Studies. The Carl Beck Papers, 905, August 1991). Also Schuyler, 27.

25. Critchlow, *Nationalism in Uzbekistan*, 61–69, 77–91.

26. *Ibid.*, 90–91.

27. Lester R. Brown, Worldwatch Institute, in Foreword to Feshbach and Friendly, *Ecocide in the USSR*, xii.

28. Rahmanbek Rahimbekov, "Who Does Not Know the Land Does Not Know the People," *Ozbekistan adabiyati va san"ati*, December 11, 1992, 2.

29. "'The Aral Catastrophe,'" *Ozbekistan adabiyati va san"ati*, October 9, 1992, 8.

30. *Pravda Vostoka*, December 22, 1992, 1.

31. "Regulations of the International Fund for Saving the Aral Sea," in The World Bank, *The Aral Sea Crisis: Proposed Framework of Activities* (Washington, D.C.: The World Bank, 1993), Appendix D.

32. Eric Sievers, *Ecostan News: Ecological News from Central Asia*, 1,1 (September 1, 1993), 6.

33. The World Bank, *The Aral Sea Crisis.*

34. United Nations Environmental Program, The Aral Sea: Diagnostic Study for the Development of an Action Plan for the Conservation of the Aral Sea (New York: United Nations Environmental Program, 1993).

35. Glantz, Rubinstein and Zonn, "Tragedy in the Aral Sea Basin."

36. Joan DeBardeleben, "Introduction," in DeBardeleben, ed., *To Breathe Free: Eastern Europe's Environmental Crisis* (Washington, D.C.: The Woodrow Wilson Center Press and the Johns Hopkins University Press, 1991), 1.

37. Gore, *Earth in the Balance*, 295–360.

9

The Environmental Impact of Estonia, Latvia and Lithuania on the Baltic Sea Region

Juris Dreifelds

Baltic environmental consciousness reached a peak in the late 1980s in tandem with a similar peak in most industrialized countries of the world. Almost in lock-step with the dissipation of this consciousness in the world, after 1990 the Baltic republics also experienced environmental mobilization fatigue. While in the West this surge of green concern affected the rhetoric and policies of decision-makers and even helped change ruling political parties, in the Baltics the environmental issue was responsible for much more fundamental political changes. It helped usher in the period of awakening which propelled the three Baltic republics to independence.

By 1993 most environmental activists had been diverted by concerns of bare economic survival; however, the issues which triggered their initial involvement remain unresolved, despite advice, technical help, and limited financing proffered by neighboring countries. The geographical location of the three republics on the shores of the Baltic Sea, shores shared by such relatively wealthy and modern countries as Sweden, Denmark, Finland, and Germany, has provided unexpected leverage for Balts in their assault on pollution sources. At times this leverage might be classified as a form of environmental blackmail or a type of danegeld – protection money paid by wealthy neighbors for a policy of containment against foreign pollutants. Almost all streams and rivers of the Baltic republics eventually carry their water and attendant heavy load of pollutants into the Baltic Sea. It has become clear that the Sea is also the major receptacle for airborne pollution and could be endangered by nuclear fallout and other types of radioactivity. At one time the Baltic Sea was vying for the title of the most polluted sea in the world. The perceived threat of its imminent death during the late 1960s mobilized the Scandinavian countries and West

Germany into a program of serious pollution abatement. Much progress has been made. Unfortunately the "socialist" side of the Baltic Sea, while eager in its rhetoric and legal decrees, failed to make more than cursory inroads against the problem. Indeed, one could readily claim that in the case of the Baltic republics, their achievements in the realm of pollution control resemble those of Scandinavia – but of thirty years ago.

In 1992 a joint program of the Baltic Sea states identified 132 "hot spots" of pollution, of which 47 were placed in the "priority" category, a designation of concern committing them to the first phase of investment programs to be implemented between 1993 and 1997. All of the priority areas were located in former communist countries. Only 35 non-priority hot spots were located in Sweden, Finland, Denmark and Germany (including East Germany). The three Baltic republics were the source of 38 hot spots, 16 of which were rated as top priority. The preliminary estimate for required financing for Baltic hot spots was over 2.5 billion European Currency Units (ECUs), of which about 753 million was to be financed by outside sources.[1]

The Baltic Sea: Its Natural Features

There are several features of this water body that present special dangers in its protection. It has been described as "an almost stagnant sea" because water exchange with the North Atlantic occurs very slowly through three relatively shallow narrows between the large islands of Denmark. It takes about 30 to 50 years for the Baltic water to be exchanged.[2]

The Baltic Sea is also very shallow and has a unique layering of water created by two different sources of replenishment. The saltier and heavier water from the North Sea lies near the bottom and especially in the deeper parts of the basin. The freshwater flowing from the surrounding rivers collects closer to the surface. Under such conditions there is a marked halocline at a depth of 60–80 meters in the Baltic proper (excluding the gulfs) which prevents the mixing of the bottom layers by more oxygenated waters at the top. Thus for much of the area of the Baltic Sea only the inflow of new oxygenated salt water from the North Sea can renew the oxygen levels at greater depths. This exchange, however, is hampered by the sills and depressions of the bottom topography, hence a true scouring effect of the stagnant and oxygen-depleted deeper layer occurs when there are truly powerful North Atlantic gales which channel vast amounts of new sea water throughout the basins or deeps of the sea bed.

The unique gradient of salinity, the relatively cold temperatures and the short supply of light during long winter and fall periods have helped create a sea with a very small number of plant and animal species which are nevertheless present in great numbers. As a Nordic Council report points out: "The water is too fresh for the true marine species, and too saline for the true freshwater species," and many animal species have to expend much energy adjusting and surviving under such conditions.[3] Thus we see a naturally created stress factor which leaves a diminished margin in many animals and plants for buffering or coping with pollutants. Furthermore, the limited number of species creates simple food chains which can be easily disrupted or destroyed. The entire ecosystem suffers serious repercussions if any of the species are subjected to serious negative natural or man-made disturbances. Indeed there are many severe environmental disturbances that are of great concern. Almost one half of the bottom of the Baltic proper measuring about 100,000 square kilometers is virtually a dead zone where oxygen has been depleted and where poisonous hydrogen sulphides from anaerobic decay kill most life processes. Such a situation was quite common in large areas of Lake Erie several decades ago. The formerly clear waters of the Baltic are becoming ever more turbid, limiting the penetration depth of light. Widespread eutrophication is occurring as a result of a massive increase of nutrients such as phosphorus and nitrogen from agricultural run off, municipal and industrial waste waters and from the atmosphere. The abundance of nutrients has encouraged widespread algal blooms, some of which are poisonous. One unsightly result of algal growth is the widespread explosion of slimy green algae which adhere to rocks and cliffs and destroy the recreation value of beaches and seashores. In different areas of the Baltic Sea, scientists have measured high concentrations of heavy metals, chlorinated organic material, dioxins and oil.

One of the more positive changes of the last two decades has been the decrease of DDT/DDE and PCB concentrations. As a result, some of the previously threatened predator species, such as osprey and eagles which feed on Baltic fish, have been able to avert extinction and to experience a modest comeback. The shallowness of the Baltic Sea and the periodic scouring of the sea bottom by gale-induced massive sea water penetration from the North Atlantic present an opportunity for a new start. Many of the present problems can indeed be washed away and the sea can be regenerated if the sources of man-induced pollutants can be averted. Unfortunately, while the pollution legacy of the last half century may be removed by natural forces, much of the threat is only diluted somewhat as it circulates within a bigger sink, the North Atlantic.

Threats to the Sea: Estonia, Latvia, Lithuania

During the Soviet period the Baltic republics became urbanized, and heavily industrialized. In 1989 urban dwellers accounted for 72 per cent of the population in Estonia, 71 per cent in Latvia and 68 per cent in Lithuania. The total population of the republics is only 7.5 million. Industries were constructed to serve planning strategies of the entire USSR and hence were much larger than one would normally expect in such relatively small countries. Moreover, the emphasis on economic expansion far outpaced the ability and willingness of either the all-union ministries or republican organs to contain pollutants associated with this growth.

Among the most common quantitative measures of water pollutants of the Baltic Sea are such nutrients as nitrates and phosphorus, oil products and biological oxygen demand (BOD). See Table 9.1.

There is as yet no available systematic comparative data on other more noxious types of water pollutants pouring into the Baltic Sea from the Baltic republics such as toxic chemicals and heavy metals. In 1989 Lithuania claimed to emit 1,000 tons of heavy metals. That same year Estonia contributed 523 tons of phenols, most of which originated from the Oil Shale Chemical Production Association at Kohtla-Jarve.[4] Health-threatening bacterial pollution varies from locality to locality and has forced the closing of most Baltic Sea beaches and other water-based recreational areas and has affected the quality of drinking water.[5] A major problem also arises from air pollutants (Table 9.2) that may be deposited into the sea directly or may be washed away to nearby streams which flow into the sea.

From the above it is clear that Latvia has a much smaller problem from stationary sources than either Estonia or Lithuania. Between 1986 and 1989 the volume of air pollutants from such sources in Latvia decreased by 25 per cent in large part because of the introduction of natural gas to replace oil in thermal power plants.[6] While the control of dust particles has made much headway in Latvia, only three per cent of gases and evaporated liquids were being successfully treated in 1990, leading one critic to claim that "the atmosphere receives the most harmful chemical substances."[7]

The sources of pollution receiving the greatest attention in the Baltic republics are sewage and the energy industry. Various other industrial objects, especially pulp and paper mills, as well as chemical and cement plants, have caused many problems. Agriculture has been a serious source of nutrients and pesticides. Waste disposal, especially of toxic substances, is rarely discussed but may be a time bomb for the future welfare of Baltic society.

Sewage Purification

One of the greatest differences between the countries of the east shore of the Baltic and the rest is their approach to sewage control and purification. Most of the major cities and all three capitals of the Baltic republics are still dumping damaging sewage either directly into the Baltic Sea or into waterways that flow into this sea. Sewage problems were involved in 17 of the 38 hot spots in the Baltic republics (Lithuania 9, Estonia 5, Latvia 3).

TABLE 9.1 Load of Nutrients, Oil and BOD to the Baltic Sea from Estonia, Latvia, Lithuania, 1989[8] (in tons)

	Nitrates	*Phosphorus*	*Oil Products*	*BOD (1990)*
Estonia	10,350	588	240	44,000
Latvia	7,155	944	640	51,000
Lithuania	7,770	881	540	59,000

TABLE 9.2 Air Pollutants Emitted in the Baltic Republics, 1989[9] (in 1000 tons)

	Estonia	*Latvia*	*Lithuania*
From traffic	474	426	ca. 570
From stationary sources	576	159	431
of this			
a) solid particles	261	38	44
b) sulfur dioxide	210	59	188
c) nitric oxides	23	12	44
Total	1,050	585	ca. 1,000

In 1989 Estonia discharged the highest volume of waste water requiring treatment but it also claimed the highest rate of success in purifying waters within sufficient levels by Soviet standards, i.e., 52.4 per cent (Table 9.3). Latvia was able to cope satisfactorily with 30 per cent of discharges while Lithuania achieved only 25.4 per cent. The actual volume of treated and untreated sewage in Estonia was 246 million cubic meters, in Latvia 258 and in Lithuania 335.[10]

It should be noted that existing sewage treatment plants in almost all instances are not equipped to deal with nutrients (phosphorus, nitrogen) or with heavy metals, and various industrial chemicals. Sophisticated chemical treatment plants can be obtained only in the West and are extremely expensive. Moreover, the majority of industrial plants flush their wastes into the commercial sewage system and create hazardous conditions for biological treatment facilities. With the economic rupturing of the USSR many of the relatively affordable chemicals used in treatment, as well as new equipment or spare parts to maintain existing treatment plants, have become difficult to obtain from the East; local procurement of these items is inadequate and foreign purchases are expensive.

Tallinn

Every year Tallinn ejects over 140 million cubic meters of waste water into the Gulf of Finland, much of which receives only primary mechanical treatment.[11] Industrial waste contaminated by oil, phenols and other unsafe chemicals mingle with the communal sink and toilet detritus produced by half a million people. The lack of progress thus far has been explained by the failure of construction organizations, and by deficits in materials, and finances.[12] The estimated price tag for effective purification devices is over 96 million ECUs, a sum which cannot as yet be carried by Estonia alone. In addition to Tallinn other sewage-related hot spots in Estonia include Kohtla-Jarve, Haapsalu, Parnu and Paide.

Riga

Riga sewage is particularly dangerous because most of it is flushed directly into the Daugava River below the Riga hydro-electric dam. The dam operates only a few hours a day, thus creating conditions where waste volume overwhelms the natural waters of the river and quashes almost all processes of self-purification.[13]

Until the end of 1991 only a minute quantity of the 160 million cubic meters of Riga city effluent was purified within acceptable limits. Not surprisingly, Riga accounted for 61 per cent of the total of untreated sewage in Latvia in 1989.[14] In 1992, a new biological treatment plant was erected carrying part of the total waste by pipeline several kilometers into the Gulf of Riga. It is ironic that the first plans for dealing with Riga's water pollution envisaged a resolution of the problem between 1971 and 1975. This construction process took so long that by 1987 the original plan was deemed to be obsolete and existing unfinished structures had to be demolished. New plans were designed in cooperation with German waste specialists. The completion of the first phase of the project, which was expected to purify 350,000 cubic meters a day, was officially declared in the Fall of 1991. It was to treat a load composed of 60 per cent municipal and 40 per cent industrial waste water and also to purify nitrogen and phosphorus.

TABLE 9.3: Sewage Discharge and Treatment in the Baltic Republics 1989[15] (in million cubic meters and percentage)

	Estonia	*Latvia*	*Lithuania*
1. Treated within Soviet standards	271/52.4%	110/29.9%	114/25.4%
2. Partially treated	192/37.1%	143/38.9%	124/27.6%
3. Untreated	54/10.5%	115/31.2%	211/47.0%
Total needing treatment	517/100.0%	368/100.0%	449/100.0%

In spite of the media hype and the victorious declarations about the successful completion of the first phase, it turned out that only 110,000 cubic meters per day could actually be treated because major sewage pipes, collectors and pumping stations required for the first phase had not even been constructed.[16] In June 1993, the volume of treated waste water had increased to about 200,000 cubic meters per day.[17] Phase II of the Riga sewage treatment project will provide an additional capacity of 350,000 cubic meters per day. This second plant has been registered as a priority hot spot requiring 62.5 million ECUs. A major problem being experienced under phase I is that the treated water is "dirtier" than expected largely because the incoming wastes from industry are two to three times more polluting than the set norms. Only 10 per cent of industrial wastes are pre-treated before being discharged into the sewage system. Consequently, extremely toxic substances and heavy metals are seriously damaging the biological processes of the new treatment plant.[18] The other two hot spot sewage polluters are Liepaja and Daugavpils.

Vilnius and Kaunas

The two largest cities of Lithuania, Vilnius and Kaunas, accounted for 177 million cubic meters or 53 per cent of all dirty waste waters in 1989. At that time Kaunas had no treatment facilities whatsoever, and Vilnius provided only mechanical treatment.[19] In the fall of 1993, Vilnius was close to having completed its purification plant mode with claims that only "final touches" were remaining. Kaunas has also started to build its waste water cleaning structures. Both cities flush their wastes into adjoining rivers, the Nemunas and its tributary the Neris. Indeed, the Nemunas river basin is the recipient of wastes from 13 hot spots, two of which are located in Kaliningrad and one in Belarus. The river also has a hydro-electric dam which works only at peak hours and interrupts normal flow and processes of self-purification. The Nemunas has become the main sewage carrier of Lithuania, winding its way to the Kursiu Bay on the coast of the Baltic Sea. In 1989 this bay had extremely high concentrations of mercury, phenols, DDT, HCH, ammonia ions and nitrites.[20] In addition to the two largest cities, sewage problems are found in the following hot spots: Siauliai, Kedainiai, Panevezys, Marijampole, Alytus, Klaipeda and Palanga.

While the construction of new facilities has been retarded, the breakdown of old facilities continues at a rapid pace. In Lithuania, only 58 per cent of treatment plants performed effectively in 1990. The main causes for this poor performance included faulty or shoddy construction, lack of trained personnel, and overloading. In addition, there was a tendency to mix industrial and communal sewage, with many industries not providing required preliminary treatment.[21] Toxic wastes thus often harm the biological purification systems. In Latvia and Estonia a similar pattern prevailed.

Energy Industry

All three republics face hard choices in their selection of energy supplies. Baltic decision-makers now realize that almost all energy sources bear a high environmental or monetary price tag. While energy can be imported from neighboring countries, its cost within the framework of dramatically decreased personal, communal and state budgets and precarious industrial production sets limits to choices: either to be unemployed and freeze in the dark or to countenance further pollution of the environment and potential threats to individual health and safety. In the long term more and better pollution purification devices can be erected and energy conservation measures can be introduced. However, efficient purification devices are prohibitively expensive. Conservation measures require the reorientation and expensive replacement of much of the existing heat production and relay equipment and of electricity guzzling facilities. Energy, undervalued in the communist period, now requires full accounting. The introduction of personal consumption meters for gas and for heat will have to be initiated.

Estonian Oil Shale

Oil shale in Estonia is located on the northeast coast adjoining the St. Petersburg region of Russia. Vast tracts of the mineral lie at a depth of only about 100 feet, thus facilitating open-pit mining which accounts for one half of exploitation. The other half is extracted through underground mining, a process which is somewhat less damaging to the environment but is more wasteful of resources. The mining of oil shale affects 7.5 per cent of the surface area of the republic.[22]

Oil shale has a relatively low heat value, comparable to one fifth of that derived from crude oil and about one third of that from good-quality coal. About one half of oil shale is inorganic, hence 100-meter high mountains of ash have been created near the power facilities with about 10 million tons of ash added every year. Only a small fraction of the residual ash is utilized. The best oil shale has already been reclaimed and the oil content of much of the remainder is comparatively low. As a result, greater volumes of oil shale are required to maintain a stable electricity output and proportionately more ash is produced for every unit of electricity. In 1991 the total production of oil shale was 19.6 million tons, somewhat less than the 26 million tons produced in 1975.[23]

There is a broad range of chemical products that can be derived from oil shale, but in Estonia the greatest part of this fuel has been utilized for the production of electricity at two enormous thermal-electric power plants, one of which is located at Narva and the other twenty-five kilometers south, both alongside the Russian border. These two power stations rank among the ten biggest sources of air pollution in Europe and provide Estonia with about 75 per cent of its main air pollutants from stationary sources and with some of the highest per capita figures in the world for emissions of sulfur dioxide, nitrogen oxides, carbon dioxide and dust. They also emit oxides of alkali, alkaline-earth metals, fly ash and heavy and toxic metals such as lead (50 tons a year), mercury (30 tons), zinc (30 tons) and copper (20 tons), and over 8,000 tons of toxic organogenic compounds such as hydrocarbons, benzene and toluene.[24] While 90 per cent of these compounds and elements are deposited within 30 kilometers of the power stations, a significant portion lands in Finland and Russia. In view of the total lack of desulfurization mechanisms and processes it may appear surprising that the sulfur problem in flue gases is not more acute. The special properties of oil shale, however, have significantly mitigated the acid ejection problem. Oil shale has a high content of calcium oxide which fixes or neutralizes about 80 per cent of total sulfur during the combustion process. The remaining 20 per cent of sulfur is still a formidable problem.[25]

With the advent of independence, Estonia has acquired the right to cease or decrease oil shale production. However, economic pressures, the need for local electricity and demands for electricity purchases by neighboring Latvia have limited this option. Estonia, however, is not alone in its concerns with pollution. Neighboring Finland is now seriously involved in the technical research and partial financing of programs to reduce sulfur dioxide emissions by 70–90 per cent. This will involve equipping twenty-four new boilers with desulfurization plants and replacing entirely another 18 old boilers with modern units.[26] The estimated cost of neutralizing this most expensive point-source hot spot of the joint program list is estimated at over 1 billion ECUs, over 80 per cent of which is to be financed by Estonia.

Further rationalizations and even privatization of the electric power plants are being discussed as they might generate resources for purification equipment and lower costs of production. Such moves would most surely entail the reduction of plant workers. Most of the workers, however, are Russians who came to Estonia after World War II. Hence, any moves in this direction could entail ethnic tensions of a different order from those created when production of oil shale was increasing and migrant Russian labor was being recruited from outside the republic.

Atomic Power in Lithuania

An article in the Toronto *Globe and Mail* of October 9, 1993 captured the essence of the problem worrying many people in Lithuania and elsewhere about the Ignalina nuclear power station: "Lithuania's Looming Chernobyl." The Ignalina power station was originally planned to house four graphite-block reactors (RBMK), but currently it has only two, both of which are akin to those of the Chernobyl reactor that exploded in 1986. The technology used for the construction of the reactors was chosen in part for reasons of cost effectiveness. The first reactor began operation in 1984 and the second in 1987.

There are several factors which make Ignalina potentially even more dangerous than Chernobyl. It lies close to a tectonic fault zone which experienced severe earthquakes in 1908 measuring a high of 7 on the Richter Scale. The earth around the station is already shifting. The station is close to the Latvian border and its watershed is joined to the Daugava River. This river, of course, is the same one which flows through the center of Latvia's capital city of Riga, and alongside several other cities, towns and villages. The coolant for the station comes from the adjoining Lake Druksiai which is the largest in Lithuania. Its ecology has been changed dramatically as a result of significant heating. Now the variety of types of plankton has dropped from 100 to 20, and only coarse fish remain. The heating has further created problems of increased evaporation and the lowering of the lake's water levels.[27]

The dangers of Soviet-style nuclear reactors have made most European countries very nervous. Swedish studies in 1993 found over 200 defects in each of the Lithuanian reactors with 100 serious pipe fractures longer than 15 millimeters in Ignalina I. The chief inspector of Swedish nuclear stations admitted that no Swedish station would be allowed to work one hour further given such hazardous conditions.[28] A Danish representative came back from Ignalina in total shock in the Spring of 1993:

> What I saw was more catastrophic than I expected. Everything is controlled by hand. There are no computers in the control room. Holes in the cement around pipelines are plugged with cardboard. There is no means of controlling the steam which collects in the upper levels of the reactor.[29]

He also noted that there were no automatic systems to shut down the system quickly in case of accidents such as fires or earthquakes. There are also no fire alarm systems.

Lithuania itself has estimated that it would require $136 million to install needed safety measures over the next decade. Under conditions of economic penury the republic evidently cannot afford such large sums. Shutting the two reactors down would involve tremendous economic losses. In 1991 the Ignalina station provided 60 per cent of Lithuania's produced energy of which 40 per cent was exported. Even if it were shut down, moth-balling of the stations alone would entail expenses of over $500 million.[30]

The European Bank for Reconstruction and Development has offered a grant of $35 million taken from the Western emergency Nuclear Safety Account. Remembering the problems and costs involved in dealing with the fallout from Chernobyl, Sweden also has donated $20 million. Ignalina is much closer than Chernobyl and only 400 kilometers away from Stockholm. Unfortunately, the Swedish aid to improve Ignalina's fire safety systems has not yet borne fruit because of questions of insurance and liability. Lithuania has refused to sign the Vienna Convention which would force Lithuania to accept liability and provide compensation in case of accidents. In addition, Lithuania cannot afford the high insurance rates required. As a consequence of this uncertainty, equipment destined for Ignalina from Sweden, such as new fire fighting systems, fireproof doors, fire and gas alarm systems, are in storage in Swedish warehouses. Even the aid from the European Community has not been utilized for similar reasons.[31] This gridlock should change soon, but it does indicate the types of unexpected obstacles facing the improvement of safety at this location.

The most pressing need at the power station is a medium-term facility for the spent radioactive fuel rods which formerly were transported to Russia. But this facility, as well, is estimated to cost up to $50 million.[32]

Ignalina has been accident prone in its relatively brief period of existence. It has suffered numerous fires, leaks and breakdowns. The Lithuanian report to the Rio UNCED Conference in June 1992 describes the problem of accidents:

> Although safety measures were added following the Chernobyl disaster, accident risk is still high as proven by occurrence of numerous fires and various accidents. Ignalina also lacks automatic control, confinement and safety systems common to Western reactors. If an error occurs in a typical

> gas-cooled Western reactor, staff have six to seven hours response time to correct the problem. Ignalina's RBMK reactors allow only one minute for correction before the situation becomes critical.[33]

The planned construction of the third reactor at Ignalina became the catalyst that precipitated a huge swell of environmental activism in 1989. As a consequence the third reactor was not begun.

Other Sources of Energy

Other sources of energy have faced problems and popular opposition. In 1986, Lithuanians were successful in stopping the drilling for oil in the vicinity of Kursiu Nerija or Courland Spit, a narrow 98-kilometer peninsula or sand bar of the Baltic Sea off the Lithuanian coast.[34] Lithuanians were also successful in preventing the erection of an oil refinery in Jurbarkas, adjoining the river Nemunas in 1966.[35] Ultimately a petroleum refinery and a thermal-electric plant were constructed at Mazeikiai near the Latvian border on the watershed of the Venta, a river which flows through Latvia. The Mazeikiai plant, located just south of the Latvian border, is creating serious air pollution problems for Latvia and has been placed on the hot spot list. As a result of new economic orientations, Mazeikiai will require oil from the West and a marine terminal to collect this oil. However, major controversy has erupted from the Latvian side over the proposed plan to have this oil terminal at Butingas on the Lithuanian sea coast just three kilometers below Latvia's borders and several kilometers away from the shore, guaranteeing that the prevailing winds will blow any oil spills directly onto Latvian beaches.[36] While the latest available technology is promised, accidents do happen. The Latvian oil terminal at Ventspils has already had a history of endemic spills but costly control strategies and equipment have been put in place and a modern ballast cleaning purification system is being constructed by a Turkish firm.[37] Latvians are willing to build an oil pipeline to Mazeikiai in Lithuania from Ventspils and to give Lithuania the right to its own docking and handling facilities in the Latvian port. As yet, internecine squabbling and considerations of economic upmanship have prevented any agreements. Regardless of where the terminal is built, the transportation of oil by tankers is fraught with danger, and each of the Baltic republics has experienced major oil spills.[38]

Hydro-electric power, once the choice of environmentalists because of the absence of emissions and the renewable nature of the resource, is now considered to have serious shortcomings. Hydro mega-projects from James Bay in Canada to the Chang Jiang (Yangtze) River in China are now vociferously opposed by concerned environmentalists. In Latvia, as well, the planned construction of a fourth hydro-electric station (HES) on the Daugava River at

Daugavpils in 1987 precipitated nation-wide opposition. As a result the construction of the 300 MW capacity station was discontinued.[39] The proposed high-voltage electric cable line from Ignalina to Liepaja was also stopped by environmentalists in 1988. Latvians were faced with a Moscow-planned proposal to build a nuclear power plant north of Liepaja on the shores of the Baltic Sea. This project did not materialize because of opposition.[40]

In view of the Latvian energy shortages and the tremendous costs of imported electricity from Estonia and Lithuania, the Latvian Minister of Energy argued in 1992 for the completion of the Daugavpils HES, albeit in a modified and less damaging form, the construction of the Jekabpils HES, another dam originally planned in the Daugava River "cascade," and even the construction of a nuclear power station using western technology and safety features.[41]

The oil-fired, thermal-electric stations, providing heat and electricity in each of the three republics, are another source of pollution. While some stations have switched to cleaner natural gas, cost factors have now brought back the once popular peat – a fuel with almost no sulfur component but high dust emissions. Feasibility studies have been made for a coal-fired power station at Liepaja.[42] Burning of fuels, however, also produces carbon dioxides, one of the chief "greenhouse" gases, as well as nitrogen oxides and sulfur. As a way out of the energy impasse Latvian environmentalists have proposed the increased use of wind power, especially on the coasts of Kurzeme on the Baltic Sea. Many proposals have been made about renewing the once popular mini power stations on smaller streams. Biogas and biomass burning are other avenues of potential energy. In the long term the greatest gains are going to be made by energy saving and increased efficiency in the production, distribution and use of energy. In the short term, the major Latvian decreases in energy use are caused by the shut-down of production units for non-payment of electric and heating bills.

Other Pollution Sources

Industrial Sources

Various industries have been the focus of attention by environmentalists particularly in the following sectors: pulp and paper, chemicals, cement and construction, and food processing. The pulp and paper mills at Sloka (in Latvia), Kehra and Tallinn (in Estonia) and Klaipeda and Grigiskes (in Lithuania) are mostly blamed for still unacceptably high pollution levels. According to the joint action program, the costs of Sloka pollution abatement at 72 million ECUs surpass the costs of all the other mills combined. The Sloka mill has received the greatest publicity because its effluent is ejected into the Lielupe River 28 kilometers away from the mouth of the river which adjoins the seaside resort beaches of Jurmala. While expensive primary and biological purification systems were constructed in 1975 and 1978, the tertiary chemical complex which was planned and even ordered was never begun. The primary pollutant problems in 1989 included BOD, methanols, nitrogen, suspended solids and smaller quantities of oil, phosphorus and phenols. The major concern of the Nordic Project, which was investigating the mill, was the 763 tons of lignosulfonates or "black liquor" ejected into the river. They conclude with the observation that "the mill should either recover the waste liquor and regenerate its own pulping chemicals, partially change its profile or close down."[43] Ironically the Sloka Mill did close down for the major part of 1993, but because of economic reasons such as labor problems and high production and energy costs, rather than pollution concerns.

The Tallinn mill has problems with BOD and suspended solids which according to a Finnish study would require a new evaporation plant and the upgrading of the waste water filtration plant to reduce the given pollutants by 75–85 per cent. The Kehra mill, which is also close to Tallinn, has problems with sulfur dioxide emissions.[44] Both Estonian mills have been forced to shut down for extensive periods in 1993 for economic reasons. The Lithuanian mills are criticized for high levels of BOD and the Klaipeda cardboard mill for nitrogen emissions.[45]

The chemical industry in Estonia is concentrated in the Kohtla-Jarve area because oil shale is used as a base. In Latvia, Ventspils is the primary petrochemical fabrication base. Its facilities were constructed with the help of Occidental Petroleum from the USA, and its raw materials are imported mainly from Russia. The primary problem is the threat of explosions rather than of pollutants. Olaine is a more sophisticated pharmaceutical drug production complex which produces toxic wastes now languishing in open holding pools. In Lithuania, the fertilizer plant at Jonava has received much publicity as a result of its accidents in 1977 and 1987. The latter accident killed seven people and did much damage to the environment.[46] Another chemical plant is located in Kedainiai. Of the above chemical production industries only Ventspils is not on the hot spot list. Cement plants in all three republics eject unacceptably high quantities of dust and lead into the atmosphere, but they were not considered as critical by the Joint Program of the Helsinki Commission (see below p. 172).

One industry in Estonia which would most certainly be on the list, the phosphorite mining and processing plant at Maardu, was shut down in 1991 because of environmental concerns voiced by a broad section of the population.

Agriculture

A combination of high precipitation levels, frequently sloping and hilly terrain and the introduction of large unbroken fields after collectivization have produced severe problems of soil erosion. Heavy run-off from fields results in serious silting of rivers. In addition, this run-off washes away large quantities of chemical fertilizers and pesticides which enter the water system and create serious problems for water organisms, fish and ultimately, man. Such "non-point" sources of pollution are extremely difficult to neutralize and only prophylactic methods such as increased soil conservation and reduced use of chemicals can ameliorate the problem. The advent of tens of thousands of private farms may limit quantities of fertilizer and pesticides, but they may bring problems of maximum land utilization right up to the banks of streams and lakes. Not surprisingly, the four agricultural run-off programs on the Baltic hot spot list are among the most expensive items, totalling 510 million ECUs.

Wastes

The problem of toxic waste dumps is only now being investigated. Only a minute quantity of hazardous waste is properly disposed. According to a study by the Nordic Project in Latvia, industrial enterprises generated 247,647 tons of hazardous waste a year, most of which was dumped untreated alongside household waste landfills or in "other unsuitable areas," thus damaging soil, ground water and atmosphere. In their estimation, about 20–70 thousand tons of "extremely hazardous waste" should be treated every year. At present they acknowledge that Latvia has neither the knowledge, technical facilities nor financial wherewithal to deal with this problem. They recommend that a chemical waste management center be constructed near Riga which would include an incineration plant, physio-chemical treatment plant and a residuals repository. The capital costs alone have been estimated at over $130 million. Joint Danish and Latvian organizations are attempting to develop toxic waste collection, transportation and utilization systems modeled on the Danish experience.[47] The other two Baltic republics are in a similar predicament with respect to wastes. In Lithuania a part of toxic wastes is disposed of by burning in the Akmene cement plant.

Another waste problem is the legacy of World War II. Southwest of the city of Liepaja, the Soviet Army dumped 2,000 tons of as yet undetermined chemical substances originating from Nazi military stockpiles. The rusting canisters are too fragile for probing analyses. Their degree of danger is not known.[48]

Cross Border Pollutants

In line with world experience, pollution exported to countries or jurisdictions appears to arouse fewer concerns than when the experience is reversed. Latvia in particular suffers because over 60 per cent of its river water is collected outside the republic. Thus, the Lielupe and Venta have already been polluted in Lithuania before reaching the Latvian border. The river Daugava has been particularly subject to general nutrient pollution and to toxic waste incidents created by the chemical plants at Novopolotsk in Belarus.

The most serious case of such trans-boundary pollution occurred in November 1990, when a polymer complex in Novopolotsk in Belarus accidentally spilled 127.9 tons of hydrocyanic acid and the extremely dangerous poison "acetone cyanhydride" (both derivatives of cyanide) into the upper reaches of the Daugava (Western Dvina) River. For three days, downstream inhabitants, who use the Daugava as a source of drinking water, were not warned by the chemical plant or its controlling ministry of the danger. Only the appearance of dead fish alerted Latvian authorities to the danger, leading one Latvian official to wonder about the deadly consequences to people's lives if the river had been frozen and the dead fish had floated invisibly under the ice.[49] In March 1993, once again no warning was relayed to Latvian authorities when 14,000 cubic meters of wastes were spilled by the same city. Latvians have now instituted a continuous water monitoring system on the border with their neighbor.[50] Lithuania in turn has to contend with the pollution of the Nemunas River in its upper reaches by the city of Grodno in Belarus and in its lower reaches closer to the sea by two pulp and paper mills in Kaliningrad, Russia.

Air pollution in the Baltic is dissipated northeast because of prevailing winds. Latvia receives the pollutants from Lithuania's thermal-electric plant at Mazeikiai, the cement factory at Naujoji Akmene and the fertilizer plant at Jonava. If Ignalina has a serious eruption, the direction of the radioactive air most probably will be towards Latvia and Belarus. Estonia's emissions from its two shale-fired power plants affect Finland and Russia. Estonia itself is concerned by the Sosnovyi Bor nuclear reactor station in St. Petersburg which is similar in construction to the fateful Chernobyl reactor and is located less than 100 miles from the Estonian border.

Lithuania receives unwanted air pollutants from Poland. As noted earlier, the Scandinavians have been at the receiving end of pollution from all the former socialist countries including the Baltic republics, hence they are also the ones who have initiated serious programs for pollution abatement and are contributing sums of money to help achieve their goals of a clean Baltic littoral.

Environmental Management Challenge

During the Soviet period the efforts of environmental protection were checkmated by the quiet but effective decisions and foot dragging of all-union ministries. Symbolic fines were set but in general the organizations to protect the environment were weak and disorganized. The declaration of sovereignty of the three republics allowed the strengthening of state environmental initiatives. Each of the Baltic republics passed a new fundamental or framework law setting out basic principles of nature protection (Estonia on February 23, 1990; Latvia on August 6, 1991 and Lithuania on January 21, 1992). All three envisioned the need for environmental impact assessment for new industrial initiatives and the application of the "polluter pays" principle.

The organs of environmental management at first received much attention, new offices, new equipment and increased financing. In Latvia and Lithuania, the key structures for protection were subordinated to the legislature for greater leverage against ministries and the Council of Ministers. Estonia, on the other hand, created a Ministry of the Environment which sat in the Council of Ministers. After the June 1993 elections in Latvia, the Environmental Protection Committee was disbanded and a joint Ministry of Environmental Protection and Regional Development took over its functions. This ministry is now part of the cabinet and has a full minister as well as a minister of state for environmental protection. The Baltic republics have opted for decentralization and given much power to regional environmental administrators and inspectors. All three legislatures also have commissions specializing in questions of the environment.

There are still some basic problems to overcome. The functions of nature protection are still divided. There is a serious deficit of laboratories and precise monitoring and measuring equipment and facilities. Financial constraints limit the scope of activities. One of the most elementary problems, the inventory of pollution sources, is slowly being achieved with the help of Scandinavian countries and the United States. Large information gaps still exist, especially with regard to industries which dump their pollutants into communal sewage systems and threaten the fragile biological purification systems.

The Baltic republics have introduced natural resource and pollution taxes. The accumulated funds from these sources and from fines are used for various environmental projects at the local and national level.

Post-Independence

Environmental activism was one of the factors facilitating the advent of independence of the Baltic republics. In Latvia, the mobilizing issue was the proposed construction of the Daugavpils hydro-electric station which was ordered stopped by Moscow in 1987. The initiator of this campaign, Dainis Ivans, became the first leader of the Latvian People's Front. In Estonia, the pollution-prone phosphorite mine at Maardu, ten kilometers east of Tallinn, and the proposed start of phosphorite mining in 1987 in Rakvere, halfway between Tallinn and Narva, precipitated a wave of protest which resulted in the cancellation of the new project in the fall of 1987. Maardu was closed in 1991. Rein Taagepera has characterized this first phase of the awakening period as the "phosphate spring."[51] In Lithuania, the green movement was a "major expression" of the Lithuanian national renewal.[52] During 1987 protests over the drilling of oil in the Kursiu Nerija were successful. The focus of protest by large masses of people was the construction of the third reactor at Ignalina. Over a million signatures were collected. Plans for the third reactor were canceled.[53]

Without a doubt environmental activism was a key item of politics in the period 1987–1990, as it was for most of the industrialized world. This wave of activism subsided in the Baltic republics as it did in the rest of the world.[54]

After 1990 the environment received little publicity in the Baltic republics. Nevertheless, actual gains were being made in the decrease of pollutants. Part of the reason for this decrease has been the slowdown in industrial production. Several major polluters have scaled back their output of products as well as of pollutants. Some firms, such as the Maardu phosphorite plant in Estonia, have been shut down because of their threat to the environment and health. New anti-pollution equipment and facilities, often from the West and using Western specialists, are being brought on line. Broken-down facilities are being repaired or upgraded. Soviet military bases and objects are decreasing; thus a major source of toxic wastes and chemicals is no longer growing, but can be addressed by environmental specialists.

Some new dimensions of pollution have also appeared, however. The poorly controlled trade in fuel oil has allowed unscrupulous importers to sell toxic waste-laced oils to cash-strapped municipalities. Poor-quality leaded gas is sold to motorists and many more cars have appeared in the Baltic, almost all without catalytic converters. The biggest potential threat is in the import of wastes from Europe. Porous borders and widespread corruption and graft make it easier for unprincipled operators to bring in wastes and dispose of them in local dumps. Very few controls are yet in place to check the content of wastes being discarded in these dumps. Western traditions such as the "not in my backyard syndrome" have also appeared with the advent of private property. Perhaps one of the harbingers of progress has been the periodic opening of certain sections of Baltic beaches to swimmers in 1993 in contrast to the almost universal bans present in previous years.

International Cooperation

Poverty and the tremendous pressures to satisfy the minimal needs of survival have placed environmental concerns at the back of the line for governmental attention and budget allocations. The major hope must rest with the generosity, concern, and cooperation from neighboring countries of the Baltic Sea littoral.

The main vehicle of regional cooperation is the Baltic Marine Environmental Protection Commission or Helsinki Commission (HELCOM). HELCOM was established in 1974 and was reorganized in 1980 with the entry into force of the Convention on the Protection of the Marine Environment of the Baltic Sea Area (the Helsinki Convention). This convention delves into all aspects of pollution prevention and abatement and the protection and enhancement of the marine environment of the Baltic Sea area. The USSR was a member and represented the Baltic republics. In 1992–1993 the three republics were able to sign the Convention independently and sit on the Secretariat of the Commission which is located in Helsinki. Each participant has a vote and all decisions have to be unanimous.

On September 3, 1990, all Prime Ministers of the participating countries met at the Baltic Sea Environment Conference in Ronneby, Sweden and signed a Baltic Sea declaration. As a result, a joint Comprehensive Environmental Action Program was developed to implement the Helsinki Convention and HELCOM recommendations. It worked out details of pollution levels and financing required for 132 hot spots in the Baltic Sea basin which were presented publicly in April 1992.

The participation by Scandinavians and Germans in providing comprehensive pollution data and strategies for the Baltic republics has been their most useful contribution so far. The major financing proposed in the program, however, has been gravely affected by the serious economic recession in the West and so far only moderate sums have been donated. In November 1993 Sweden, for example, indicated that it would provide about $12 million for the construction of waste water treatment plants in three hot spots: Haapsalu in Estonia, Liepaja in Latvia, and Klaipeda in Lithuania.[55] Within the Baltic republics, credits are difficult to obtain and priorities of economic survival only allow for minimal funding of the projects on the hot spot list. With the advent of an economic upturn there is hope that serious financing will reappear. The Scandinavians and Germans cannot avoid the problem of pollution of their sea and any investments into the Baltic republics will provide a ten-fold impact compared to the effect of equal sums on their own territories. While the financial aspects of the proposals have not yet been met, the HELCOM and the Comprehensive Environmental Action Program have provided the Baltic republics with a forum for contacts, exchanges of experts and for the mediation of grievances caused by trans-boundary pollution. Such membership support has also helped obtain financing of loans and grants from the European Community.

Conclusion

Environmental pollution in the Baltic republics may be somewhat less acute than in the industrialized areas of Eastern Europe, Russia and the Ukraine. One of the most positive aspects is the fact that this pollution in most cases is reversible, a possible exception being the northeastern section of Estonia. Even the heavily polluted Baltic Sea can be rejuvenated through natural processes of water exchange with the North Sea. However, the socialist legacy has left poorly constructed and now seriously crumbling systems of purification. To renew existing systems and construct new ones is extremely expensive. Even if the entire annual budgets of the Baltic republics for 1993 were devoted to this issue alone they would still be insufficient to fully rectify the situation.

The Baltic republics, with respect to the environment, are in a similar situation to the Scandinavian countries in the mid-1960s. They lack sufficient data. They have yet to work out realistic programs of monitoring and implementation. In addition, they have not yet begun to debate seriously the issues of acid rain, CFC's, greenhouse gases and sustainable development. The help from Scandinavian countries is pushing the Baltic republics towards a speedier resolution of their pollution problems. However, these recently independent nations have to cope with so many pressing problems of survival that little attention and resources can be allotted for the cause of a clean Baltic Sea. The Latvian report to UNCED at Rio de Janeiro in 1992 pointed out that only 1.6 per cent of Latvia's gross national product went to environmental protection, but that it would require "at least five times more money than presently available to stabilize the environmental situation."[56]

Notes

1. The ECU is a combined basket of 12 European currencies worth about U.S. $1.17. The list and characteristics of the 132 hot spots as well as the details of the Joint Comprehensive Environmental Action Program can be found in "Diplomatic Conference on the Protection of the Marine Environment of the Baltic Sea Area, Background Document for the Baltic Sea Environmental Declaration," Helsinki, Finland, April 9, 1992 (Conference Document No. 5/2). The conference was sponsored by the Helsinki Commission and the document was published by the Conference Secretariat in cooperation with the Ministry for Foreign Affairs of Finland and the Ministry of the Environment of Finland. Hereafter cited as Joint Program.

2. Information on the Baltic Sea can be gleaned from several sources. Britt Aniansson, *Northern Europe's Seas: Northern Europe's Environment* (Stockholm: Nordic Council, 1989), 150–69; Anders Virdheims, *Baltijas Jura* (Riga: Latvijas Universitates Ekologiskais Centrs, 1992); Aina Zarins, "The Baltic Sea: A Pointer for the United Nations Law of the Sea Conference?" *RFE/RL Report*, August 9, 1977; Nordic Report Fund, *Study of Environmental Protection: Estonia and Partly Latvia and Lithuania* (Helsinki, 1989). The monthly journal *Ambio*, published in Sweden in English has many detailed articles on the pollution of the Baltic Sea.

3. Aniansson, *Northern Europe's Seas*, 159.

4. *Economic Survey of the Baltic Republics: Draft* (Stockholm: Swedish Ministry of Foreign Affairs, 1991), 277.

5. Authorities recommend that water in most cities be boiled at least five minutes before consumption. Over 1,000 people contracted viral hepatitis "A" from Riga drinking water in 1988. "Dabas un Cilveka Veseliba," *Zinatne un Tehnika*, 3 (1989), 12.

6. *Economic Survey of the Baltic Republics*, 278.

7. Latvijas PSR Valsts Statistikas Komiteja, *Latvija Sodien: Socialekonomisku Aprakstu Krajums* (Riga, 1990), 223.

8. *Economic Survey of the Baltic Republics*, 277.

9. *Ibid.*, 278

10. *Ibid.*, 273–74.

11. Matthew R. Auer, "Environmental Restoration, Economic Transition and Nationalism in Estonia," *Journal of Baltic Studies*, 23, 4 (Winter 1992), 381.

12. *Ibid.*; Mare Taagepera, "Ecological Problems in Estonia," *Journal of Baltic Studies*, 14, 4 (Winter 1983), 311.

13. Juris Dreifelds, "Participation in Pollution Control in Latvia, 1955–1977," *Journal of Baltic Studies*, 14, 4 (Winter 1983), 274.

14. *Economic Survey of the Baltic Republics*, 275.

15. *Ibid.*, 273.

16. *Rigas Balss*, July 8, 1992.

17. *Rigas Balss*, June 7, 1993.

18. *Rigas Balss*, March 12, 1993; Carl Bro a/s, *Pre-Feasibility Study of the Gulf of Riga and the Daugava River Basin, Volume 2: Technical Report* (Copenhagen, June 1992), 67.

19. *Economic Survey of the Baltic Republics*, 275.

20. Lithuania Environmental Protection Department, *Lithuania: National Report, United Nations Conference on Environment and Development* (Vilnius: Spauda, 1992), 70. Hereafter cited as UNCED Lithuania.

21. *Ibid.*, 73.

22. *Economic Survey of the Baltic Republics*, 384; Ministry of the Environment, Republic of Estonia, *National Report of Estonia to UNCED 1992* (Tallinn, 1992), 15. Hereafter cited as UNCED Estonia.

23. UNCED Estonia, 15; "Soviets Admit Troubles in Oil Shale," *Oil and Gas Journal*, October 6, 1975; Mare Taagepera, "Pollution of the Environment and the Baltics," *Journal of Baltic Studies*, 12, 3 (Fall 1981), 260–74.

24. UNCED Estonia, 26.

25. *Economic Survey of the Baltic Republics*, 277–78.

26. Auer, "Environmental Restoration," 379.

27. *Elpa*, March 26, 1991; *The Globe and Mail*, October 9, 1993 and August 29, 1986; UNCED Lithuania, 54–55; Augustine Idzelis, "The Socioeconomic and Environmental Impact of the Ignalina Nuclear Power Station," *Journal of Baltic Studies*, 14, 3 (Fall 1983), 247–54.

28. *Diena*, October 26, 1993.

29. *Die Tageszeitung*, April 26, 1993, as quoted in *Diena*, October 26, 1993.

30. *Diena*, October 26, 1993; *The Globe and Mail*, October 9, 1993.

31. *Ibid.*

32. *The Globe and Mail*, October 9, 1993.

33. UNCED Lithuania, 55.

34. Saulius Girnius, "Protests Against Oil Drilling in the Baltic Sea," Radio Free Europe Research, *Baltic Area Situation Report*, December 9, 1986, 37–39; *Izvestiya*, June 14, 1987 as translated in *Current Digest of the Soviet Press*, July 15, 1987, 11.

35. Idzelis, "Socioeconomic and Environmental Impact," 253.

36. *Diena*, August 25, 1993.

37. *Diena*, December 2, 1992.

38. The Antonio Gramsci dumped 9,000 tons of naphtha near Ventspils in 1979. The tanker Globe Asimi caused an estimated $100 million damage to the resort beaches of Lithuania when it ran aground near Klaipeda on November 19, 1981 and spilled 16,000 tons of heavy oil. More recently in January 1993 the oil tanker Kihnu ran aground during a heavy storm four kilometers from Tallinn harbor. While quantities of diesel fuel reached the sea, the bulk of the load was pumped out and a specially equipped ship from Finland helped clean up the spill. *Diena*, August 28, 1993; Radio Free Europe/Radio Liberty, *This Week in the Baltics*, January 22, 1993.

39. Juris Dreifelds, "Two Latvian Dams: Two Confrontations," *Baltic Forum*, 6, 1 (Spring 1989), 11–24.

40. *Padomju Jaunatne*, June 3, 1988.

41. *Diena*, July 29, 1992.

42. *Ibid.*

43. Nordic Project Fund, *Environmental Situation and Project Identification in Latvia* (Helsinki, May 1991), 40–42. Hereafter cited as Nordic Project Latvia.

44. Ministry of the Environment Finland, *Environmental Priority Action Program for Leningrad, Leningrad Region, Karelia and Estonia: Synthesis Report* (Helsinki, September 1991), 20.

45. K-Konsult, et al., *Baltic Sea Environment Program: Pre-Feasibility Study of the Lithuanian Coast and the Nemon River Basin* (August 1991). Prepared for the Baltic Marine Environmental Protection Commission.

46. "Adamkus on Lithuanian Environmental Issues," *Baltic Forum*, 6, 1 (Spring 1989), 25–26; Augustine Idzelis, "Institutional Response to Environmental Problems in Lithuania," *Journal of Baltic Studies*, 14, 4 (Winter 1983), 296–306.

47. Nordic Project Latvia, 44–59; *Diena*, May 29, 1991.

48. *Latvijas Jaunatne*, October 6, 1993.

49. *Elpa*, January 1, 1991, and March 12, 1991.

50. *Latvijas Jaunatne*, March 19, 1993.

51. Rein Taagepera, *Estonia, Return to Independence* (Boulder, Colo.: Westview Press, 1993), 120–21.

52. UNCED Lithuania, 99.

53. Evaldas Vebra, "New Directions in Environmental Protection Management in the Baltic States," in Barbara Jancar-Webster, ed., *Environmental Action in Eastern Europe* (Armonk, N.J.: M.E. Sharpe, 1993), 84.

54. Heightened environmental consciousness waves also developed in the Baltic in the period 1970–1973, replicating a world trend and indicating the presence of a type of reflected global resonance.

55. *Baltic Observer*, November 19–25, 1993.

56. Environmental Protection Committee, Republic of Latvia, *National Report of Latvia to UNCED 1992* (Riga, 1992).

Glossary of Acronyms and Terms

AES:	atomic energy station.
AMAP:	Arctic Monitoring and Assessment Program, one component of the international agreement called the Arctic Environmental Protection Strategy, signed by the eight Arctic countries in 1992.
Apparat:	the administrative apparatus of the Communist Party of the Soviet Union; the party functionaries in the apparat were called apparatchiki.
ASTs:	atomic power station for heat supply only.
ATETs:	atomic power station that supplies both heat and power.
BOD:	biological oxygen demand.
CIS:	Commonwealth of Independent States, a loose grouping of 12 of the former republics of the Soviet Union created in December 1991, including Armenia, Azerbaijan, Belarus, Georgia, Kazakhstan, Kyrgyzstan, Moldova, Russia, Tajikistan, Turkmenistan, Ukraine and Uzbekistan.
CFCs:	chlorofluorocarbons, ozone-depleting, industrial chemicals used, *inter alia*, in aerosols and refrigeration.
CPSU:	Communist Party of the Soviet Union.
CTBT:	Comprehensive Test Ban Treaty.
DDT:	dichlorodiphenyltrichloroethane, a powerful insecticide in the class of chemicals called organochlorines.
ECU:	European currency unit, the value of which is based on a basket of 12 European currencies.
G-7:	The Group of Seven countries, including Canada, France, Germany, Italy, Japan, United Kingdom and the United States of America.
Glasnost:	a Russian word for public disclosure or openness that was used to describe policies initiated under Soviet leader Mikhail Gorbachev that led to greater political and social freedoms.
HCH:	hexachlorocyclohexane, an organochlorine used in agriculture.
HES:	hydro-electric station.
IAEA:	International Atomic Energy Agency.

IASAP: International Arctic Seas Assessment Project, administered by the IAEA.

ISAR: a U.S.-based non-governmental organization formerly called the Institute for Soviet-American Relations.

Krai: a territorial-administrative division of the Russian Federation (and before that of the USSR), subordinate to central bodies.

LDC: London Dumping Convention or, more formally, the *Convention on Prevention of Marine Pollution by Dumping Wastes and Other Matter*, signed in 1972.

MMT: million metric tons.

MW: megawatt, the equivalent of 1,000 kilowatts.

NGO: non-governmental organization.

Nomenklatura: those persons selected by responsible Communist Party bodies for important positions in all spheres of social, economic and political life.

NPS: nuclear power station.

Oblast: a territorial-administrative division of the Russian Federation (and, before that, of the USSR) having roughly the same status as a krai (see above).

Okrug: a territorial-administrative division of the Russian Federation (and, before that, of the USSR) that was named after an ethnic group living in that region; it may be directly subordinate to central bodies or to a republic, oblast or krai.

PCBs: polychlorinated biphenyls, a toxic substance often used as a coolant in electrical generators.

Perestroika: a Russian word usually translated as restructuring, it refers to the reforms of the USSR's economic and political system during the tenure of Soviet leader Mikhail Gorbachev.

PHARE: the European Community's Program of Assistance to Poland and Hungary for Economic Reconstruction.

PTBT: Partial Test Ban Treaty.

Raion: a lower-level territorial-administrative division of the Russian Federation for both urban and rural areas.

RBMK: a Soviet-designed, graphite-moderated, nuclear power reactor, the type which exploded at the Chernobyl nuclear power station.

RFE/RL: Radio Free Europe/Radio Liberty.

RICEL: Russian International Center for Environmental Law, an environmental non-governmental organization.

SEU: Socio-ecological Union, a Russian environmental non-governmental organization.

Soviet: an elected legislative body representing cities, raions, okrugs, oblasts, krais and republics; often translated as council. Local councils were reconstituted and were no longer called soviets after the end of 1993.

SSN: nuclear-powered attack submarine.

START: Strategic Arms Reduction Talks.

UNCED: United Nations Conference on Environment and Development, held in Rio de Janeiro, June 1992; also referred to as the Earth Summit.

VVER: the Soviet-designed version of a pressurized-water nuclear power reactor.

WMP: world market price.

About the Contributors

James Critchlow is a fellow of the Russian Research Centre at Harvard University. A long-time expert on Central Asia, he has written extensively on the region for Radio Free Europe/Radio Liberty. His book *Nationalism in Uzbekistan: A Soviet Republic's Path to Sovereignty* was published by Westview Press in 1991.

Joan DeBardeleben is director of the Institute of Central/East European and Russian-Area Studies at Carleton University. She has written many articles and a book on the environmental situation in the Soviet Union and Eastern Europe. She edited *To Breathe Free: Eastern Europe's Environmental Crisis*, which was published in 1991, and is author of *Soviet Politics in Transition* (1992).

Juris Dreifelds is associate professor of politics at Brock University, St. Catharines, Ontario. He has authored many articles and chapters on the Baltic republics. He writes primarily on the political situation in the region, but has a special interest in the environment. His first degree was in Forestry.

Peter Gizewski is research associate at the Canadian Centre for Global Security, Ottawa, where he specializes in problems of nuclear, chemical and biological arms control. He has written on a wide variety of issues pertaining to international peace and security.

Barbara Jancar-Webster is a professor in the Political Science Department of the State University of New York at Brockport. She has written extensively on environmental issues in the Soviet Union and Eastern Europe. She edited *Environmental Action in Eastern Europe: Responses to Crisis*, which was published in 1993.

John M. Kramer is Distinguished Professor in the Department of Political Science at Mary Washington College, Fredericksburg, Virginia. An expert on energy issues in Eastern Europe, he has published numerous articles and books. His book, *The Energy Gap in Eastern Europe*, was published in 1990.

David R. Marples is associate professor of history at the University of Alberta, Edmonton, and senior research scholar at the university's Canadian Institute of Ukrainian Studies. He has written two books and several articles on the

Chernobyl disaster and is a regular contributor to the journal *Post-Soviet Geography.*

DJ Peterson is a Ph.D. candidate in political science at the University of California, Los Angeles, and a consultant on environmental policy at The RAND Corporation in Santa Monica, California. He has authored numerous articles on social, economic, and environmental affairs in the former Soviet Union as well as the RAND-sponsored book *Troubled Lands: The Legacy of Soviet Environmental Destruction*, published in 1993 by Westview Press.

Leigh Sarty is a foreign service officer with the Canadian Department of Foreign Affairs and International Trade. He received his Ph.D. from the Department of Political Science and the Harriman Institute at Columbia University. His publications have dealt primarily with Canadian foreign policy and international relations.

Lisa Van Buren is currently pursuing a law degree at Dalhousie University, Halifax, Nova Scotia. Her primary interest is in environmental law. Van Buren is a graduate of the Institute of Central/East European and Russian-Area Studies at Carleton University.

Index